Do It Yourself

Turbo C® ++

Do It Yourself

Turbo C® ++

Paul J. Perry

PUBLISHING
A Division of Prentice Hall Computer Publishing
11711 North College, Carmel, Indiana 46032 USA

To my parents. Thanks for your pride in me.

Quotations that appear in this book were taken from the *International Thesaurus of Quotations*, compiled by Rhonda Thomas Tripp. New York: Harper & Row.

International Standard Book Number: 0-672-30107-5

Library of Congress Catalog Card Number: 92-61572

94 93 92   5 4 3 2 1

Interpretation of the printing code: the rightmost double-digit number is the year of the book's printing; the rightmost single-digit number, the number of the book's printing. For example, a printing code of 92-1 shows that the first printing of the book occurred in 1992.

Composed in ITC Garamond and MCPdigital by Prentice Hall Computer Publishing

Printed in the United States of America

Publisher
Richard K. Swadley

Managing Editor
Neweleen A. Trebnik

Acquisitions Editor
Greg Croy

Development Editors
Stacy Hiquet

Production Editors
Jodi Jensen
Virginia Noble

Editors
Lynn Brown
Rebecca S. Freeman

Technical Reviewer
Keith Davenport

Editorial Assistants
Rosemarie Graham
Lori Kelley

Formatter
Mary Croy

Cover Designer
Dan Armstrong

Production Director
Jeff Valler

Production Manager
Corinne Walls

Imprint Manager
Matthew Morrill

Book Designer
Michele Laseau

Production Analyst
Mary Beth Wakefield

Proofreading/Indexing Coordinator
Joelynn Gifford

Graphics Image Specialists
Dennis Sheehan, Jerry Ellis
Sue VandeWalle

Production
Lisa Daugherty, Mark Enochs,
Tim Groeling, Denny Hager,
Carla Hall-Batton, John Kane,
Phil Kitchel, Bob LaRoche,
Juli Pavey, Linda Quigley,
Joe Ramon, Suzanne Tully,
Julie Walker

Indexer
Loren Malloy

About the Author

Paul J. Perry is a technical support engineer for Borland International, where he specializes in C/C++ and Windows programming. Perry received his bachelor of science degree at California State University, Chico, where he studied electronics and computer technology with a minor in business administration. He is the author of *Quicken Quick Reference* (Que, 1990), *DESQview Instant Reference* (Sybex, 1991), and the upcoming *Using Turbo Pascal for Windows* (Que).

He has also written over a dozen magazine articles on computers. If he is not writing or programming, you will find him out pedaling his bicycle, going on 15- to 25-mile bike rides daily.

Overview

Appendixes

Contents

Part II: The ABC's of C

5 Input/Output 83

6 Operators 99

7 Conditional Statements 117

8 Program Flow

135

9 Data Structures

153

10 Using Functions

177

Part III: Advanced C Topics

17 Sequential File I/O   321

18 Random Access File I/O   341

Part IV: Object-Oriented Programming

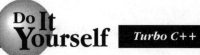

Acknowledgments

Many thanks to the great people at Prentice Hall Publishing, including development editor Stacy Hiquet, acquisitions editor Greg Croy and all the others who worked "behind the scenes." It couldn't have been done without you.

Trademarks

All terms mentioned in this book that are known to be trademarks or service marks have been appropriately capitalized. Sams Publishing cannot attest to the accuracy of this information. Use of the terms in this book should not be regarded as affecting the validity of any trademark or sevice mark.

Turbo C++ is a registered trademark of Borland International.

Introduction

Today, the C and C++ computer programming languages are used by most major PC software developers in writing many of their applications. C has rapidly become the most popular and powerful programming language in existence. Borland International is one of the companies largely responsible for popularizing C, C++, and object-oriented programming.

Borland's C++ compiler and development tools make available sophisticated programming tools on the cutting edge of technology. By providing a superior product with the tools you need, Turbo C++ is not only the greatest value available, it is one of the most powerful.

Turbo C++ includes the Integrated Development Environment, which provides the best programming environment in C and C++ for DOS. It is guaranteed to bring you up to speed programming in C and C++ quickly.

Who Should Use This Book?

Do It Yourself Turbo C++ is written for everyone with an interest in programming using the Turbo C++ compiler—from the new user to the seasoned veteran. The book is aimed at beginning to intermediate-level C programmers. This book will benefit those who have no programming experience as well as those who already have some programming background in another language, such as Pascal or BASIC.

What You Should Know to Use This Book

This book assumes that you are familiar with using DOS commands.

For example, you should be able to list directories and create, execute, copy, and erase files. You should be familiar with tree-structured directories and know how to move about within them.

Purpose of This Book

This book was written to provide an easy-to-follow tutorial for using the features provided in the Turbo C++ compiler. The book is meant to supplement the Borland manuals and is in no way meant as a replacement. Each aspect of the C and C++ language is covered in this book, as well as the extensions provided by the Turbo compiler. C and C++ are powerful languages, and Turbo C++ adds even more to the languages. This book tries to touch on many important elements of the package. Some topics are given more information than others, because of their relative importance.

What You Need to Use This Book

The title suggests that you can only use this book if you have Turbo C++. It was written with Version 3.0 of the compiler in mind. Anyone who uses Turbo C++ (or any other C++) compiler will find this book useful. Although the book does include several examples that are specific to Turbo C++, most of the book will be helpful to anybody studying the C or C++ programming languages.

Turbo C++ is currently available with or without an application framework called Turbo Vision. Turbo Vision is an object-oriented user interface package. It builds on object-oriented design methods to help you create programs that are event driven. Turbo Vision is not required to use the material found in this book.

Organization of This Book

Do it Yourself Turbo C++ is divided into four parts. Essentially, they provide an introduction to the Borland programming environment, an introduction to the fundamentals of C, advanced topics in C, and coverage of object-oriented programming. Practical sample programs are presented throughout the book.

Part I, "The Turbo C++ Programming Environment," gives an introductory explanation to the Turbo C++ programming package. Early chapters lead the beginner through the stages of installing the compiler. The design and operation of a typical C program is examined as well as using the Integrated Development Environment to quickly start creating programs.

Part II, "The ABCs of C," introduces the fundamentals of the C programming language. Topics include data types, input and output, operators, conditional statements, program flow statements, data structures, and functions, each of which form the core of the languages.

Part III, "Advanced Topics of C," includes information about operators not covered in Part II—pointers, text screen displays, the Borland Graphics Interface (BGI), and information about accessing files inside your program. Both sequential and random access file programming methods are described. The section ends with a chapter on how to debug your programs.

Part IV, "Object-Oriented Programming," deals with the object-oriented extensions specific to C++. Information is included on classes, object hierarchy, operator overloading, and streams.

Each part comprises short chapters. Each chapter tackles a single topic, so you can focus your energies on a specific goal. Every chapter contains a "Goals" list to outline the important concepts explored in that chapter and a concluding section entitled "What You Have Learned" to provide a quick reference to the important topics discussed within each chapter.

The appendixes provide a handy reference you can use while programming, including ASCII tables, quick reference to memory models, a C language summary, error messages, and runtime libraries. You will use these appendixes often while you program. The glossary gives a description of the commonly used words and phrases in the book.

Notation and Conventions

To get the most out of this book, you need to know something about how it is designed. The chapters contain bold text, italicized text, bulleted lists, numbered lists, figures, program listings, code fragments, and tables of information. All these design features should help you understand the material being presented.

Characters that you are asked to type appear in `monotype bold`. Also in lines that you must type, ***bold italic*** is used for characters that hold the place of a drive or filename, or anything else you must substitute. Any program output is in `plain monospace`.

In certain places in the book you will find the use of the backslash continuation character (|) in the program listings. This notation is used in the instances where lines have too many characters to be formatted on one line.

For example, take a look at the following line of code:

```
printf("This is aline which is way too long to fit on \
a single line and is split into two using the \
continuation character");
```

The backspace character at the end of the first line tells the compiler that the second line is a continuation of the first. When you type these lines, make sure that you use the backslash so that the compiler will recognize the code and compile it without errors.

Italic type is used to emphasize or define an important word or phrase. You should pay close attention to italicized text. It is also used to introduce new technical terms.

A boxed *note* is used to highlight a useful piece of information or a special notice.

A *warning* box is used to warn you about problems of possible unwanted results or probable data loss.

A *tip* box is used to separate programming tips and shortcuts from the rest of the text.

Bulleted lists have the following characteristics:

• Each item in this type of list is preceded by a bullet. The bullet is a special flag that draws your attention to the important material.

• The order of items in a bulleted list is not mandatory. That is, the items represent related points you should understand, but they are not in any special sequence.

- The text for items in a bulleted list is often longer than the text you see in other kinds of lists. Items in bulleted lists contain explanations, not simple actions.

Numbered lists contain actions you should perform or lists of items that must be kept in a particular sequence. When you see a numbered list, you should do the following:

1. Start at the beginning of the list. Don't skip ahead to later items in the list; the order is important.

2. Make sure that you completely understand each item as you encounter it.

3. Read all the items in the list. Don't skip any of them—each item is important.

Figures are pictures or graphics that can help you understand the text. Each figure is double-numbered, with the chapter number followed by a sequential number (numbers begin with 1 in each chapter). Thus, Figure 4.2 means that the figure appears in Chapter 4, and it is the second figure within that chapter. Figure 1.1 is a sample of a figure.

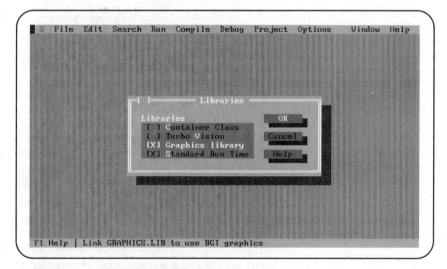

Figure 1.1. *A sample illustration.*

Program listings give the C and C++ source code for a complete program or perhaps for a program module that can be compiled separately. In either case, source code shown in a program listing, can, in fact, be compiled. Listing 1.1, for example, shows the source code for a complete program. (Most complete programs are much longer than this short sample.)

Listing 1.1. START.C. A sample program listing.

```
/***********************************************
 START.C--Show sample of a C program listing.
 Do It Yourself Turbo C++ by Paul J. Perry
 ***********************************************/

#include <stdio.h>

void main()
{
    printf("This is a test; it is only a test\n");
}
```

You should notice a couple of things about Listing 1.1:

Listings, like figures and tables, are double-numbered with the chapter and sequential number. However, the reference numbers for figures and program listings are independent. Each program starts with a comment section which instantly identifies the program and gives a brief description of its purpose.

A *code fragment* also shows C and C++ source code, but the code does not make up a complete program (the fragment cannot be compiled). Code fragments are inserted directly in the text and do not have headings, reference numbers, or line numbers. Code fragments contain enough source code to illustrate a point, but they are short (usually only five or six lines). Note that a special monospace type face is used for keywords, program listings, and code fragments.

Tables appear when rows and columns of information are suitable.

Tables also have their own headings and reference numbers—again, independent of the numbers for figures and program listings. Table 1.1 shows how a table is presented in this book.

Table 1.1. The formatting conventions used in this book.

Format Convention	*Use*
Italic	An eye-catching type style used to emphasize important words or phrases.
Bulleted lists	A list of items with a bullet flagging each item; the sequence of items is usually not important.
`Bold monospace`	Characters you are to type into a program.
Numbered lists	A list of items with numbers flagging each item; sequence is important.
`Monospace`	Output from a program or the program code itself.
Program listings	Complete programs that can be compiled.
Code fragments	A small number of source code lines that illustrate a point; code fragments cannot be compiled apart from other code.
Tables	Information arranged in columnar format; tables may or may not contain explanations or descriptions.

A Note on Programming

Many readers of this book will already have some experience in writing programs. If you have such experience, you need no further explanation about how to learn to program effectively.

If however, you are approaching Turbo C++ as your first programming language, you need to know an important point about learning C, or any programming language: It is impossible to learn C without writing code, compiling your programs, and observing the way they work (or possibly don't work).

Because practicing C programming is essential to learning the C programming language, many sample programs are included so you can type them in and see how they work. However, I urge you to try different things. It is important to experiment with a language to really learn it.

Part I

The Turbo C++
Programming
Environment

1

Getting Started

Goals

After reading this chapter, you will

- Have a background about C, C++, and the Turbo C++ package.

- Know what is included in the Turbo C++ package.

- Know the difference between a compiled and interpreted programming language.

- Be able to install the Turbo C++ package, step by step.

This chapter introduces you to the Turbo C++ programming environment. You will first learn the background of the C and C++ programming languages. You will see how C++ evolved into what it is today, and you will learn a little bit about the history of how Turbo C++ came into existence.

To get you started, this chapter leads you step-by-step through the process of installing Turbo C++ on your computer. During the process of installing the program, you will learn essential information about the package.

History of C, C++, and Turbo C++

Programming languages are not just a quick inspiration of a genius in a research lab. As the industry progresses, there are gradual progressions and changes in what a programming language can do. All programming languages evolve to meet the needs of the programmer. The experiences of a large group of people working in different situations provide a language with a rich set of capabilities. C, C++, and Turbo C++ are no exception to the rule.

About C

C was originally designed in the early 1970s and implemented in 1978 by Dennis Ritchie at Bell Telephone Laboratories, Inc. (now AT&T Bell Laboratories) and outlined in the book *The C Programming Language*, by Brian Kernighan and Dennis Ritchie. C was an outgrowth of two earlier languages, called BCPL and B, which were also developed at Bell Laboratories.

Although C is used on many different computer systems, it was first closely associated with the UNIX operating system, because UNIX was actually written with the C programming language. The language has sometimes been called a "system programming language," because of its usefulness in writing operating systems. It combines high-level language constructions with the ability to interact with the system at a close level to the operating system.

As developers began programming in C, different dialects of the language started appearing on different computing platforms. This happened because parts of the language weren't clearly defined, and they were interpreted differently by different implementers of the language. It was clear that an updated definition of the language was needed that could become an industry standard.

In 1983, the *American National Standards Institute (ANSI)* created a committee to provide a standard definition of the C programming language. The ANSI committee overlooking the standardization of the language included professors, researchers, and programmers from some of the top computer companies. In 1988, the second edition of the book by Kernighan and Ritchie (who are also known as simply K&R) was published. The newer edition included the new, standardized version of C, called *ANSI C.*

About C++

C++ (as you might imagine) is a superset of the C programming language. That is, it has all the features of C, as well as additional ones. Most importantly, C++ includes *classes,* which are the fundamentals on which *object-oriented programming (OOP)* is based. There are other object-oriented programming languages, including Smalltalk, Objective C, and Pascal with Classes. C++ is the object-oriented programming language which has gained the greatest acceptance.

In 1980, when research into object-oriented programming techniques first began, researchers wanted to base their work on a well-known programming language. At the time, the C programming language was a dominant power in the computer industry. So, it was the logical choice to base this "new" object-oriented language on C.

C++'s predecessor was a language called "C with Classes." It was based on the C programming language because C was such a powerful force in the industry at the time. By basing it on a well-known language, programmers had a foundation on which to use and understand the new object-oriented programming concepts. Thus, C programmers could make the transition to object-oriented programming by using the coding methods they were used to.

The "C with Classes" language was extended around the year 1984, and the resulting language was called C++. The C++ language came out of the laboratories and first became generally available in 1985. Many software designers recognized the powerful features of C++ and, most specifically, the object-oriented extensions to the language.

Today, the C++ language definition is found in the book *The Annotated C++ Reference Manual* by Margaret Ellis and Bjarne Stroustrup. It provides a complete definition of the language.

About Turbo C++ 3.0

Borland International first made a name for itself in 1983, with the release of the incredibly popular Turbo Pascal compiler. In 1987, the developer extended the realm of the Turbo language series with Turbo C. It included an editor, linker, and compiler, all in one complete package, known as the *Integrated Development Environment.* Turbo C proved to be a popular development platform. The package has been continuously upgraded and improved since then. Turbo C was followed with 1.5 and 2.0 versions of the product. These upgrades added integrated debugging and additional support for the C language.

In 1990, Borland released Turbo C++. It included an ANSI C and C++ compiler, a completely redesigned Integrated Development Environment, and a new project creation tool. Turbo C++'s second release upgraded the programming tools and brought additional extensions that were added to the language. In 1992, Borland introduced Turbo C++ 3.0. It is now known as the next-generation programming environment for PC-compatible computers.

Turbo C++ 3.0 is related to its big brother, Borland C++, in that it includes a similar Integrated Development Environment and language syntax. However, Borland C++ is different, because it is an expensive, professional development system that includes additional tools for software development. It also supports creation of DOS and Microsoft Windows applications, which Turbo C++ does not.

The Turbo C++ Package

The Turbo C++ package is a complete application development system for DOS. The package includes both a C (and C++) Integrated Development Environment (IDE) as well as a command-line compiler.

Turbo C++ includes the following specific features:

- An ANSI C and C++ 2.1 compiler (the two languages actually require two difference compilers).

- The IDE, which integrates the steps of editing, compiling, linking, and debugging your programs.

- A command-line compiler (however, this book uses the IDE only).

- The Borland Graphics Interface (BGI) for accessing the high resolution graphics modes available on most computers.

- A handful of valuable utility programs that make programming easier.

The Turbo C++ 3.0 package is an incredibly powerful tool that has extended the state-of-the-art in programming technology.

Compiled and Interpreted Languages

If your programming experience has been limited to BASIC, you might find some of the operations of Turbo C++ rather strange. Program development tools are divided into two broad categories: interpreted and compiled languages. BASIC is an interpreted language, whereas C is a compiled language.

A program written in a high-level language must be translated into machine language before it can be executed. Compilers (such as C and Pascal usually use) translate an entire program into machine language before executing any of the instructions. Interpreters (which is what BASIC usually is) proceed through a program by translating and then executing single instructions, one at a time.

A compiler or interpreter is itself a computer program that accepts a high-level program (for example, a C program) as input and generates a corresponding machine-language program as output. The original high-level program is called the *source code*, and the resulting machine-language program is called the *object code*. Another program takes that object code and combines it into a resulting executable file *(executable)*. This is known as *linking*.

Every high-level language must have a compiler or interpreter. If you have used GW-BASIC, BASICA, or QBASIC, you have used an interpreter.

Most implementations of C (including Turbo C++) operate as compilers. Pascal and FORTRAN are also compiled languages. Some languages have versions of interpreters and compilers available for them.

> Interpreted languages are usually more convenient to use during program development. However, once a program is error-free, a compiled version of the program will always execute much faster than an interpreted version. Most importantly, with a compiled version of the program you only need to distribute the resulting machine-language program, so your source code is not distributed.

An interpreted language requires distributing the (usually proprietary) source code of the program, and also requires the language interpreter to be present at run time to execute (or interpret) the code.

Installation of Turbo C++

Installing Turbo C++ is easy, because Borland has a superior installation program that removes most of the strain of installing a large package. This section leads you through the process of installing Turbo C++ on your system.

You must use the installation program included on the first of the program diskettes to install the package. The system files are archived (stored in a compressed form) and must be assigned to the proper directories on your hard drive. The installation program takes care of all this for you and prompts you to insert the proper diskettes at the right time.

> Before you install any application on your computer, it is wise to make backup copies of each of the diskettes. Use the DISKCOPY utility found with DOS to back up each program disk. Use only the backup copies when you install the program.

Starting the INSTALL Utility

Before installing Turbo C++, you need to check the amount of free space available on your hard drive. Turbo C++ is a large package: it requires at least 10.5 megabytes of hard disk space when all options are installed. Another 1 megabyte is required during the installation process to decompress disk files.

To begin the installation process, put the disk labeled DISK 1 in a floppy disk drive and type

n:**INSTALL**

where *n* is the floppy drive that contains the installation disk (usually A or B).

The first screen that appears (shown in Figure 1.1) welcomes you to the installation program. It also informs you about the amount of hard disk space required for full system installation. Press Enter when you are sure that the correct amount of disk space is available.

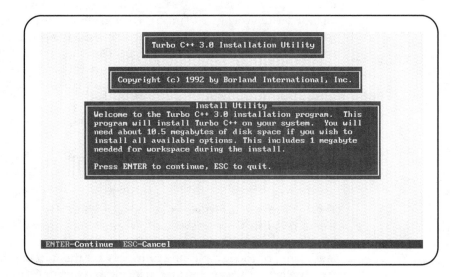

Figure 1.1. Installation program welcome screen.

The second screen (shown in Figure 1.2) asks which floppy disk drive you are using to perform the installation. To respond, just type the appropriate drive letter and press Enter.

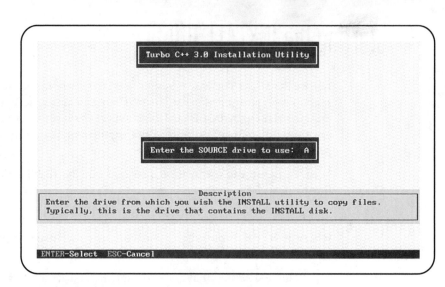

Figure 1.2. Source drive to install Turbo C++.

The third screen you see is the menu for the Turbo C++ installation utility. From this menu, you select options to specify what features will be included when you install Turbo C++ and where the files will be stored on your hard drive. Figure 1.3 shows the Turbo C++ installation utility's main menu. To modify an option on the installation menu, use the arrow keys to move the highlight bar to the option you want and press the Enter key. You are then prompted for the changes you wish to make. To return to the main menu, press the Esc key.

Using INSTALL to Customize Program Settings

The first menu item enables you to specify where the program and support files for Turbo C++ are to be placed. Although it's easier to let the installation utility place Turbo C++ program files in the default location (and some of the sample programs rely on them being there), you can specify where you want the files to be located through this menu selection (shown in Figure 1.4).

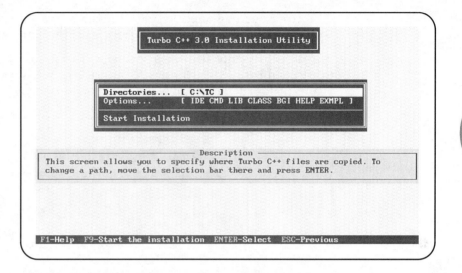

Figure 1.3. *Turbo C++ installation program main menu.*

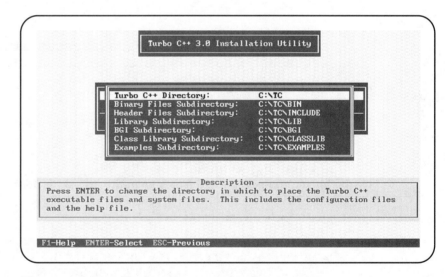

Figure 1.4. *Installation directory specification menu.*

Although most of the directory options are self-explanatory, some require extra information. The first option, Turbo C++ Directory, is the root directory for the other program subdirectories. If you modify this option, the other directories will change accordingly.

To change a subdirectory, move the cursor over the appropriate item and press Enter. Type the new directory and press Enter again.

The next option on the main menu is titled Options.... It enables you to pick and choose which parts of the package you want installed. See Figure 1.5 for an illustration of the install options menu.

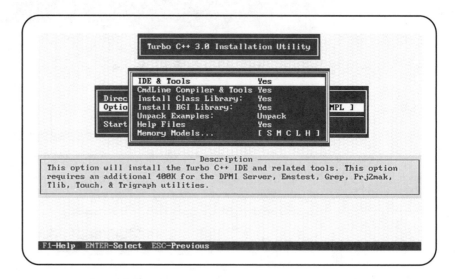

Figure 1.5. INSTALL options menu.

Unless you are working on a system with limited hard disk space, there is no reason not to install the entire package. However, if there is a specific program you know you will not use, you may prefer to conserve disk space and omit it. Each part of the package is listed. Press the Enter key when the cursor is located over an option to tell the install program not to install it. The menu options toggle between "Yes" and "No". These words indicate whether to install the option.

The Unpack Examples option may need more explanation. If you press Enter when the cursor is located over this option, it alternates between Unpack, Packed, and No. If you choose the No options, the sample programs will not be installed on your hard drive. If you choose Packed, the sample programs will be installed; however, they will be compressed. You will need to use the decompression program as a separate step to get to them. The Unpack option tells the installation program to copy the sample programs to your hard drive and decompress them all at one time. The reason you are given several choices is that the sample programs take up a large amount of disk space. Some users want to have them available but don't want to sacrifice the hard disk space for them.

Another option that requires further explanation is the Memory Models... option at the bottom of the Options... menu. When you choose this option, the installation program will ask you what memory models you want to use, as shown in Figure 1.6. If you are not familiar with memory models, this may be a confusing question.

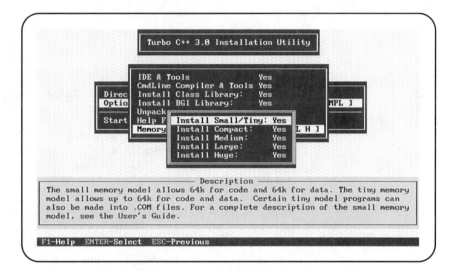

Figure 1.6. *Selecting among memory model options.*

The reason for this question has to do with the segmented architecture of the 8086, 286, 386, and 486 microprocessors. A program consists of both code and data. Code or data that fits in a single segment executes quickly. When code or data exceeds the size of a segment, which is 64K, it is accessed differently internally and as a result executes more slowly.

Depending on the type of application being developed, the programmer must select a memory model large enough to accommodate the program but not unnecessarily large because larger models reduce execution speed. Refer to Table 1.1 as you specify which memory models to install.

Table 1.1. Memory model specifications.

Memory Model	Meaning
Tiny	All code and data must reside in a single 64K segment.
Small	Your code has 64K available to it, and your data has 64K available to it.
Compact	64K is available to your code, and 1MB is available to your data.
Medium	1MB is available to your code, and 64K is available to your data.
Large	Your code has 1MB available to it, and your data has 1MB available to it.
Huge	Sizes are the same as for the large model, but address arithmetic is performed in such a way that an array can span multiple segments.

C and C++ use library routines to perform input, output, math, and other operations. Each group of library routines comes in five different versions, which correspond to each available memory model. (The tiny and small memory models use the same routines.)

You can specify the memory models you plan to use, and the installation program will copy the files containing the appropriate routines to your hard drive. The routines for all the memory models are installed by default. The files containing these routines take up considerable disk space, so you may choose to install only some of the memory models.

Most of the examples in this book can be compiled with the small memory model. So unless you know you are going to need another model, you might want to specify only the single memory model to save disk space.

Once you have entered your settings for the items in the installation utility's main menu, you can begin the actual installation. To do this, press the F9 key or position the cursor over the menu item Start Installation and press Enter. All you have to do at this point is place each disk in the drive when you see a prompt like that in Figure 1.7. The installation program takes care of the rest.

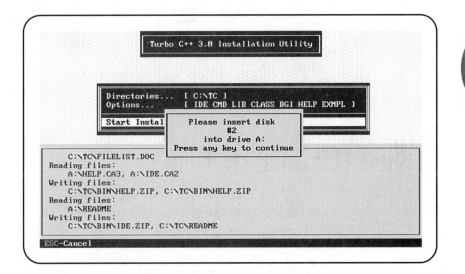

Figure 1.7. The installation program prompt for another disk.

When you finish copying files, you will be given the opportunity to view the contents of the README file. It is important to look over the file and make note of any last minute changes to the program and documentation. To make a hardcopy output of the file on your printer, type the following line from the DOS prompt:

`COPY n:\TC\README LPT1:`

(where *n:* is the letter of your hard drive where you installed Turbo C++). If you changed the name of the directory in which Turbo C++ files were installed, use that name instead of \TC. When you press the Enter key, the entire contents of the file will be printed on the printer connected to your system. If you are using a laser printer, remember to press the Form Feed button to clear the buffer internal to the printer and print any remaining pages in the printer's memory.

When the installation is complete, you need to update the number of FILES specified in your CONFIG.SYS file and modify the PATH command in your AUTOEXEC.BAT file. For example, to set the number of files in your CONFIG.SYS file, use an editor and modify the CONFIG.SYS file by adding the following line:

`FILES=20`

To change the PATH specification for your system, add the following statement to the AUTOEXEC.BAT file:

`PATH=C:\TC\BIN`

Again, change \TC if you stored Turbo C++ under a different directory name. After you reboot your computer, the revisions will take effect.

That completes the installation of Turbo C++. In the next chapter you'll explore how to use the IDE to write your first C program.

What You Have Learned

In this chapter you learned the history of the C and C++ programming languages. You found out how Borland International became a major force in the compiler business. You learned, step-by-step, how to install Turbo C++ 3.0 on your own system. The following topics were covered in this chapter:

- The C programming language was developed by Brian Kernighan and Dennis Ritchie from AT&T Bell Labs.

- The UNIX operating system was written in C. Since then, the language is available on just about every major (and minor) operating system.

- ANSI C is the standard definition of the language begun by the American National Standards Institute in 1983 and completed in 1988. It provides a basis on which all C compilers can be compared.

- C++ is a superset of the C programming language. The biggest improvement to the language is the addition of classes, which form the basis for object-oriented programming. However, there are other small features that make the language more powerful.

- Turbo C++ is the newest version of a series of language tools from Borland International. It includes an ANSI C and C++ compiler with the ability to create programs for DOS.

- Every program written in a high-level language must be translated into machine language before it can be executed. The two broad categories of software development tools are interpreters and compilers.

● In a compiled language, the high-level program instructions are called *source code*, and the resulting machine-language program is what you execute when you want to run the program.

● Compilers translate an entire program into machine language before executing any of the instructions. Programs usually take longer to develop with a compiler; however, execution speed is drastically faster than with interpreted code.

● Interpreters proceed to convert a program by translating and executing single instructions at runtime. Interpreters are easier to program in (compared to compilers), but the resulting program is slow, and the source code must be distributed for the program to be used.

● Turbo C++ is installed with the INSTALL program included with the package. It takes care of creating the necessary directories on your hard drive as well as decompressing the program files. It also copies the correct files from the distribution disks to your hard drive.

2

Programming Environment

Goals

After reading this chapter, you will

- Be able to start the Integrated Development Environment (IDE).

- Know the basic elements of the IDE.

- Understand the main menu commands in the IDE and how they are used.

- Know about the windowing system that is part of the Turbo C++ IDE and its editor window.

- Recognize the five types of controls found in a dialog box and what they are used for.

- Know what the status line is for.

● Understand what hot keys are and how to select one listed on the status line.

● Be familiar with editor operations: use of the basic cursor movement keys, functions of the clipboard, and techniques for search and replace functions.

● Know how to use the built-in help system of the IDE.

With the Integrated Development Environment (IDE) of Turbo C++, you can do all your programming work in one convenient environment. The IDE integrates all the tools you need so that you can be a productive and efficient programmer. This chapter introduces you to the IDE and helps you to start using its features immediately. You can think of this chapter as a tour guide to the IDE.

You will learn how to start the IDE. You will see what the elements that make up the Integrated Development Environment are. You will learn the main menu commands and get an idea of what they are used for. By the end of the chapter you will learn how to use an editor window. In the process, you will learn the essential hot keys and cursor movement keys that will help you get the most of the IDE. You will also learn how to access the powerful Borland help system for context-sensitive help.

The Integrated Development Environment

Starting the Integrated Development Environment is simple. To execute the IDE, simply type

TC

at the DOS prompt and press the Enter key. When Turbo C++ begins execution you will see the screen shown in Figure 2.1. This gives basic information about the product. Press the Enter key to continue.

The About box gives product information and version numbers about the product. If you press Alt+I, a scrolling marque will display a list of the programmers who created the product for you!

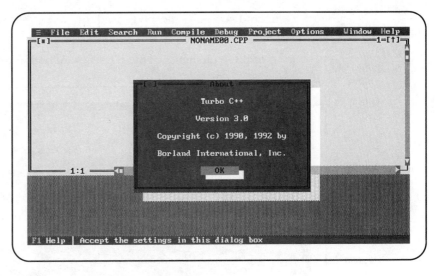

Figure 2.1. *Turbo C++ About box.*

You will next be presented with an open window displayed in the programming environment, resembling that of Figure 2.2. It consists of the following four elements:

- *The main menu bar*. The menu system gives you access to Turbo C++'s powerful tools. You use the utilities and features by selecting an option from the menu bar. The menu bar is the first line of the screen. The commands on the menu bar access each of the major groups of utilities found in the environment.

- *The editor window*. The editor window enables you to edit and modify C programs. An editor window is part of the windowing system inherent to the IDE. A variety of different types of windows are available for editing programs, debugging programs, and viewing a program's operation. When you first start Turbo C++, it creates an editor window for a file called NONAME00.CPP. Later, you will learn how to open and close your own editor windows.

- *The desktop*. The desktop is the background gray pattern on which all windows are displayed. It provides an area for you to work with multiple windows.

- *The status line*. The last line of the screen displays shortcut keys for carrying out some of the most commonly used commands in Turbo C++. The status line gives you information about what a

command you have chosen is used for, and it tells you what Turbo C++ is doing.

Each of these elements of the IDE is examined in this chapter.

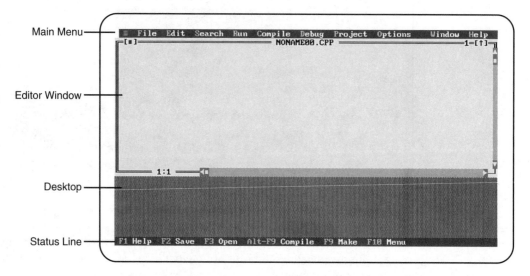

Figure 2.2. The Integrated Development Environment.

The Turbo C++ Integrated Development Environment can be operated using either the keyboard or the mouse. Although the mouse is not required, mouse support has been carefully integrated into the environment, and a mouse is certainly a useful tool in making the most of the product.

The Menu System

The menu system is used to access the features of the Integrated Development Environment. You can load or save files, set options, and access features of the compiler through the menus. The system provides commands for handling files, for editing programs, for compiling or debugging programs, for modifying options, for working with the windowing system, and for obtaining help.

If you have a mouse, you must tell your computer to recognize the presence of the mouse. You can tell that your mouse is active by moving it. If a small rectangle (the size of a single character) moves around the screen, you know that your mouse is active.

To tell your computer that you have a mouse, include a line similar to

```
DEVICE=MOUSE.SYS
```

in your CONFIG.SYS configuration file, located in the root directory of your computer. Most mouse devices sold today come with this piece of software, appropriately called a *mouse driver*. If your mouse did not come with it, check with the manufacturer of the mouse; you need the driver to use the mouse with most programs.

You can enter the menu system in three ways:

- Press the F10 key to make the menu bar active and use the arrow keys to move the menu bar to the menu option you wish to select. Then press Enter or use the Down arrow key.

- Press the Alt key along with the first letter of the command on the menu you want to select. The first letter of each menu title on the menu bar is highlighted in a different color.

- Click the mouse on the command in the menu bar you want to select.

Some menu commands are context sensitive: They are only accessible while you are doing certain tasks. Depending on the state of your work, only certain menu options are available. The unavailable options are displayed in gray and cannot be selected.

Many times a command in the main level of the menus will lead to another option. Each menu command that is followed by a series of ellipsis marks (...) displays a dialog box. You use the dialog box to set additional options. Dialog boxes such as that in Figure 2.3 pop up, enabling you to make several choices about the command you have selected.

Some menu commands are followed by an arrow (→) that leads to another popup menu. You can make further selections from that menu, which in turn often leads to a dialog box.

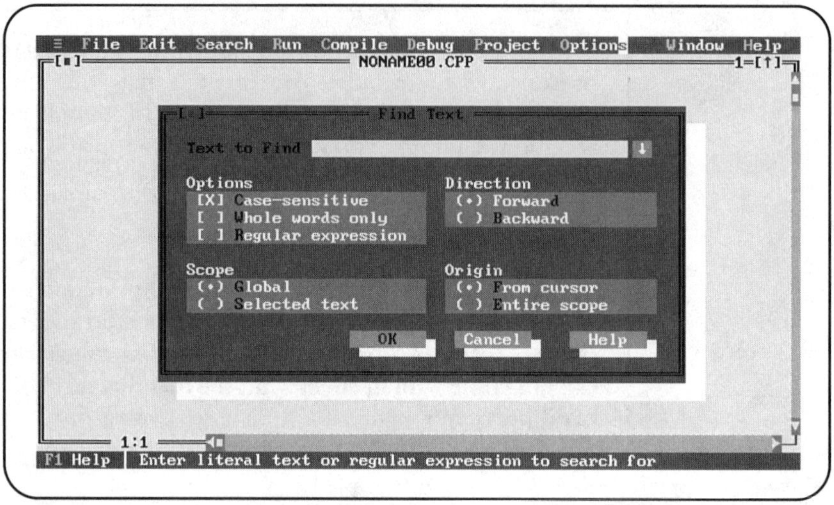

Figure 2.3. *A typical dialog box.*

You can press the Esc key at any time to hide a menu. No menu selection method is best; you will develop your own habits quickly. Many times the best selection method is to use a combination of the procedures.

Let's briefly review the main menu options:

=   Called the system menu, this clears or restores the screen and executes various utility programs either supplied with Turbo C++ or purchased separately. Press Alt+Spacebar to select this menu with the keyboard.

File   This menu enables you to create, open, save, and print program files. Through this menu you can exit the IDE.

Edit   You use this menu to cut, copy, paste, and clear text in edit windows, and to restore deleted text. You can also view the contents of the system clipboard with an option on this menu.

Search   This menu offers powerful tools for searching and replacing text in edit windows, for finding compile-time errors in your files, and jumping to specific line numbers in your files.

Run	You use this menu to run your programs and to debug your programs using the integrated debugger that is part of the IDE.
Compile	The compile menu is used to compile your programs or to make or build programs that are built on several different files.
Debug	This menu enables you to set various debugging options, including setting breakpoints, and to view variables.
Project	The project menu enables you to manage multifile programs through the project make facility.
Options	With the options menu you can change various default settings in the Turbo C++ compiler and linker as well as change the directories used by Turbo C++. The default settings are adequate for most programming tasks. For now, simply accept the default settings. As you use Turbo C++ more, you will learn how to customize it through this menu.
Window	The Window menu contains options used to manage various windows within the IDE. This menu is especially helpful if you are not using a mouse. Options enable you to arrange the windows on the desktop and to access specific windows from a list.
Help	The Help menu contains a powerful online help system. You can obtain help on every aspect of the Turbo C++ IDE, including information on the C and C++ programming languages.

The Window System

Turbo C++ performs most tasks inside a window. The IDE is based on the concept of windows. A window is a specific portion of the screen. All windows have similar characteristics. Several kinds of windows are available. They provide areas in which you can write your programs, see program output, debug problem code, and display status information. Figure 2.4 shows a typical editor window.

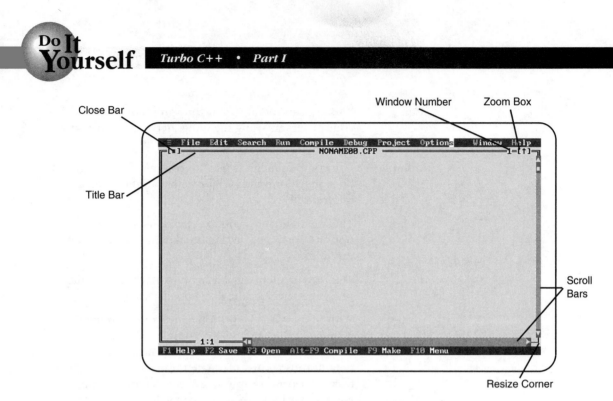

Figure 2.4. Features of a typical editor window.

A number of editor windows can be open on the desktop at a single time; the number is limited only by the amount of memory you have on your computer. The window you are working with is called the *active window*. The active window appears on top of all the other windows and is enclosed with a double-lined border.

When multiple editor windows are open, you can move between windows using both the keyboard and the mouse. To make a window active, use the mouse and click anywhere in the window. Using the keyboard, you will select List from the Window menu and choose the description of the window you wish to make active.

An editor window is made up of the following elements:

- *Title bar*. The title bar, located at the top of the window, describes what the window is used for. Editor windows contain the filename of the file currently being edited in the window. To move a window, move the mouse pointer so that it is on the top border of the window. Press and hold the left mouse button and drag the window to its new location. A window that is enlarged to full screen size cannot be moved.

- *Close box*. The close box is located in the upper left corner of the window and is identified by a small square inside brackets. Clicking the close box with the mouse removes the window from the desktop. To close a window by using the keyboard, choose the Close command from the Window menu.

- *Zoom box*. The zoom box, located in the upper right corner, consists of an up-arrow character. It is used to enlarge the size of a window. Once a window is enlarged to the full size of the desktop, the zoom box appears as a double-sided arrow. Clicking it again reduces the window to its previous size. The menu-equivalent command is Zoom from the Window menu.

- *Window number*. The window number, to the left of the zoom box, helps you identify open editor windows. At any time you can press the Alt key in combination with the window number to make that window active. This works for the first nine windows you have open. If you have more than this amount opened, you should use the List All option on the Window menu (or press Alt+0) to choose from a list of windows.

- *Scroll bars*. Vertical and horizontal scroll bars enable you to scroll text in a window using the mouse. Vertical scroll bars move through a file one line at a time by clicking the Up or Down arrow. A slider box moves along the scroll bar, indicating the relative position in the file. You can click the scroll bar, and the text in the window will page up or down depending on which side of the scroll bar you clicked.

- *Resize corner*. You can drag any resize corner to change the size of the window. To change the size or position of a window using the menus, select Window and choose the Size/Move option. Now, using the arrow keys, you can move the window around the screen. To change its size, hold down the Shift key along with one of the arrow keys.

Dialog Boxes

Menu selections that are followed with an ellipsis (...) will cause a dialog box to be displayed, as Figure 2.5 illustrates. A dialog box "pops up" for

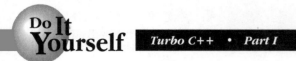
some of the menu commands, enabling you to make several choices about the command you have selected. Most dialog boxes contain one or more of the following items:

- Radio buttons

- List boxes

- Input boxes

- Check boxes

- Action buttons

```
 ≡  File  Edit  Search  Run  Compile  Debug  Project  Options    Window  Help
┌─[■]──────────────────────── NONAME00.CPP ════════════════════════1=[↑]─┐
│       ┌─[ ]──────────────── Open a File ──────┐                         │
│       │ Name                                  │                         │
│       │ D:\TC\*.C                      ↓│   ┌─────────┐                  │
│       │                                   │   Open    │                  │
│       │ Files                          └─────────┘                  │
│       │ BGI\                           ┌─────────┐                  │
│       │ BIN\                           │ Replace   │                  │
│       │ CLASSLIB\                      └─────────┘                  │
│       │ DOC\                                                         │
│       │ EXAMPLES\                                                    │
│       │ INCLUDE\                       ┌─────────┐                  │
│       │ LIB\                           │ Cancel    │                  │
│       │ ..\                            └─────────┘                  │
│       │ ◄                          ►  ┌─────────┐                  │
│       │                                │ Help      │                  │
│       │ D:\TC\*.C                      └─────────┘                  │
│       │ BGI         Directory  Mar 4,1992    6:54pm                  │
│       └─────────────────────────────────────────┘                  │
│    1:1                                                                  │
├─ F1 Help │ Type for incremental search: lower for files, upper for directories ─┤
```

Figure 2.5. *Sample Open a File dialog box.*

Radio buttons are a list of mutually exclusive options. That is, you can only choose one item from a group of commands. A radio button list takes the following form:

( ) Option 1

(o) Option 2

.

.

.

( ) Final Option

To select a radio button, tab to the list or click one of the buttons. Next, use the arrow keys to change the selection or click on the desired selection using the mouse.

A *list box* provides a list of items from which you can choose. To activate the list box, press Tab until the box is active or click on it using the mouse. Once the list box is activated, select the item you want by moving the highlight to the appropriate item and pressing the Enter key. You can also double-click the item using the mouse.

An *input box* lets you type text into a box and use the basic editing keys to work with the text you enter. If the input box is followed by a down-arrow character, a history list is associated with the input box. The history list contains entries you have previously used in the input box. This feature is useful if you want to repeat or modify a previous command.

To activate the list box, press Tab until the box is active or click it. When the box is activated, select the item you want by moving the highlight to the appropriate item and pressing Enter (or by clicking the item). You activate the history list by pressing the Down arrow key when you are in an input box, or by clicking the down-arrow symbol. If you don't want to use any of the selections in the history list, press Esc to cancel the list.

Check boxes are used to turn an option on or off. A check box looks similar to this:

[X] Option Name

[ ] Another Option

[X] Still another Option

If the check box contains an X, that option is turned on. If the check box does not contain an X, that option is turned off. Often, several check boxes are grouped together when they apply to the same topic. To change the state of a check box, tab to the box and use the arrow keys to select a particular check box, then press the Spacebar to toggle the option. With a mouse, clicking the check box toggles it on or off.

Action buttons trigger an immediate action when you select them. There are two types of action buttons: standard and default. The default action button (there can only be one) is highlighted differently and is automatically selected when you press the Enter key in a dialog box when the cursor is located over any control other than another action button.

To activate an action button, press the Tab key until the action button is highlighted, then press Enter. If you use a mouse, simply click the appropriate button.

Most dialog boxes have action buttons for OK, Cancel, and Help. OK is used to accept the new dialog box settings. Cancel is used to abort the dialog box entirely. Help opens up a help window that describes how to use the dialog box.

There may be other action buttons in a dialog box that relate to the specific function of the dialog box.

The Status Line

The line on the bottom of the screen is called the *status line,* because it displays a short comment relating to whatever you are currently doing. The status line changes as you switch windows or change activities.

When you have selected a menu command, the status line changes to display a summary of the function relating to the selected menu item. For example, when the File main menu option is selected (press F10 to select it now), the status line displays the following:

```
F1 Help ¦ File-management commands (Open, Save, Print, etc.)
```

The value of the information displayed on the status line is that it provides a visual clue about the meaning of whatever is the current focus of the IDE.

One of the most common status lines is the one you see when you're using an editor window. It looks like this:

```
F1 Help  F2 Save  F3 Open  Alt-F9 Compile  F9 Make  F10 Menu
```

The line shows the hot keys available while you are working in an editor window. Turbo C++'s most common operations can be activated directly without going through the menu system.

These operations are activated by hotkeys, which are various key combinations that are displayed to the right of various menu entries. You can move the mouse cursor over the status line and click on the associated hotkey item to carry out. Table 2.1. summarizes the hotkeys available while you are working in an editor window.

Table 2.1. Hotkeys available in an editor window.

Key	Description
F1	Display Help screen
F2	Save file
F3	Load file
F4	Execute program to location where cursor is positioned
F5	Zoom the active window
F6	Make the next window the active one
F7	Execute single line of program code
F8	Procedure step through code
F9	Compile current program
F10	Make menu bar active

Using the Editor

When the IDE begins executing, an editor window is created and made active. An editor window enables you to type in and modify program code. The title bar contains the filename of the file currently being edited. As mentioned earlier, when you first start the IDE, an editor window is created with the filename NONAME00.CPP.

At the bottom left of the editor window, the number of the current line and column position of the cursor are displayed. If a file has been modified, an asterisk (*) will appear to the left of the column and line numbers.

When an editor window is active and you are not working with menus or in a dialog box, the window is ready to accept input. You can start typing text, and text will appear in the editor window at the current location of the cursor. When you start, the cursor should be positioned in the upper left corner of the editor window.

The editor starts out in *insert mode*. This means that as you type text, it will be inserted at the cursor's current location. An alternate mode is called *overwrite mode*. This mode enables you to write over existing text. You toggle between the two modes by pressing the Insert key. The shape of the cursor identifies the current editor mode. Insert mode is identified by an underscore character for the cursor. Overwrite mode is identified by a large rectangle cursor.

Using the editor is quite easy and rather intuitive. What you type appears on the screen at the current cursor location. Pressing the Enter key inserts a new line and moves the cursor to the start of the next line. The Backspace key deletes the character to the left of the cursor. The Delete key removes the character directly under the cursor.

Pressing the PageUp or PageDown key scrolls the window up or down a screen at a time. To move through text quickly, you can combine the action of several keys with the Ctrl key. Pressing Ctrl-Left arrow or Ctrl-Right arrow moves the cursor to the beginning of the previous or next word. Pressing Ctrl-PageUp moves the cursor to the beginning of the file. Ctrl-PageDown moves the cursor to the end of the file. Table 2.2. summarizes the commonly used editing commands.

Table 2.2. Common cursor keyboard commands.

Key	*Description*
Arrow keys	Move cursor one unit in appropriate direction
PageUp	Scroll window one screen up
PageDown	Scroll window one screen down
Home	Move cursor to beginning of line
End	Move cursor to last character of line
Enter	Insert line, move to beginning of next line
Backspace	Removes character to the left of cursor
Delete	Removes character under the cursor
Insert	Toggle between insert and overwrite mode
Ctrl-Left arrow	Move cursor left one word
Ctrl-Right arrow	Move cursor right one word

Key	Description
Ctrl-PageUp	Move cursor to beginning of file
Ctrl-PageDown	Move cursor to end of file
Ctrl-Y	Delete current line

To gain experience with using the editor, make sure that an editor window is active (by choosing the File New menu command), and start typing some text. If you make a mistake, you can use the previously mentioned keys to correct it. Now try inserting a line of text. Remember to place the editor in insert mode and press Enter. Then type the line of text you want to insert. Don't worry about saving the file; this is just your experiment.

The Clipboard Commands

The editor enables you to manipulate a block of text. Once you have selected a block of text, you can easily copy it to a new location, move it, or delete it. The Edit menu gives you access to the set of options for working on blocks of text.

There are several ways to mark a block of text. The easiest method is to move the cursor to the beginning of the area you want to work on, hold down the Shift key, and move the cursor. At the end of the text you wish selected, let go of the Shift key. The highlighted text is now the selected block. To use the mouse for selecting text, move the mouse cursor to the beginning of the text you wish to mark and press and hold down the left mouse button. Move the mouse cursor to the end of the text and let go of the left mouse button (this operation is known as *dragging*). The block should now be highlighted.

At this time, several options on the Edit menu become active, as shown in Figure 2.6. The Cut option removes the text from the cursor location and stores it in the clipboard. The *clipboard* is the location of memory that is used to temporarily store a block of text. The Copy menu option copies the highlighted text and stores it in the clipboard. The Clear command deletes the currently selected text but does not store it in memory.

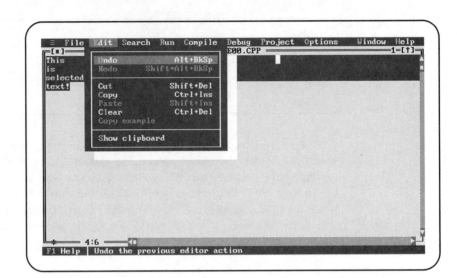

Figure 2.6. The Edit menu.

You can use the Show Clipboard command found on the Edit menu to view or modify the contents of the clipboard (see Figure 2.7). Selecting this option displays the Clipboard window with the currently selected clipboard contents. To return to the window you were working on, close the window using the Close option on the Window menu or click the close box.

To insert the text currently in the clipboard into an edit window, you choose the Paste command on the Edit menu. The result is the current contents of the clipboard are copied and inserted at the location of the cursor in the active editor window. The text will still be in the clipboard, so you can copy the contents of the clipboard as many times as you like by selecting Paste.

You can use the Cut option on the Edit menu to remove currently highlighted text from an editor window and insert it to the clipboard. This step is useful if you need to move text rather than copy it.

Sometimes, when copying large amounts of text to the clipboard, you may want to clear the clipboard before continuing your editing operation to give your program more memory. The easiest way to delete the clipboard contents is to select a single character (like a space). When you copy that text to the clipboard, the previous clipboard contents are removed.

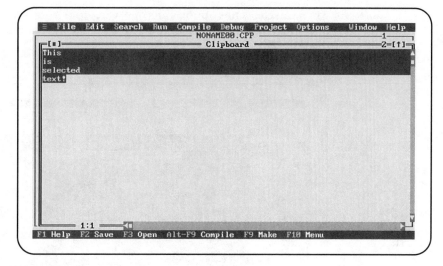

Figure 2.7. *The Clipboard window.*

Searching Operations

To find a specific sequence of characters, use the Find option on the Search menu. The dialog box shown in Figure 2.8 will prompt you to type the string you wish to search for and to specify any of the various search options. The default settings cause the search to begin from the current cursor position and move forward. The default search is also case sensitive.

You can change these Find settings so the search moves in the opposite direction by selecting the Backward option. You can also have the search start at the beginning of the file by choosing the Entire scope option. When the search is case sensitive, it means that upper- and lowercase characters are treated separately, and the search will find only the case you use to type the characters in the dialog box. However, you may sometimes want to do a case-insensitive search to find all instances of the characters whether they are upper-, lower-, or mixed case. For a case-insensitive search, make sure the Case-sensitive option is not selected.

If the Whole words only option is checked, it tells the editor to search for a character that is not part of a full word. In other words, distinctions will be made between strings contained in other strings. For example, when you check this option and your searching string is Rem, just instances of *Rem* are found, not the three characters inside another string, such as *Rembrandt*.

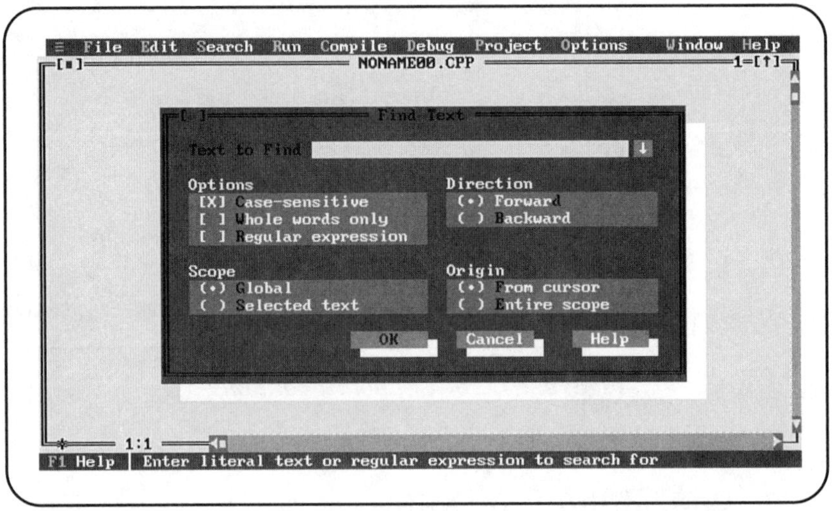

Figure 2.8. Find Text dialog box.

If you check the Regular Expression box, you can use wildcard characters in your searches. You can confine the search to a currently selected block by selecting the Selected text option.

You repeat a search using previously entered options by choosing the Search Again option from the Search menu. A simpler method is to press the Ctrl-L key combination. This is a convenient method to use when you want to search through a file quickly and there are multiple copies of the string you are searching.

You can do a search and replace operation by choosing the Replace option on the Search menu. This displays the Search and Replace dialog box, which is shown in Figure 2.9. Its options are similar to those in the Find Text dialog box. Besides entering the text to find, you also enter the text you want to replace the previous text with.

```
 ≡ File  Edit  Search  Run  Compile  Debug  Project  Options    Window  Help
┌─[■]─────────────────────── NONAME00.CPP ══════════════════════════1═[↑]┐
│  ┌─[▪]────────────────── Replace Text ──────────────┐                  ▓│
│  │                                                  │                  ▒│
│  │ Text to Find  ┌─────────────────────────────┬↓┐ │                   │
│  │               └─────────────────────────────┴─┘ │                   │
│  │ New Text      ┌─────────────────────────────┬↓┐ │                   │
│  │               └─────────────────────────────┴─┘ │                   │
│  │ Options              Direction                   │                   │
│  │ [X] Case-sensitive   (•) Forward                 │                   │
│  │ [ ] Whole words only ( ) Backward                │                   │
│  │ [ ] Regular expression                           │                   │
│  │ [X] Prompt on replace                            │                   │
│  │                                                  │                   │
│  │ Scope                Origin                      │                   │
│  │ (•) Global           (•) From cursor             │                   │
│  │ ( ) Selected text    ( ) Entire scope            │                   │
│  │  ┌────────┐ ┌────────────┐ ┌────────┐ ┌──────┐   │                   │
│  │  │   OK   │ │ Change All │ │ Cancel │ │ Help │   │                   │
│  │  └────────┘ └────────────┘ └────────┘ └──────┘   │                   │
│  └──────────────────────────────────────────────────┘                  ▼│
├─*───── 1:1 ──────◄■────────────────────────────────────────────────────┤
│ F1 Help │ Enter literal text or regular expression to search for         │
└──────────────────────────────────────────────────────────────────────────┘
```

Figure 2.9. *Search and Replace Dialog Box.*

> Before any of your code is changed, the editor will prompt you to
> make sure you want to carry out the operation.

You can turn this option off by deselecting (clicking again) the
Prompt on replace option.

Getting Help

When you select the Help menu option by pressing Alt+H, you see various
menu selections for obtaining help. The IDE includes an extensive help
facility. It gives you information about the IDE itself, the C language, and
the runtime library routines. The Help menu leads to six menu options.

Selecting a menu option leads to a help window. You can move,
resize, zoom, and close help windows just like editor windows. You will
find hot keys associated with several help commands for instant access to
valuable information.

The Contents option displays the table of contents to the help system, some of which appears in Figure 2.10. You can leave an open help window on the desktop, so you can refer to it while programming.

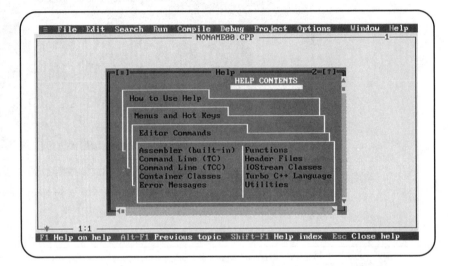

Figure 2.10. Help table of contents.

Help screens often contain highlighted keywords that you choose to get more information. You press Tab to move to a keyword, and press Enter to get more information. With a mouse, you double-click the left mouse button on a keyword and the information for that item will be displayed.

The Help Index option displays a list of help topics like those in Figure 2.11. You scroll the list using the cursor movement keys or with the mouse and the scroll bars. You can search the list by typing letters from the keyboard. When you type a letter, the help system goes to the help topics that begin with that letter. If you continue typing letters, it will try to find a specific help topic. To display the information on an item, press Enter.

For example, in the index list type the letter **P**, then watch as the list jumps to the beginning of entries that start with that letter. Typing more characters narrows the search down. Type **r**, and the search moves to the word starting *pr.* You will find the help index an invaluable method of obtaining information. It is even easier than searching through manuals, because the computer does the search for you.

The Topic Search option gives help on the word on which the cursor is currently located. If an item is not in the help system, the help index displays the closest match.

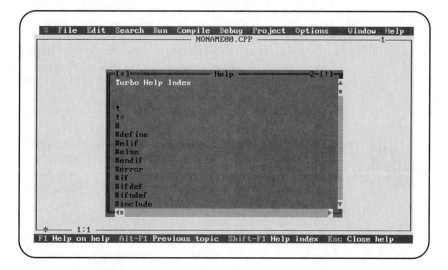

Figure 2.11. *Help index window.*

Several hot keys make using the help system easy. Pressing F1 anytime displays a help window. Pressing Shift+F1 displays the help index, enabling you to type in additional characters to narrow the search. To conduct a topic search, press Ctrl+F1. It makes it easy to move the cursor over a keyword in an editor window and instantly to display help for that topic. Finally, Alt+F1 redisplays the help text you viewed last. You can go back through a maximum of 20 previous help screens.

Exiting Back to DOS

To leave the IDE, select the File option and choose the Quit (or press Alt+X). If the file or files you have been working on have been modified, a message prompts you to save the file to disk before exiting.

Before you quit, the IDE creates a desktop file, updates it, and writes it to disk. This desktop file (with the extension .DSK) keeps track of the editor windows currently open. In this way, when you restart the IDE, those same files that were on the desktop when you exited will display in the same location with the exact same size. This makes it easy to pick up where you left off and continue working efficiently.

You have taken a full tour of the IDE in this chapter. You learned how to use menus, how to manipulate windows, and how to gain access to the help system. Now that you know how to use the IDE, the next chapter will start you in writing a program.

What You Have Learned

This chapter presented the elements of the Turbo C++ IDE. You became acquainted with many useful functions found in the environment. In particular, the following topics were covered:

- The Integrated Development Environment is started by typing **TC** at the DOS prompt and pressing the Enter key.

- The IDE is made up of the following elements: the main menu bar, editor windows, the desktop, and the status line.

- The main menu is used to access the features of the IDE. To select a menu you press F10 and use the arrow keys to move to the appropriate menu selection, or you press Alt along with the first letter of the main menu command you want to access. To use the mouse, click on the command in the menu bar you want to select.

- The windowing system makes up a large part of the interface between the IDE and the user. Each window has certain attributes that make using the environment easier.

- Dialog boxes enable you to enter additional information that you cannot enter through the menu system. Dialog boxes are made up of controls. The five types of controls include radio buttons, list boxes, input boxes, check boxes, and action buttons.

- The status line is located on the bottom of the screen and displays short comments relating to whatever you are currently doing.

- Hotkeys are keys that carry out Turbo C++'s most common operations directly from the keyboard, without having to go through the menu system. Hotkeys are usually displayed to the right of menu commands and on the status line.

- The editor has two modes: insert and overwrite. Insert mode sandwiches new text between the previous and subsequent text at the current cursor location. Overwrite mode writes over characters that are located at the cursor. Switch between the two modes using the Insert key.

- A variety of methods are provided for moving the cursor in an editor window. Table 2.2 provides a list of the most commonly used ones.

- The clipboard is a temporary location in memory that enables you to store information you want to copy, cut, or paste to a new location.

- You can use the Find option on the Search menu to locate a specific string of text in an editor window. The Replace option searches for a string and replaces another string with it.

- The IDE help system is called up with the F1 key and gives help on just about every part of the environment.

3

C Program Structure

Goals

After reading this chapter, you will

- Know what steps are involved in writing a computer program.

- Be able to edit, link, and compile a simple C program using the Turbo C++ IDE.

- Recognize the fundamental parts of a C program.

- Know what character set (type of characters) is recognized by the C compiler.

- Understand what an identifier is and what keywords are used for in a C program.

- Know what the C preprocessor is and how to use a preprocessor directive.

- Know what the main( ) function is used for. The reader will begin to see how functions form the basis of C programming.

- Recognize a C++ comment and know how to create one.

Now that you have installed Turbo C++ and have become familiar with the basic layout of the Integrated Development Environment (IDE), you are ready to start programming in C. You need to know what components are necessary to create a C program, and how to enter and run a program in Turbo C++.

This chapter presents a simple program and explain what it does. You will learn about the fundamental program structure of the C programming language. You will learn how to create a stand-alone program of your own.

First, you can gain an overview of programming by following the breakdown of a C program into steps and examining each one separately.

Five Steps to a C Program

The steps in this section will guide you through the process of writing a complete program. The checklist breaks the process of writing a C program in Turbo C++ into five distinct steps.

Step 1. Analyze the Problem

Begin with a clear idea of what you want a program to do. Most programs are written to solve a problem. Clearly outline what problem the program must solve. Consider what sort of input the program needs to work with and what the program will provide as output. As you analyze the problem, it is usually best to get pen and paper (or word processor and keyboard) together and write down on paper exactly what the program is going to do.

Step 2. Design the Program

Decide how the program will work. Choose what the user interface will be like. Will it use a text-based or graphical interface? Will it be command-line or menu driven? These fundamental decisions affect your choices for how the program will operate. Work out any algorithms required by the program. If you are writing a program to compute compound interest, make sure you have the formulas you will need so you can turn them into instructions to the compiler.

Step 3. Implement the Program by Writing Code

With a clear idea of what you want the program to do, design the code to carry out the goals of your program description. This is where you use the C language to make your program description a reality. Your knowledge of the language is most important at this step. You will use both your analysis of the problem and your program design documents you created in steps 1 and 2.

To implement the program you need to know the C programming statements and instructions that are compiled by the Turbo C++ system.

This is the step in which you start using the IDE to type in and edit the source code for the program.

Step 4. Compile and Run the Program

Before you can actually execute the program, you must compile it. Because the IDE has the compiler integrated into it, the compilation step is fast and easy. This is the stage where the C language code is converted from high-level source code to the machine-level instructions actually recognized by the computer's microprocessor.

The compiler also makes sure that the program you typed in is grammatically correct. Just as the English language has rules of grammar and structure that are correct, the compiler has rules of grammar and structure it understands. Unlike humans, however, who can understand

language that isn't absolutely perfect, the compiler requires adherence to the C++ rules of grammar and structure.

To execute the program, you usually type its filename from the DOS prompt. However, after compiling and linking your program, the IDE will automatically execute the program, so you can see the results of your program without exiting to DOS.

Step 5. Test and Debug the Program

Now that you have a running program, you must make sure it works as you expected. For simple programs, this step can be as easy as executing the code once and making sure the results are acceptable. On larger programs, you may wish to obtain the help of others to test your program in a number of different situations. This program testing stage is usually referred to as "beta testing." Beta testing can be a valuable time in program development, because you get feedback from people who are going to be using your program. Several rounds of changes may be necessary to isolate and resolve program "bugs." Thus, this revision process has been dubbed "debugging."

The result is a program that performs as expected. Sometimes your final program is released to other people and you will find that it is not working correctly. If this happens, you must go back and change the code that is causing the error and then replace all the operating copies of the program. Obviously, it's preferable to address errors before the code is distributed as final.

The five programming steps are outlined in Figure 3.1.

✓ Analyze the Problem
✓ Design the Program
✓ Write the Code
✓ Compile and Run
✓ Test and Debug

Figure 3.1. *The steps in program development.*

Programming is not always a straightforward process as just described. Sometimes you will skip a step, and other times you will go back and forth between steps. For example, after you have laid out a description of what you want the program to do and you have started programming, your customer (or boss or co-worker) might add another requirement to the project. At this time, you must go back and add this to the description of the project and work it into the design of the program.

Develop the habit of planning your project before you begin coding. It is smart to write down the objectives of your program and outline the design before you start coding. If you shortcut these steps, you will run into problems later. If you do follow the steps, you will reap rewards down the road in time saved and deadlines met.

A Simple C Program

This section shows you what basic components are necessary to execute a C program. You will learn how to edit, compile, link, and run a simple C program. Later, the chapter examines this program in detail.

The first time you look at a C program, it may appear cryptic and confusing. After you get used to looking at C code, you will know that this brief syntax is what makes C so flexible and powerful. Even though their code lines look confusing, all C programs follow the same basic structure. Once you know the language, C programs will take on a simpler appearance.

Entering the Program

To start a new program, you must open a new file. Start the IDE by typing

`TC`

at the DOS prompt. Choose the File menu and select the Open option. Type the name FIRST.C in the Open a File dialog box shown in Figure 3.2.

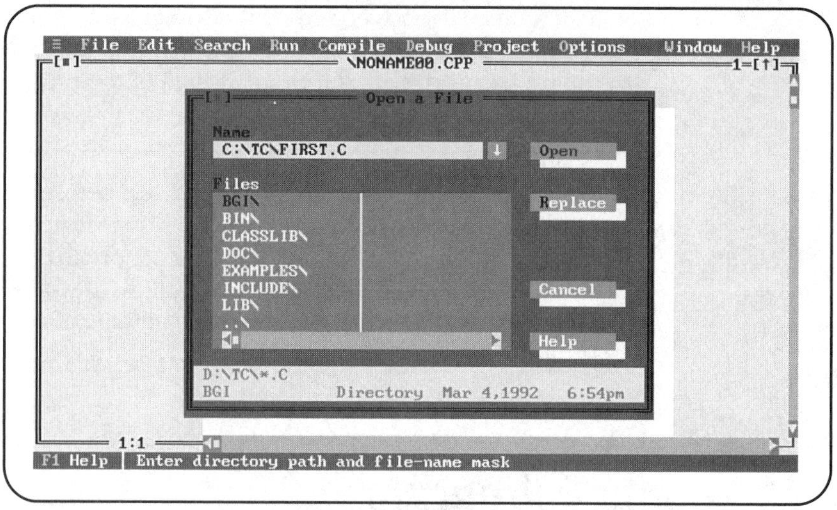

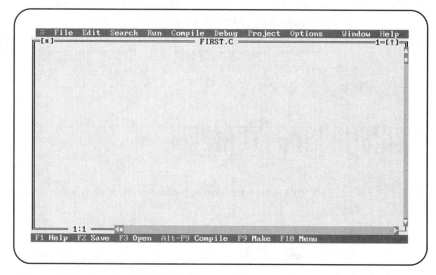

Figure 3.2. *The Open a File dialog box.*

Because this file does not already exist, it must be created (if it existed, it would now load). The IDE opens a window with the filename appearing in the title bar. The editor window is active with the cursor flashing in the upper left corner, as Figure 3.3 shows.

Figure 3.3. *IDE with FIRST.C in an editor window.*

Type in the program FIRST.C in Listing 3.1 or, if you have obtained the disk that contains all the programs in this book, simply open the program's file. (For more information about the accompanying disk, see the offer at the back of the book.) Remember to use the editing features discussed in Chapter 2. Type the program exactly as it is printed. Make sure to use the same upper or lower case characters and include all punctuation.

Listing 3.1. FIRST.C program.

```
/**************************************************
FIRST.C--Beginning sample C program
Do It Yourself Turbo C++ by Paul J. Perry
**************************************************/

#include <stdio.h>

void main()
{
    printf("First there was the earth, and that was good\n");
}
```

As you type the program, notice that words are colored or shaded differently than usual on your screen. This is a helpful feature of the Turbo C++ environment. We will see shortly what the different highlights mean. For now, remember that different types of program code are highlighted and colored differently. We will take a look at what this program does shortly. First, we'll get the program to run.

After you enter Listing 3.1, you should save it to disk. To do this, open the File menu and select the Save option. The file FIRST.C will be written to the current directory. To change the filename of the program, you would use the Save As option and enter a new filename. When you save a file, the IDE automatically appends the file extension .CPP. This stands for C plus plus. At this time, because we are writing straight C code, you should save it with the .C file extension. The file extension actually tells the IDE which compiler to use: the C or C++ compiler.

Compiling and Running the Program

Now that you have created your program's source file, you are ready to run it. In order to run the program, you must first compile and link it. Turbo C++ enables you to compile and link a program by choosing the Compile menu and selecting the Make option (or simply by pressing the F9 hotkey).

A status box appears, as shown in Figure 3.4. It tells you how much progress the compiler has made on the program. The program is first compiled and then linked. It all takes place somewhat transparently to you once you press the F9 hotkey.

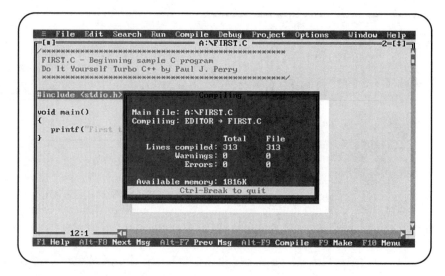

Figure 3.4. Turbo C++ compiler status box.

The status window contains a variety of information. Including the filename of the file being compiled, the number of lines already compiled, the number of warnings and errors which have occurred, and the amount of memory available. With this program, the status box should only appear for a short amount of time. Longer programs require more time to compile.

The Linking Process

Once compiling has been completed, the linking process begins. The status window will display a message telling you that linking is taking place. If you watch closely, you will notice that several file names will flash on the screen. These are the files that are being linked with the source code object file.

Although the compiling and linking process seems like a simple task, a great many processes happen when it occurs. During compilation, the compiler converts your source code into an object file with the extension .OBJ. The linker then combines this file with various other files. When the linking process is finished, your program is ready to run. The result of linking is the file named FIRST.EXE. The edit, compile, and link process is illustrated in Figure 3.5.

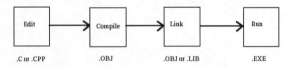

Figure 3.5. The edit, compile, link, and run processes.

Before any code is compiled and linked, the project "Make" facility looks at the creation time and date on the files that you are compiling. If any other source files use code from another source file, that code is recompiled. All updates to dependent files are automatically carried out by the compiler.

In complex programs, many files are used to store program source code. By checking the time and date, you can avoid unnecessary recompilation of source code files. This speeds up the program development process.

Running the File

There should not have been any errors during compilation of the sample program. If there was a typing mistake, we'll explore what to do in a moment.

Assuming that there were no errors during the compiling or linking process, you are ready to execute FIRST.C. To run the program, open the Run menu and select the Run option (or press Ctrl+F9). When you do this, the desktop will disappear and the screen will flash momentarily. Then the desktop will be redisplayed.

You may wonder what happened. The answer is your program was executed and you were returned to the IDE. Open the Window menu and select User screen (or press Alt+F5). You will see one line of text like that in Figure 3.6 that FIRST.C displays at the top of the screen. Pressing any key brings you back the IDE.

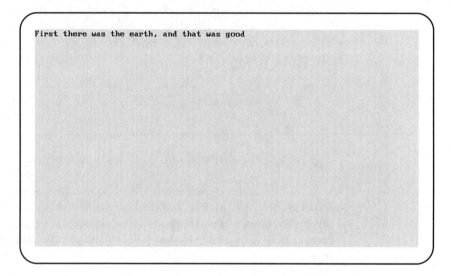

First there was the earth, and that was good

Figure 3.6. The user screen.

Your user screen may look somewhat different from the example. This is because the user screen includes any interactions with DOS that you may have had before you started Turbo C++. Therefore, you will probably at least see the command line you used to load Turbo C++.

At this point, if you exit to DOS or choose the DOS shell option on the File menu and enter the DIR (directory) command, several new files have been created. Of course you will find the .C file, as well as the .OBJ. You would also find the .EXE file that is the stand-alone executable file of the program. You can run this directly from DOS by typing its name and pressing the Enter key. It runs independently of the Turbo C++ IDE.

Working with Errors

It is possible that your first attempt to edit, compile, and link a C program was not successful. One of the best features of the Turbo C++ IDE is that when errors are located, you can interactively fix them. After compilation, if errors were detected, you will see a list of the errors in the message window at the bottom of the screen. You'll see the edit window with your program in it at the top of the screen. The message window will have one line highlighted.

Suppose that you left out the beginning quote before the phrase "First there was the earth, and that was good". If there are several errors in the message box, move the highlight bar over the specific error using the up and down arrow keys. As you move the highlight bar in the Message window, a corresponding highlight will move in the editor window.

Move the cursor over the first error in the message window and press the Enter key. At this point, the editor window will be made active. The cursor will be positioned at the appropriate location in the editor window near where the compiler found the error. And you can make a change to the program.

At this point, you can type in the opening quote. Try recompiling the program. You may recompile and run the program in one step by pressing Ctrl+F9. If there were other error messages, go back and correct them through the same process.

Warning and Error Messages

The C programming language is quite flexible. There are many program statements in which the compiler will find grammatically acceptable, however your program won't work correctly. To help you with your programming, Turbo C++ provides two types of messages: warning and error messages.

Warnings are displayed in cases where something you entered looks like it might not execute correctly, however what was entered is syntactically correct. It is just a guess on the part of the compiler that a possible problem exists. Error messages are displayed when a definite problem has been found.

> To execute your program, the compiler must not generate any error messages. That is, error messages will prevent your program from being executed. However your program will compile and link, even if warning messages are displayed. And you may execute it (although, if the compiler generates warning messages, it is a good idea to keep your eye open and remedy the situation). The best situation is to make your program compile without any warning messages.

To force the compiler to generate a warning message, remove the key word void in the source code and try to recompile. You should get the message `Warning A:\FIRST.C 12: Function should return a value` (as shown in Figure 3.7). You will notice that you will still be able to execute your program. Add the word void back to the program.

Consider warning messages a sign that something may be incorrect with your code and it should be checked. If you run into error messages, on the other hand, your code must be changed to begin running the code.

Now that we have entered the program and executed it, we will look at parts of the program and see what they do.

Elements of a C Program

Several basic components are necessary to create a C program: preprocessor directives, variables, declarations, function declarations, and the `main()` function. All C programs follow the same basic structure. Even a large, complex C program generally has the same layout as a short one.

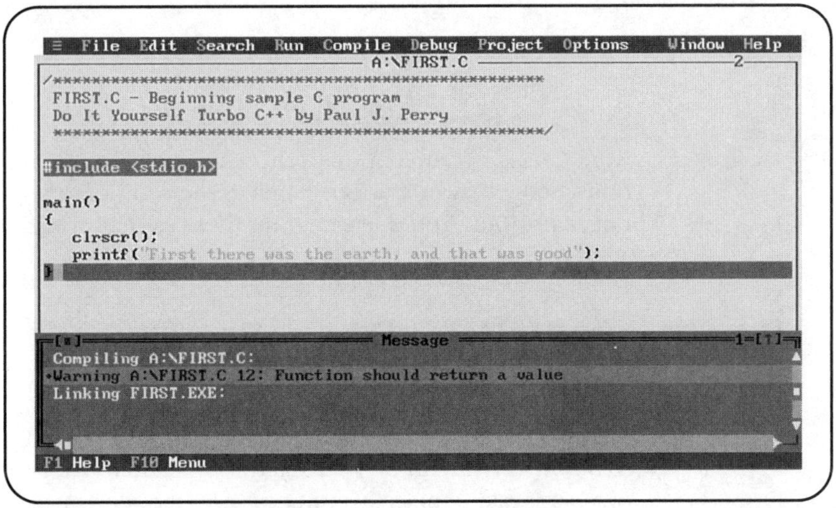

Figure 3.7. Warning message.

Case Sensitivity of C

It is important to understand that C is case sensitive. This means that upper and lowercase letters are treated as separate characters. For example, the names SUM, sum, Sum, and suM are all treated as different names. Languages such as BASIC and Pascal are not case sensitive and would treat the names exactly the same.

When you enter a C program, be careful to use the proper case. If you don't, the compiler will not recognize your code and it won't be processed correctly.

The C Character Set

C uses the uppercase letters A to Z, the lowercase letters a to z, the digits 0 to 9, and the following special characters:

        [ ] { } < > ( )

```
!  *  +  =  "  '  .  ?
#  / \  &  %-      _ ^
~  | ;  :  ,  @  $  '
```

C uses a combination of these characters to represent special operations. Some may be obvious (such as the addition operator, +); others are not as obvious. You'll learn about them as they come along.

Comments in Your Program

A *comment* is any additional text that you add to your code for clarification of what is taking place. Comments are frequently used to jog the mind of the programmer after he or she has been away from the program and returns to perform maintenance on it. Comments are an important part of any program. They help the person writing a program, and anyone else who must read the source file, to understand what's happening. All comments are ignored by the compiler, so they do not add to the file size of the executable program. Neither do they affect the execution time of the executable program.

> A comment is not a required part of a program. It does not perform any programming task. Comments may be used freely throughout your program to make the code easier to understand.

In C, comments begin with the sequence /* and are terminated by the sequence */. Everything within the sequence is ignored. In the FIRST.C program, the first three lines of the program are comments, as follows:

```
/***************************************************
FIRST.C - Beginning sample C program
Do It Yourself Turbo C++ by Paul J. Perry
***************************************************/
```

Helpful information to include at the beginning of your program in a comment is your name (the author), the date the program was written, and any revision notes.

Preprocessor Directives

You can include various instructions to the Turbo C++ compiler in the source code of your program. These instructions are called *preprocessor directives.* Although they are not part of the C language, they expand the scope of C beyond the basic definition. All preprocessor directives begin with the pound (#) character.

The preprocessor directives are interpreted before the compilation process begins. Preprocessor directives usually appear at the beginning of a program and are grouped together with other directives (although this is not required). The directives apply to the portion of the program following their appearance.

The fifth line of the FIRST.C program,

```
#include <stdio.h>
```

tells the compiler to include information about the standard input/output library. If you take a look at the STDIO.H file (usually located in the \TC\INCLUDE subdirectory) you will see that it is actually program code, just like what would appear in your own program. This line appears at the beginning of many C source code files.

The `#include` directive instructs the compiler to include another source file in the one that contains the directive. The name of the source file to be included is enclosed between angle brackets. The file is searched for in the directory specified in the Include input line of the Options Directories dialog box.

In C, the file that is included within your code (in this case STDIO.H) is called a *header file* or *headers* for short. This naming convention is due to the fact the declarations are usually found at the beginning of a program.

The `main()` Function

Notice the name `main()` in line 7 of the program. The section of code starting with `main()` and enclosed in braces is called a *function*. All C programs are divided into small, separate units, known as *functions*. Most high-level computer languages break programs into small units like this. Sometimes, these smaller units are called *subprograms*.

FORTRAN and BASIC use subroutines. Pascal, being somewhat more closely related to C uses, procedures, and functions. There are obvious differences between how other languages operate, but the main idea is the same. Functions, subroutines, and procedures enable the programmer to separate code into smaller units.

A C program is a collection of functions. Each program is one or more functions that have been put together. Each function contains one or more C statements. Usually a function is written to carry out a single task. Each function has a name and a list of values that the function will receive. Usually, you can give a function any name you want. As you will see shortly, the `main()` function is a special case.

A C program can have almost an unlimited number of functions. No matter how many functions there are in a program, the `main()` function is the one to which control is passed from the operating system when the program begins to run. Because it controls the program operation, all C programs must have a `main()` function. It is executed first when your program begins to run. Your program can only have one `main()` function. If you used more than one, the compiler would not know which version to start with. If you feel experimental, create more than one `main()` statement in a C file and try to compile the program.

A *function definition* is used to tell the compiler the name of the function. Later, when you learn more about functions, you will see that functions interact with values being used in the program. In the FIRST.C program, the function definition is

```
void main()
```

The keyword void tells the compiler that the function does not return a value. We will get into return values and functions later in the book. The word `main()` is the name of the function, and the parentheses tell the compiler that this is the definition of the function.

Some programs have only one function (like the FIRST.C sample program). Large programs have too much code to fit inside a single function. The large program breaks up tasks into logical steps, each can be carried out inside a function. Then, calls to the separate functions are found inside `main()`.

Following the function definition are braces that signal the beginning and end of the function. The opening brace, {, signifies that a block of code is about to begin. The closing brace, }, terminates a block of code. In C, braces perform a similar function to the `Begin...End` statements in Pascal. In essence, braces mark the body of a function.

The FIRST.C program has only one statement inside its body, as follows:

```
{
printf("First there was the earth, and that was good\n");
}
```

This line is actually a call to another function. It is the formatted print or `printf()` routine. The `printf()` function takes the text in quotes and outputs it to the standard output device. Because we included the STDIO.H file (which defines standard input and output), the string is displayed on the video display.

The \n at the end of the line is called an *escape character*. It is used to send a carriage return and line feed combination to the screen. This character causes your program to move the cursor to the next line on the screen. Turbo C++ comes with an extensive set of built-in library functions that help you write your programs. The `printf()` function is one of these library functions. By providing a number of ready-to-run library functions, the compiler can be used more quickly than if you had to write your own function to display text on the screen. It is important to note that these library functions don't make up the standard definition of the language. This grants as much versatility as possible to the programmer.

Notice that the line beginning with the `printf()` statement is terminated with a semicolon (;). This is an example of a *statement*. In C, statements are separated with the semicolon. It is this semicolon which separates the statement from the next one.

> The C programming language does not recognize "whitespace" characters. This includes carriage returns, tabs, and spaces. You can put as many whitespace characters in your program as you like. It does not matter to the C compiler. In fact, the whitespace characters are invisible to the compiler.

The FIRST.C program will compile and run exactly the same if it had been entered in the following format:

```
#include <stdio.h>

void
main()
{
printf
("First there was the earth, and that was good\n");
}
```

Similarly, the program will run the same if it had the following format:

```
#include <stdio.h>

void main(){printf("First there was the earth, and that was good\n");}
```

Although the two preceding examples are treated the same by the compiler, the code in each obviously looks different from the other to the programmer. The second version is grouped together resulting in making it hard to see program structure. The way the program was first listed (in Listing 3.1) is easier for humans to understand.

Because the compiler is so flexible, C programmers have come to use a particular style while entering their programs. You will see all programs conform to a similar style throughout this book. The most important point is to align matching pairs of braces. This makes it much easier to ensure that each opening brace (and by extension, each section) has a closing brace that marks a block's conclusion. Also, the program is usually spaced to make it easier for you to understand the full meaning.

Exiting the IDE

To exit the IDE, choose the Quit option from the File menu (or press Alt+X). If you have not saved the latest revision of your program, Turbo C++ gives you a chance to save your file (as shown in Figure 3.8).

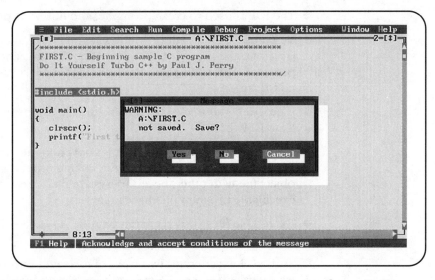

Figure 3.8. *Message displayed by Turbo C++ as you choose Quit.*

In the first part of this book, you installed the Integrated Development Environment, learned how to use it, and saw how to create and execute a C program. The second part covers other important parts of using the C language. For now, go ahead and take a rest. You deserve a break!

What You Have Learned

In this chapter, you learned how to create, compile, link, and run C programs. You learned the basic structure of a typical C program and saw how this structure contributes to the flexibility and convenience of the C programming languages. You learned about the following topics:

● Creating a C program requires some advance thought. The best way to create a program is to (1) analyze the problem, (2) design the program, (3) write code to implement the program, (4) compile and run the program, and (5) test and debug the program.

- The IDE is used to create, compile, and link your programs.

- You must open an editor window before you can enter the source code into the compiler. You then compile, link, and execute the program. This can be done by pressing the F9 key from within an editor window.

- A program's source code contains the file extension .C for regular C or .CPP for C++.

- When a program is compiled, it is converted into an object file, with the extension .OBJ. Next, the linking process combines the object file with other, necessary system files to create a resulting executable program file that can be run.

- Executable files you create can be run on systems that don't have Turbo C++.

- Turbo C++ generates two types of messages during compilation: warnings and errors. *Warnings* are messages which the compiler generates when it thinks something may be wrong, but is not sure. A program may still be executed if warning messages are generated. *Error messages,* on the other hand must be corrected before your program will compile. They are usually a result of an error in entering the source code.

- Elements of a C program include preprocessor directives, variable declarations, function declarations, and the `main()` function. The `main()` function is passed control from DOS when the program begins to run. Furthermore, there can only be one `main()` function in every program.

- The C programming language is case sensitive. That is, it treats upper- and lowercase letters separately. The identifiers LANGUAGE, Language, languagE, and LaNgUaGe are each unique and different to C.

- Comments are used to help humans understand what is happening in the code. Comments are ignored by the compiler. They begin with the sequence /* and end with the */ characters.

- Preprocessor directives begin with a pound sign (#) and are instructions to the C preprocessor. That is, they are acted on before the compiler does anything to the program. The `#include` preprocessor directive is used to include a file within another file. The included file is usually called a header file.

● Braces signal a block of code. The opening brace, {, signifies the beginning of a block of code. The closing brace, }, terminates a block of code.

● Every statement in a C program is terminated with a semicolon (;) character. "Whitespace" characters (carriage returns, tabs, and spaces) are not recognized by the C programming language as terminators.

Part II

The ABCs of C

Data Types

Goals

After reading this chapter, you will

- Be familiar with the term *data type*. The reader will learn what numeric data types are available in C.

- Know what an integer variable is and how much space it takes to store in the PC's memory.

- Know the three basic types of floating-point variables found in C.

- Tell the difference between an integer and a floating-point variable.

- Know what a character variable is and how to declare, define, and assign one.

● Recognize the difference between a variable and a constant, and be familiar with the types of constants available in C.

● Know how to modify the basic variable declarations with type modifiers and how these type modifiers affect the values stored in a variable.

● Be familiar with the programming terms *visibility* and *lifetime*, and how they apply to C programs.

In the previous chapters, you learned how to use the Integrated Development Environment (IDE) and how to write a basic C program. This chapter focuses on the foundations of the C language. You learn about the basic types of numeric variables found in the C language. You will learn how to define and access these different variables.

A C program consists of variables and functions. Variables are the fundamental part of any computer language. A *variable* is a symbolic name that can be assigned different values. A *function* is a section of code that carries out a particular operation. (Functions are discussed in detail in Chapter 10.)

A variable is stored in the computer's memory. When a variable is given a value, that value is placed in the memory space designated for the symbol corresponding to that variable. Different types of variables require different amounts of memory for storage. As with most computer languages, C supports several different types of variables. Unlike other computer languages, C allows for great versatility in declaring variables.

Using Variables

All variables in C must be declared before you use them. Pascal is another language that has this requirement. The declaration is necessary because the compiler must know what type of data a variable is before it can properly compile other statements that rely on the variable. This is part of what gives a C compiler great efficiency compared to languages such as BASIC, which does not require variables to be declared before they are used.

A *data type* is a set of values that represent a particular variable in memory. The C programming language has five basic data types: integer (`int`), floating point (`float`), double-precision (`double` and `long double`), and character (char). These basic data types can be further expanded with type modifiers.

> When designing your program, you must take into account what the variable will hold and declare it appropriately. The data type of a variable tells what kind of data the variable can contain as well as the range of values the variable can store.

The general form of a variable declaration statement is as follows:

```
VariableType NameList;
```

Here, **VariableType** is a valid C data type, and **NameList** is one or more identifier names separated with commas. In the Turbo C++ IDE on a color monitor, keywords are colored bright white and variable names are green by default. This color system helps your eye follow the code easier. It also helps prevent typographical errors. If you expect a certain color for a keyword, and it is not displayed in that color, you are likely to check the word for errors.

Examples of variable declarations follow:

```
float total_sum;
int x, y;
double a, b, radius;
char ch;
```

The first declaration defines a variable, total_sum, to be of type float (floating point). The second declaration creates two integer variables named x and y. In C, it is legal to declare multiple variables on one line. Such a declaration saves space and typing time. The third declaration creates three variables of type double. The last declaration creates a variable named ch of type char (character).

A variable name can consist of letters and digits. However, the first character must be a letter or the underscore character (_). Both upper and lowercase identifiers are permitted. You can use the underscore character (_) in a variable declaration, and an underscore is often used in the middle of an identifier to make the identifier easier to read.

In Turbo C++, the first 32 characters of variable names are significant. Keywords cannot be used for variable names.

The next section looks at the types of variables that C provides. You will find out the difference between constants and variables, and you will find out what a type modifier is. Finally, the last section of the chapter explores the visibility and lifetime of variables.

Integer Variables

Integers consist of any valid combination of digits along with a plus or minus sign. An integer is a number that does not contain a decimal point. The set of integers in mathematics are whole numbers and can be negative or positive. Examples of integers include

```
1676, -49, 0, 66841, -123
```

Notice that integers can be positive or negative. If a plus sign (+) is not declared, the variable is assumed to be positive. To declare a number negative, it must include the (–) symbol. The number 0 is included in the set of integers.

Sample integer variable declarations include

```
int loop_counter;
int x, y, center, radius;
int bikes = 12;
```

To declare an integer, you first list the reserved word int and then list the name of the variable you need to declare. The keyword int signals your program to set aside enough space for the integer and to assign the name following keyword to represent that memory space.

The third declaration sets up an integer variable by the name of bikes and assigns it an initial value. Assigning an initial value to a variable is often useful because you cannot assume that a variable will be assigned any value when you first declare it. If you want it to be a certain value, you must explicitly do it yourself. When a variable is declared but not assigned a value, it contains whatever value happened to be in the memory location that was assigned to the variable when it was declared. Using an unassigned variable can be disastrous, so make sure you assign a value to a declared variable before you attempt to use it.

Listing 4.1 declares an integer variable and gives it a value. When the program is run, the variable is created and an integer value is assigned to it. When you execute the program, remember to display the contents of the user screen by choosing the Window menu and selecting the User Screen option. The value of the integer variable is displayed on the video screen.

Listing 4.1. NUMB.C—Example of using an integer number variable.

```
/***************************************************
NUMB.C—Uses an integer number.
Do It Yourself Turbo C++ by Paul J. Perry
***************************************************/

#include <stdio.h>

void main()
{
    int x;

    x = 123;                            /* assign value to x */
    printf("The value of x is %d\n", x); /* output new value */
}
```

Notice the assignment statement, which assigns the value of 123 to the variable x (line 12). The = is the assignment operator and gives the variable on the left side the value of the constant on the right side.

The printf() statement may arouse your curiosity, because of some rather strange notational conventions. You already know that the printf() function displays output on the video display. What is different in this example is the %d characters, along with another argument passed to the printf() function (the variable name).

The %d is called a format specifier. It tells the printf() function where to put a value in a string and what format to use to print the value. The %d tells the compiler to format an integer value. Later you will learn about more format specifiers.

4

Every integer variable requires 2 bytes of memory and holds numbers in the range –32,768 to 32,767. You will see how this compares to the memory requirements of other variable types as we discuss them in this chapter. You will see that 2 bytes is a rather small amount of memory. For this reason, integers are commonly used as counters in program loops and temporary variables.

Floating-Point Variables

Floating-point variables are used when a fractional component is required in the numbers your program uses or when your application requires extremely large or small numbers. Floating-point variables represent numbers with a decimal place. Examples include

`3.1415927, .00001676 and 49.4949`

There are three basic types of floating-point numbers: `float`, `double`, and `long double`. The difference between them is the magnitude of the largest (and therefore smallest) number they can hold. Let's first take a look at type `float`, the smallest of the floating-point variable types.

Type `float`

Variables defined as `float` can be in the range 3.4×10^{-38} to 3.4×10^{-38} and occupies 4 bytes of memory. Precision is set at seven digits of accuracy.

Floating-point variables require more memory to store than other types of variables. As a result, the computer takes longer to process information with a variable declared as a `float` or a `double`.

Choosing the correct data type is an important aspect of creating optimized programs that run quickly and efficiently. The following examples show several floating-point variable declarations:

```
float diameter;
float principal, interest;
float distance = 25.05;
```

The first declaration is the simplest. It declares a single variable with no initial value. The second declaration shows how to declare multiple variables on a single line. The third declaration shows the assignment of an initial value to the variable.

Listing 4.2. gives an example of using a floating-point variable in a program. It prompts the user to enter the radius of a circle. It then displays the area of the circle.

Listing 4.2. AREA.C—Calculates the area of a circle.

```
/*****************************************************
 AREA.C—Calculate area of a circle, given the radius.
 Demonstrates using floating-point variables.
 Do It Yourself Turbo C++ by Paul J. Perry
 *****************************************************/

#include <stdio.h>
#define PI 3.1415927

void main()
{
    float radius;
    float area;

    printf("Enter radius of circle:");
    scanf("%f", &radius);

    area = PI * (radius * 2);
printf("Area of circle with radius %f, is equal to %f\n", radius,
area);
}
```

Here's a sample interaction with the program:

```
Enter radius of circle:2
Area of circle with radius 2.000000, is equal to 12.566371
```

Some new concepts are used in this program. Line 8 is an example of a preprocessor directive: the #define statement. The scanf() function is used in line 16.

The #define statement tells the preprocessor to scan the program and replace any instances of the characters PI with the number 3.1415927. The #define statement is different from a variable. You cannot change the value of the identifier during execution. To the compiler, it is treated as if you had entered the number straight into the code. It is handy to the programmer, because if the value of pi changes, it only needs to be changed in one place, not in several places throughout the program.

The scanf() statement in line 16 is an input statement. It prompts the user for the radius value and stores that result in the variable named radius. Line 18 does the actual calculation for the program. Line 19 displays the output on the video screen using format specifiers, which we will discuss later.

Type **double**

The second type of floating-point value is double. Variables of type double require 8 bytes of memory to store and can hold numbers in the range 1.7×10^{-308} to 1.7×10^{308}. Precision is set at 15 digits of accuracy. The larger size gives better precision and range but also uses more memory. Because they can hold larger values, numbers of type double are often used in scientific and financial calculations.

Examples of double variable declarations follow:

```
double value;
double pi = 3.2425927;
```

The first line creates a double variable with the name value. The second creates a double variable with the name pi and assigns it an initial value.

Type **long double**

A long double requires 10 bytes of memory and can store values in the range 3.4×10^{-4932} to 3.4×10^{4932}. Some sample declarations include

```
long double very_big_number;
long double variable1, variable2;
```

Notice that this variable type requires two keywords. The `long` keyword is actually a type modifier that modifies the basic definition of the `double` type. Besides providing a greater array of values that can be stored, a `long double` provides more precise values. A long `double` has 19 digits of precision.

Character Variables

Most variable types are numeric, but there is one that isn't. It is the character (or `char`) type. A character is a single letter surrounded by single quotes (actually, apostrophes). Character variables are used to hold 8-bit ASCII characters, such as "A", "P", "1" or any other 8-bit quantity. A character variable uses 1 byte in memory. ASCII stands for the American Standard Code for Information Interchange. It is a universal standard used to represent alphanumeric characters.

Character variables are used to represent the ASCII character set. An ASCII code is actually just a number used to represent a symbol. You will find times that variables of type `char` and type `int` are similar and can be used interchangeably.

To declare two character variables, use the following statement:

```
char letter1, letter2;
```

Listing 4.3 uses a character variable to query a single-character value from the user.

Listing 4.3. DSPCHAR.C—Requests character from user.

```
/***************************************************
DSPCHAR.C—Display character variable.
Do It Yourself Turbo C++ by Paul J. Perry
***************************************************/

#include <stdio.h>
```

continues

75

Listing 4.3. continued

```
void main()
{
    char grade;

    printf("Enter your grade on the test (A, B, C...): ");
    grade = getche();
    printf("\nYou earned the score %c.\n", grade);
}
```

Notice the use of the getche() function. It waits to get a single character value from the keyboard and then echoes it (displays it) to the screen. In our program, the value is then assigned to the variable grade. We will see other functions that get input from the user later in the book.

You may wish to assign special control codes to characters. For example, C defines certain codes that can be used to assign a control code to a variable. Table 4.1. displays the special character constants.

Table 4.1. Special character constants.

Code	Description
'\\'	Backslash
'\b'	Backspace
'\r'	Carriage return
'\"'	Double quotes
'\f'	Formfeed
'\n'	Newline
'\0'	Null value
'\''	Single quote
'\t'	Tab
'\v'	Vertical tab

To assign a backslash character to a code, you would use the following line of code:

```
char ch = '\\'
```

The other special codes are used similarly.

This ends our discussion of the five basic data types in C. Table 4.2 summarizes the information about the size and range of values for the basic data types in C.

Table 4.2. Variable sizes and ranges.

Type	Size	Range of Values
int	2 Bytes	−32,768 to 32,767
float	4 bytes	3.4×10^{-38} to 3.4×10^{38} (7-digit precision)
double	8 bytes	1.7×10^{-308} to 1.7×10^{308} (15-digit precision)
long double	10 bytes	3.4×10^{-4932} to 3.4×10^{4932} (19-digits precision)
char	1 byte	−128 to 127

Constant Values

Constants are identifiers that cannot change during execution of your program. A program can have constants of any of the five basic data types.

There are integer constants, floating-point constants, and character constants.

A constant is declared using the reserved word const and assigning the identifier a value. Examples of constant declarations include

```
const int speed = 55;
const float pi =    3.1415927;
const double diameter = 899.567;
const char ch = 'P';
```

Notice that the only difference between variable declarations and constant declarations is the reserved word `const`. All the constants are given a value that cannot be changed during the execution of a program. Remember the earlier discussion of giving a variable a beginning value that could be changed during program execution.

Constants are similar to `#define` preprocessor directives that we learned about earlier. However, constants are easier to use during the debugging phase. Constants are usually better to use then `#define` declarations. The reason that `#define` declarations are still around is because the original C language definition had no constant definition in the language. Therefore, programmers had no choice. But now, you have a choice, and I recommend using constants rather than `#define` statements.

Constants cannot be changed during program execution (try it if you need convincing). If you try, you will receive an error message: `Error 9: Cannot modify a const object`. Listing 4.4 gives an example of using constants in the C programming language.

Listing 4.4. CONSTS.C—Sample constant program.

```
/*****************************************************
 CONSTS.C—Sample program to use constants.
 Do It Yourself Turbo C++ by Paul J. Perry
 *****************************************************/

#include <stdio.h>

void main()
{
    const char letter = 'X';
    const float pi = 3.1415927;
    const int value = 12345;
    char wait;

    printf("The constants include:\n\
        character =\t\t%c\n\
        floating point =\t%f\n\
        integer =\t\t%d\n", letter, pi, value);
```

```
        printf("Press any key to return to Turbo C++\n\n");

        wait = getch();  /* causes compiler to generate warning */
}
```

Lines 10 through 12 declare constant values. They are displayed on the video screen starting at line 15. Notice the use of the ending backslash in lines 15 through 17. This notation tells the compiler to combine physical lines into one. In this program, lines 15 through 17 appear as a single line to the compiler.

Type Modifiers

Type modifiers enable us to extend the basic data types. Type modifiers give great flexibility to C programmers in what variable types can be declared. The extended data types are derived from the basic types using special reserved keywords. The modifiers are short, long, unsigned, and signed. Let's start by looking at the different types of integer variables created with type modifiers.

Normally, the range of values that can be held by an integer is from –32768 to 32767. Sometimes you don't need negative values. A variable can be declared as an unsigned int, which can contain values ranging from 0 to 65535. The unsigned keyword is called a *type modifier.* Here is a sample declaration:

```
unsigned int positive_number;
```

To get an even larger integer number, a variable can be declared as a long int. A long integer can contain values from –2147483648 to 2147483647. If the long integer does not need to contain negative numbers, it can be declared as an unsigned long int, in which case its range of values is from 0 to 4294967295.

You can also declare a short int. In Turbo C++, a short integer is the same as a regular integer. Other implementations of C and C++ may have a different size for a short integer.

C++ has a signed type modifier, but because integers are by default signed, it is unnecessary to use the signed modifier on an int. The size of the integers stays the same whether the type is signed or unsigned. Following are some examples of declarations for integer types:

```
unsigned int top;
long int l;
unsigned long int = 4294967290;
short int;  /* Same as type int */
```

Type modifiers can also be applied to character types. An unsigned char holds variables that can be in the range of 0 to 255. You already saw type modifiers assigned to double-precision numbers. Table 4.3. summarizes the data types created with the use of type modifiers.

Table 4.3. Derived variable types.

Type	Size	Range of Values
unsigned char	1 byte	0 to 255
short int	2 bytes	–32,768 to 32,767
long int	4 bytes	–2,147,483,648 to 2,147,483,647
unsigned int	2 bytes	0 to 65,535
unsigned long int	4 bytes	0 to 4,294,967,295

Visibility and Lifetime

A variable's *visibility* describes where within a program it can be accessed. A variable can be referred to by statements in some parts of the program and in other parts of the program it cannot. The *scope* of a variable is that part of the program where the variable is visible.

You can designate a variable to be associated with a certain part of your program. Such as variable is invisible outside its scope.

In general, the variable declaration's position in the program determines the scope.

The time between creation and destruction of a variable is called its *lifetime*. Although we won't go into great detail about these two terms here, they will come up again. When we look at extending the C language with functions, we will discuss them in more detail. It is good to at least have heard the terms at this point.

What You Have Learned

This chapter introduced the notion of data types in a program. The following topics were covered:

● A data type is a set of values that represent a particular variable in memory. C includes five basic data types: integer (`int`), floating-point (`float`), double-precision (`double`), `long double`, and character (`char`).

● A variable name can consist of letters and digits. The first character must be a letter. The first 32 characters of a variable name are significant. You can also use the underscore (_) to help improve readability of variable names.

● An integer variable is one that does not contain a decimal point. They are declared with the reserved word `int`.

● Floating-point variables are those that have a decimal point. They are also used when a number must be extremely large or small.

● There are three types of floating-point numbers: `float`, `double` and `long double`. The difference between them is the size of the numbers they can hold and the precision of the number.

● Character variables are represented by a single character that is surrounded by a single quotes. They are defined with the reserved word `char`.

- Constant values are identifiers that don't change during execution of a program. A constant can be any of the five basic data types.

- Type modifiers allow an extension of the basic data types. The four type modifiers are `signed`, `unsigned`, `long`, and `short`.

- A variable's visibility describes where within a program it can be accessed. The lifetime of a variable is the time between creation and destruction of the variable.

5

Input/Output

Goals

After reading this chapter, you will

- Possess the background information necessary to understand keyboard input and video output in the C programming language.

- Know what character input/output is and the functions used to access character I/O with C.

- Understand what is meant by formatted I/O.

- Know what the five standard streams are and how they are defined in Turbo C++.

- Be familiar with the `printf()` and `scanf()` formatted I/O functions—how they are accessed and the format specifiers used for many C data types.

- Know how to align decimal points in output when you are using the `printf()` function.

Chapter 4 briefly used the `printf()` and `scanf()` functions to display output on the screen and to get input from the user. This chapter takes a close look at input and output using these functions as well as others. The main focus of the chapter is the transfer of information between the computer and the keyboard/video display.

We will first look at character I/O and then at formatted I/O. You will learn what a format specifier is and how these format specifiers are used in formatted I/O.

Getting Input and Output

Input and output operations are not provided for directly by the C language itself. Input and output is accomplished through the use of library functions. Turbo C++ defines a complete set of input and output functions that handle I/O operations.

An I/O function is accessed from anywhere within a program by writing the function name, followed by a list of arguments enclosed in parentheses. The arguments represent data items that are sent to the function. Some I/O functions do not require arguments, although empty parentheses must still appear in the function call.

To access the input/output functions, a collection of header files is provided by Turbo C++ that provide the necessary information in support of the various types of I/O functions. As a rule, the file required by the standard input/output library functions is called STDIO.H. It will be used in most of your programs.

Character I/O

Single characters can be entered using the C library function getch(). The getch() function is a part of the console I/O library routines. The console I/O routines use the keyboard and video display to input and output information with the user. Therefore, the compiler requires the CONIO.H header file for prototype information. A prototype tells the compiler what types of variables are to be passed to a function. The getch() function returns a single character from a standard input device (usually the keyboard). The function does not require any arguments, although a pair of empty parentheses must follow the function name.

In general, the function is referenced as follows:

```
character_variable = getch();
```

where character_variable refers to some previously declared character variable.

The counterpart to the getch() function is the putchar() function. It displays a single character on the monitor. The putchar() function is part of the standard C language I/O library. It outputs a single character to the standard output device (the video display). The character to be displayed is represented as a character type variable. The character is expressed as an argument to the function, enclosed in parentheses. In general, a reference to the putchar() function is

```
putchar(character_variable);
```

where character_variable refers to some previously declared character variable.

Listing 5.1 shows how to use the getch() and putchar() functions. It waits for you to enter a keystroke. It then displays that keystroke on the screen.

Listing 5.1. Character I/O example.

```
/****************************************************
CHAR_IO.C--Input and output a character variable.
Do It Yourself Turbo C++ by Paul J. Perry
****************************************************/
```

continues

Listing 5.1. continued

```c
#include <stdio.h>        /* for putchar() function */
#include <conio.h>        /* for getch() function */

void main()

{

    char c;
    c = getch();
    putchar(c);

}
```

Notice the two header files included in the beginning of the program. The STDIO.H file defines standard input and output for the PC computer (it is required in almost every program). The other file, CONIO.H defines console input and output for use with the getch() function. As your programs become longer, it will not be uncommon to include a long list of header files at the beginning. It would be rare not to have at least several.

In line 13 of the program, a character variable is declared. Line 14 waits for the user to enter a character with a call to the getch() function. When the user makes the entry, it is stored in the variable named c, and then displayed with the putchar() function.

As is typical with any flexible programming language, C gives us another way to allow the user to enter a character variable and to display it. The getche() function waits until you press a key and then returns its value, similar to the process that the getch() function uses. In addition, the function also echoes (or displays) the key that is pressed on the screen automatically (that is what the ending e stands for).

Listing 5.2. performs the same task as the previous example with less code using the getche() function.

Listing 5.2. Shorter character I/O example.

```c
/****************************************************
CHAR_IO2.C--A shorter character I/O sample.
Do It Yourself Turbo C++ by Paul J. Perry
****************************************************/
```

```
#include <conio.h>
void main()
{
    char c;
    c = getche();    /* creates warning message */

}
```

When you compile CHAR_IO2.C, the compiler will display a warning message: `Warning CHAR_IO2.C: 'c' is assigned a value that is never used.` Remember that warning messages are not fatal, and the compiler is just telling us that we did not make use of the variable in the program (which we already know). In a larger program, we might not have known about it.

The program does the same as CHAR_IO.C, except it is shorter, using the single `getche()` function to input a character variable and display it on the display at the same time. The program only needs to include a single header file for this function, adding to its shortness.

Now that we have taken a look at character I/O, we will examine formatted I/O. It will then be time to take a look at the `printf()` and `scanf()` functions in detail.

Formatted I/O

Before you can start using the formatted keyboard and screen I/O functions, you need to know how C handles input, output, and data. Turbo C++ uses streams to represent the data that moves in and out of a program. A stream is just a method of showing how information flows in a program. Input and output information are often referred to as *streams.* The idea is that input flows in a stream into the program and can be directed to an output device (the screen or the printer).

Turbo C++ streams let you use your computer's I/O devices without worrying about low-level control of your computer (such as might be required in assembly language). It is through streams that you do most I/O with the system. Later you will see how disk files are accessed through streams.

Streams are a portable way to handle input/output tasks. They are used for all types of input and output, including manipulation of data files. The power of using streams with C lies in the *portability* it grants to code; that is, streams make code transferable to different compilers on other computer systems.

This feature may not seem powerful if all you care about is writing programs for your PC, but large system houses may use C entirely for this benefit. When they want to write a program for a different computer, they can just transfer the C code to the new system and make small changes. If they had to rewrite the program, it would take more time and energy.

Turbo C++ automatically provides several predefined streams for use in your programs. Whenever you write a C program, you automatically have access to the following standard streams:

Stream Name	*Description*	*Device*
stdin	Input Stream	Keyboard
stdout	Output Stream	Video Display
stprn	Printer Stream	Printer Port
stdaux	Auxiliary Output	Serial Port
stderr	Error Stream	Video Display

Using these standard streams is easy because you do not have to do any extra housekeeping chores (such as is required when you access disk files). Turbo C++ automatically opens the standard streams and makes them available for use when your program is executing.

Formatted I/O Functions

You have already been exposed to the two basic methods of formatted I/O functions: `scanf()` and `printf()`. When input and output are formatted, we can input data in a format that we are familiar with. For example, we are familiar with the floating-point number 3.1415. We are unfamiliar with the binary codes with which the computer stores the number in memory. Formatted I/O is basically an easier way for programmers to access and manipulate data.

Both formatted I/O functions work with formatted data. One gets input from the user, the other displays output to the user. When you use either function, you specify what type of data you will be working with.

Both `printf()` and `scanf()` work with C's basic data types. For example, you can use the functions to input integer data just as easily as you can use it to input floating-point data or character data.

Using `printf()`

The `printf()` function consists of two main parts: a format string and a variable argument list. The format string specifies what type of data will be output. The variable argument list supplies the data to be output.

In general terms, the `printf()` function is accessed as follows:

```
printf("control string", arg1, arg2, ..., argx);
```

where `control string` refers to a string that contains formatting information, and `arg1, arg2, ..., argx` are arguments that represent the individual output data items. The arguments can be written as constants, single variable names, or more complex expressions.

The control string is composed of individual groups of characters, with one character group for each output data item. Each character group must begin with a percent sign (%). The combination of a character group with a percent sign is known as a *format specifier*. Table 5.1 is a list of valid format specifiers for the `printf()` function.

5

Table 5.1. Format Specifiers for `printf()` function.

Format Specifier	Output Type
%d	Signed decimal integer
%f	Floating point
%e	Floating point with exponential notation
%x	Unsigned hexadecimal integer
%o	Unsigned octal integer
%c	Character
%s	String

The simplest form of the `printf()` function is without the variable argument list. The variable argument list for the `printf()` function is not required. It is perfectly legal to use the function without specifying the argument list, as in,

```
printf("This will be displayed on the screen\n");
```

This line of code simply uses the `printf()` function to print a message on the screen.

If you make use of format specifiers you must make sure that the conversion specifications match the variables you provide. A mismatch between the format string and the variable argument list causes strange program behavior.

Following is a sample line of code that uses a format specifier as follows:

```
printf("The value is %d", result);
```

When the compiler interprets this line, it replaces the value of the variable `result` inside the string where the format specifier is located. For example, if `result` is equal to 5, the output would look like this:

```
The value is 5
```

The replacement of the %d with the value of result is done automatically by the compiler.

You can insert many special escape codes in a control string to control output. These enable you to output characters that you could not communicate easily with the keyboard. Table 5.2 lists the special escape codes that you can use in a string.

Table 5.2. Special escape sequences.

Code	Description
'\\'	Backslash
'\b'	Backspace
'\r'	Carriage return
'\"'	Double quotes
'\f'	Formfeed
'\n'	Newline
'\0'	Null value
'\''	Single quote
'\t'	Tab
'\v'	Vertical Tab

The most frequently used control sequence is the \n or newline code. It is used to separate output lines between subsequent `printf()` calls. It separates lines of output. For example:

```
printf("One\nTwo\nThree");
```

would be output as follows:

```
One
Two
Three
```

The \n code therefore tells the `printf()` function to separate the output lines and insert a carriage return and line feed sequence every time the \n code is located in the control string.

Listing 5.3. shows an example of using the `printf()` function in a program. The program, PRINTF.C requests the user to enter a number in inches. It then converts the value to centimeters and displays the result on the video display.

Listing 5.3. Inches-to-centimeters conversion program.

```
/****************************************************************
PRINTF.C--Sample program showing use of the printf() function.
Converts inches to centimeters.
Do It Yourself Turbo C++ by Paul J. Perry
****************************************************************/

void main()
{
    float inches, cent;            /* variable declarations */

    printf("How many inches? ");
    scanf("%f", &inches);          /* get input from user  */
    cent = inches * 2.54;          /* calculation  */
    printf("%.2f Inches is %.2f Centimeters\n",inches, cent);

}
```

The following is a sample execution of Listing 5.3,

```
PRINTF.C:

How many inches? 3.5
3.50 Inches is 8.89 Centimeters
```

The screen displays the conversion of 3.5 into 8.89 centimeters. (Now you know the dimension of 3-1/2-inch diskettes in the metric system. It's fortunate that an American company named them; it would be a mouthful to call them "eight and eighty-nine one-hundreths centimeter" diskettes.

The program uses the scanf() function to prompt the user for the number of inches (we will discuss it in the next section). It then does the calculation. Finally, line 14 uses the printf() statement to demonstrate the use of the %f format specifier to display the values. The line looks a little different than what Table 5.2 shows. It uses a field-width specifier to format the data:

```
printf("%.2f Inches is %.2f Centimeters\n",inches, cent);
```

The number entered into the program above was 3.5. However, it was later displayed as 3.50. The %.2f format specifier tells the printf() function to use the format specifier for floating point numbers. It also stuffs a .2 in between the % and the f. This code enables the programmer to control how many characters will be printed following the decimal point. In this example, it always displays two characters. That is why the 3.5 was displayed as 3.50.

The programmer can also control how many spaces should be printed before the decimal point. A digit preceding the decimal point in the fieldwidth specifier controls the width of the space to be used to contain the number when it is printed. This is helpful in lining up tables of numbers with a decimal point. Here is a code example:

```
printf("%8.2f%8.2f%8.2f\n", 1.6, 49.01, 1600.2);
printf("%8.2f%8.2f%8.2f\n", 1600.2, 1.6, 49.01);
```

This is what would be output by the function:

```
   1.60   49.01  1600.20
1600.20    1.60    49.01
```

Although the format specifiers may be confusing, the output is formatted nicely.

In summary, the format specifier in the printf() function determines the interpretation of a variable's type, the width of the field, the number of decimal places printed, and the justification.

Using **scanf()**

Input data can be entered into the computer from a standard input device by means of the C library function scanf(). This function can be used to enter any combination of numerical values and single characters. The function returns the number of data items that have been entered successfully.

When a program uses the scanf() function to get data, the user must press the Enter key after the data has been entered. This is different from the getch() family of character input functions, which wait for a single character and resume execution when it is pressed without the press of any other key.

In general, the scanf() function has the following parameters:

scanf(*control string, arg1, arg2, ..., argx*);

where *control string* refers to a string containing certain required formatting information, and *arg1*, *arg2*, ..., *argx* are arguments that represent the individual input data items. Actually, the arguments represent pointers that indicate the addresses of the data items within the computer's memory. You'll learn about pointers later, in Chapter 14.

The control string comprises individual groups of characters, with one character group for each input data item. Each character group must begin with a percent sign (%). In its simplest form, a single character group consists of the percent sign, followed by a conversion character that indicates the type of the corresponding data item.

Within the control string, multiple character groups can be adjacent, or they can be separated by whitespace characters (blank spaces, tabs, or carriage returns). If whitespace characters are used to separate multiple character groups in the control string, then all consecutive whitespace characters in the input data will be read but ignored. The use of blank spaces as character group separators is common. Table 5.3. is a list of the scanf() conversion codes.

Table 5.3. scanf() **conversion codes.**

Character	*Description*
%c	Single character
%d	Signed decimal integer
%e	Floating-point value in exponential format
%f	Floating-point value
%h	Short integer
%i	Integer
%o	Octal integer
%s	String pointer
%u	Unsigned decimal integer
%x	Hexadecimal integer

Listing 5.4. is an example of using the scanf() functions.

Listing 5.4. Sample scanf() program.

```
/****************************************************
SCANF.C--Sample program using scanf() function.
Do It Yourself Turbo C++ by Paul J. Perry
****************************************************/

void main()
{

    float age, days;

    printf("How many years old are you? ");
    scanf("%f", &age);
    days = age * 365;
    printf("\nYou are %.1f days old.\n", days);

}
```

As you can see, the format specifiers for the scanf() function look very much like that for the printf() function. As with printf(), the first argument is a string that contains the format specifiers. In this case there is only one (%f). The following parameters are variable names. This program introduces a new symbol: the ampersand (&) appended to the beginning of variable arguments.

As mentioned earlier, the arguments to the scanf() function are actually the addresses of variables, rather than the variable themselves. This is an important concept in C programming. It is one that we will take up in more detail later in the book. Listing 5.5 is a short example that shows the difference between a variable and an address.

Listing 5.5. Difference between an address and a variable.

```
/****************************************************************
ADDR.C--Shows difference between a variable and its address.
Do It Yourself Turbo C++ by Paul J. Perry
****************************************************************/
```

continues

Listing 5.5. continued

```
#include<stdio.h>

void main()
{
    int value;
    value = 23;

    printf("Actual value=%d, and address=%d",value, &value);
}
```

Here is the output from the program:

```
Actual value=23, and address=834
```

On my computer, the address where the variable is stored is 834. On your computer, it is almost certainly different. It is a result of differences on the computer you are running on as well as other things. Knowing the address of a variable will turn out to be very important in C programming, as you'll learn when we get to the chapters on pointers. In the meantime, what you need to remember about the scanf() function is that you need to precede variable names with the ampersand character.

This chapter has taken a look at three types of input and output. We first looked at both input and output for character variables. You learned about the getch() and putchar() functions to accomplish this. We then looked at formatted input and output operations. We were able to take a close look at how to use the printf() and scanf() functions to tailor how the output will be displayed, or to tailor what information we will get from the user.

The next chapter looks at operators. It examines some of the math features of C and how operators are used in the language.

What You Have Learned

In this chapter you looked at fundamental input and output operations. The chapter focused on the interaction between the computer and the keyboard or monitor. In particular, the following topics were covered:

- Input and output operations are not provided for directly by the C language. Library functions must be used to access any type of I/O device, including the keyboard, the video display, the parallel printer port, and any other I/O devices on your computer.

- Turbo C++ provides several functions that perform character input and output. You saw how to get a single character from the user and then display it on the video display. You then learned about the getche() function, which both got a character from the keyboard and echoed it to the video display.

- Turbo C++ provides several predefined streams for use in your programs. Streams enable you to automatically have access to the keyboard, the video display, the printer port, the serial port, and a standard error stream that is usually routed to the video display.

- You use the scanf() function to input formatted data. This function enables you to specify the type and format of data to be input. The function expects you to supply a format string argument specifying data types to input, and a list of addresses indicating where input data will be stored.

- You use the printf() function to output formatted data. This function enables you to specify the type and format of data to be output. The printf() function enables you to specify the type and format of data to be output. The function expects you to supply a format string argument specifying data types to output, and a list of variables to be output.

6

Operators

Goals

After reading this chapter, you will

- Be familiar with the basic operators available in the C programming language.

- Know how an assignment operator is used to assign a value to a variable.

- Understand how automatic type conversions work to convert data types when you use the assignment operator.

- Know how the five arithmetic operators in the C programming language operate.

- Know the precedence of operators in C.

● Know how to use parentheses to force the compiler to evaluate an expression in a certain order.

● Be familiar with the six types of relational operators in the C programming language.

● Understand how the increment and decrement operators work.

● Differentiate between the prefix and postfix operators.

● After reading this chapter, the reader will know how logical operators are used while programming in C.

Operators are words or symbols that cause a program to do something to variables. The C programming language includes a large number of operators that fall into several different categories. In this chapter, we examine several of these categories in detail. Specifically, we will see how assignment operators, arithmetic operators, relational tests, and logical operators are used to form expressions.

Assignment Operators

You have already seen the use of the assignment operator used previously in this book. An example follows:

```
int num;
num = 11;
```

The first statement declares an integer variable. It is given a name (num) and a type (int). The second statement uses the assignment operator (=) to assign the variable a value. This operator has the same function as the := operator in Pascal or the = operator in BASIC.

Assignment expressions that make use of the = operator are written in the form

```
identifier = expression;
```

where *identifier* usually represents a variable, and *expression* represents a constant, a variable, or a more complex expression. Listing 6.1 shows an example for the use of the assignment operator.

Listing 6.1. Sample assignment operators program.

```
/****************************************************
 ASSIGN1.C--Demonstrate assignment operator use.
 Do It Yourself Turbo C++ by Paul J. Perry
 ****************************************************/

#include <stdio.h>              /* standard I/O header file */

void main()
{

    int x,y;
    x=5;
    y=10;
    x = y;
    printf("x is equal to %d", x);
}
```

The output of the program looks like this:

```
x     is equal to 10
```

Let's take a closer look at what the program does. The first statement (line 11) declares two integer variables (x and y). The second and third statements assign the variable x with the value 5 and the variable y with the value 10. The fourth statement assigns the value of y (which was just defined to be equal to 10) to the variable x. The result is x is equal to 10.

Independent Assignment Statements

Assignment expressions are often referred to as *assignment statements*, because they are usually written as complete statements. However (as you will see later), assignment expressions can also be written as expressions that are included within other statements.

101

Automatic Type Conversion

Let's take another look at an example of an assignment expression with a little different scenario. Type and execute Listing 6.2.

Listing 6.2. Second assignment operator example.

```
/*****************************************************
 ASSIGN2.C--Assignment operator with two data types.
 Do It Yourself Turbo C++ by Paul J. Perry
 *****************************************************/

#include <stdio.h>          /* standard I/O header file */

void main()
{
    int num1;
    float num2;
    num2 = 3.2425;
    num1 = num2;
    printf("num1 is equal to %d", num1);
}
```

Listing 6.2 declares two variables, one of type int and the other of type float. This time, we try to assign the integer variable (num1) to be equal to the floating-point number (num2). There is a fundamental problem, because as we learned, integer numbers are different than floating-point numbers.

The compiler automatically takes care of the conversion for us. In the previous example, the program outputs the following line:

```
num1 is equal to 3
```

What happened was that the value of the number to the right of the decimal point was dropped and the compiler converted the remaining number to an integer type. This conversion of variable types is called *automatic type conversion*.

The entire expression then becomes the same type. Under some circumstances, this automatic type conversion can result in an alteration of the date being assigned. Certain rules follow:

- An int (integer) quantity may be altered if it is assigned to a shorter integer identifier or to a character identifier.

- A float (floating-point) value may be truncated if it is assigned to an integer identifier (as was the case in Listing 6.2).

- A double (double-precision) value may be rounded if it is assigned to a floating-point identifier.

Be careful in your use of type conversion. It is frequently a source of errors among beginning C programmers. It can sometimes cause sneaky things to happen to your data if you are not aware of it.

The next group of operators we will explore is that concerned with arithmetic.

Arithmetic Operators

You have already seen uses for arithmetic operators (there are some operators you cannot get around using when you try to teach the basics). C provides five arithmetic operators, which are summarized in Table 6.1.

Table 6.1. Arithmetic operators in C.

Operator	Purpose
+	Addition
-	Subtraction
*	Multiplication
/	Division
%	Remainder (modulus operator)

The C programming language uses the four arithmetic operators that are common in most other programming languages, including BASIC and Pascal. It also uses one, the remainder operator, that is not as common.

The operands acted on by the arithmetic operators must represent numeric values. Thus, the operands can be integer, floating point, or character (because character variables are actually represented as integer quantities). Following the laws of mathematics, the division operator (/) requires the second operand to be nonzero.

Division of one integer value by another is referred to as *integer division.* The % operator is the remainder after dividing integer values. It is sometimes referred to as the *modulus operator.* It requires that both operands be integer variables, and that the second operand be nonzero. Integer division always has the effect, in a result, where the decimal portion of the quotient is dropped.

Chapter 5 included several sample programs that demonstrated the multiplication (*) operator. Listing 5.3 (PRINTF.C) included the following statement:

```
cent = inches * 2.54;
```

This statement multiplied the value of the variable inches by 2.54 and assigned that resulting value to the variable cent.

Another example was in Listing 5.4 (SCANF.C) with the following line:

```
days = age * 365;
```

Similar to the previous example, this one multiplied the value of the variable age (which was assumed to be in years) by the integer value 365 (the number of days in a year) to tell users how old they are in days.

Both of the previous examples use simple multiplication. The C programming language can easily handle more complex expressions. Listing 6.3 is an example of a program that converts temperatures from Fahrenheit to centigrade.

Listing 6.3. Math expression example to convert Fahrenheit temperatures to centigrade.

```
/****************************************************************
FTOC.C--Convert Fahrenheit temperature to centigrade.
Do It Yourself Turbo C++ by Paul J. Perry
****************************************************************/

void main()
{
    int faren, cent;
```

```
    printf("Please enter temperature in degrees Fahrenheit: ");
    scanf("%d", &faren);
    cent = (faren-32) * 5 / 9;
    printf("%d degrees Fahrenheit is equal to %d degrees centi- \
grade",
                faren, cent);

}
```

Here's some sample interactions with the program:

```
Please enter temperature in degrees Fahrenheit: 68
68 degrees Fahrenheit is equal to 20 degrees centigrade.

Please enter temperature in degrees Fahrenheit: 0
0 degrees Fahrenheit is equal to -17 degrees centigrade.
```

This program uses the standard formula for converting temperatures between Fahrenheit and centigrade. It asks the user for a temperature in Fahrenheit. It then subtracts 32 from the Fahrenheit temperature and multiplies the result by five-ninths. The formula was entered into the computer as follows:

```
cent = (faren-32) * 5 / 9;
```

> You will notice that some parts of the formula have extra spaces around them, and others don't. As was mentioned in earlier chapters, the compiler disregards spaces surrounding your operators. You are free to arrange the expressions however you like. The following expression is considered the same as the previous one:
>
> ```
> cent = ( faren - 32)*5/9;
> ```

The other point to notice about the formula is the use of parentheses. The reason parentheses are used is that we want 32 subtracted from faren before we multiply by 5 and divide by 9. Because multiplication is usually carried out before addition and subtraction, we use parentheses to ensure that the subtraction is carried out first. The parentheses are used to force Turbo C++ to evaluate an expression in a specific order.

Relational Tests

Relational operators are symbols used to compare two values. If the values compare correctly according to the relational operator, the expression is considered true; otherwise, it is considered false. There are six relational operators in the C programming language. They are listed in Table 6.2.

Table 6.2. Relational operators.

Operator	Full Name	Example(s)	
<	Less than	5 < 10	5 is less than 10
>	Greater than	10 > 5	10 is greater than 5
==	Equal to	10 == 10	10 is equal to 10
!=	Not equal to	9 != 10	9 is not equal to 10
<=	Less than or equal to	5 <= 5	5 is less than or equal to 5
		5 <= 10	5 is less than or equal to 10
>=	Greater than or equal to	10 >= 10	10 is greater than or equal to 10
		20 >= 10	20 is greater than or equal to 10

The resulting expressions of the true-or-false type comparisons represent an expression of type integer, because true is represented by the integer value 1 and false is represented by the integer value 0.

For example, the expression 10 > 9 (10 is greater than 9) results in a true value. However, the expression 9 > 10 (9 is greater than 10) is a false expression. Listing 6.4 provides an example of the relational operators.

Listing 6.4. Working with relational operators.

```
/****************************************************************
  RELATION.C--Sample to test relational operators.
  Do It Yourself Turbo C++ by Paul J. Perry
 ****************************************************************/

#include <stdio.h>

void main()
{
    int i;

    i = 7;
    printf("i is equal to: %d\n\n",i);
    printf("i < 5 is %d\n", i<5); /* False */
    printf("i > 4 is %d\n", i>4);/* True */
    printf("i == 6 is %d\n", i==6);/* False */
    printf("i != 7 is %d\n", i!=7);/* False */
    printf("i <= 10 is %d\n", i<=10);/* True */
    printf("i >= 6 is %d\n", i>=6);/* True */
}
```

The program declares a variable and assigns it a starting value. A series of relational tests is then carried out. The output of the program should look similar to this:

```
i    is equal to: 7

i    < 5 is 0
i    > 4 is 1
i    == 6 is 0
i    != 7 is 0
i    <= 10 is 1
i    >= 6 is 1
```

Each `printf()` statement includes a relational operator. It returns a value of 1 (true) or 0 (false). The tests themselves are pretty self-explanatory.

Chapters 7 and 8 discuss conditional statements and program flow, and use relational operators to help make decisions about how a program should operate.

Unary Operators

The C programming language includes some rather unique unary operators. The operators we have looked at so far work on two variables. Next we are going to look at *unary operators,* which act on a single variable at a time. Although only two of C's unary operators are covered now, they are the ones that are most interesting. The unary operators act on a single operand to produce a new value.

Increasing and Decreasing Operand Values

The two unary operators we are going to work with are called the *increment operator* (++), and the *decrement operator* (- -). The increment operator causes its operand (or the variable it is next to) to be increased by one, where the decrement operator causes its operand (or variable it is next to) to be decreased by one. These two operators work only on a single variable.

An example follows:

```
int i;
i = 0;
++i;
--i;
```

This code causes the integer variable i to be initialized to zero and then incremented by 1 (in statement 3) and decremented by 1 (in statement 4). It is equal to the statement:

```
int i;
i = 0;
i    = i + 1; /* same as ++i */
i    = i -1; /* same as --i */
```

Prefix and Postfix Operators

The increment and decrement operators are used in different ways, depending on whether the operator is written before or after the operand.

If the operator precedes the operand (as in ++i), the operand will be altered in value before it is used within the program (so the operator in this case is the *prefix operator*). If, the operator follows the operand (as in i++), then the value of the operand will be changed after the variable is used (so the operator is called the *postfix operator*).

At this point, it may not seem important whether the operand is altered before or after it is used. Listing 6.5 gives a demonstration of the increment operator with both prefix and postfix notation. This example should clear things up for you. Type the program in and run it now.

Listing 6.5. Increment operator example.

```
/**************************************************************
UNARY.C--Show the use of the increment operator.
Do It Yourself Turbo C++ by Paul J. Perry
**************************************************************/

void main()
{
    int val;
    val = 10;

    printf("i = %d\n", val);
    printf("i = %d\n", ++val);
    printf("i = %d\n", val);
    printf("i = %d\n", val++);
    printf("i = %d\n", val);
}
```

This program's output looks like this:

```
i    = 10
i    = 11
i    = 11
i    = 11
i    = 12
```

The program declares an integer variable and assigns it a value of 10. The starting value of the variable is displayed in the first printf() statement. The next statement increments the value of the variable and displays its output. It uses the prefix increment operator. The next line displays the new value of the variable (which is the same as what is displayed in the previous line).

Now we use the postfix version of the increment operator in line 14. Notice that the printed output for the fourth line is the same as for the previous line. However, we know the variable was incremented, because when we display the final value (in line 5), it is what we expect. This is due to the use of the postfix version of the increment operator.

This example demonstrates the power of the increment (and indirectly the decrement) operators. They enable the programmer to have complete control of when the operator modifies the value and what value is returned in a program.

The increment and decrement operators are examples of operators in the C programming language that other programming languages don't have. As we continue, you will discover other features of C that just aren't available in other programming languages.

Logical Operators

In addition to the relational and equality operators, C contains two logical operators. They are presented in Table 6.3.

Table 6.3. Logical operators.

Operator	Description	Explanation
&&	AND	Result is true if both expressions are true.
¦¦	OR	Result is true if either expression is true.
!	NOT	Result reverses the condition of the expression.

The logical operators are rather unique because they usually work on operands that are themselves logical expressions (although not always).

The result is to combine individual logical expressions into more complex conditions that are either true or false.

> To place this in the context of everyday living, we would call an expression such as "If it is sunny, I will go swimming" a simple expression. Another simple expression might be "If I have time, I will go swimming." We can combine these two simple statements and say, "If I have time *and* if it is sunny, I will go swimming." This result is a complex statement.

Before looking at complex statements, we will get an overall feel for the use of logical operators.

The logical AND, as well as logical OR operators work on two operands to return a logical value based on the operands. The logical NOT operator works on a single operand. Tables 6.4, 6.5, and 6.6 show the results of the logical tests. Notice that every logical value is represented as x and y values. The result signifies how the logical operator is evaluated.

> A *truth table* is a way to picture the result of a logical expression. The x and y refer to two different variables. The result shows what happens when the logical function is applied to the variables with the corresponding values.

Table 6.4. Logical AND (&&) truth table.

x	y	Result
1	1	1 (true)
1	0	0 (false)
0	1	0 (false)
0	0	0 (false)

Table 6.5. Logical OR (¦¦) truth table.

x	y	Result
1	1	1 (true)
1	0	1 (true)
0	1	1 (true)
0	0	0 (false)

Table 6.6. Logical NOT (!) truth table.

x	Result
1	0
0	1

To explain logical operators, several examples follow:

```
1 && 1
0 ¦¦ 0
!1
```

The first statement is an example of the AND operator. If you look in the truth table, it should return a value of 1. This is the only case that the AND logical operator returns a true value. All other times it returns false.

The second statement shows the use of the OR operator. It returns a false condition. This is the one condition that the OR operator would return false. In all other cases it only returns true. The last statement demonstrates the NOT operator. It only takes one operator, and returns a logical expression that is the opposite of what it operates on.

Listing 6.6 is an example of a program that uses complex statements. Type it in and execute it now.

Listing 6.6 Example of complex logical statements.

```
/*****************************************************************
LOGIC.C--Test the logical operators.
Do It Yourself Turbo C++ by Paul J. Perry
*****************************************************************/
```

```
void main()
{
    int a,b;

    a = 1;
    b = 2;
    printf("Beginning values:\n");
    printf("a = %d\nb = %d\n", a,b);
    printf("Tests\n:");
    printf("a == 1 is %d\n", a==1);
    printf("b != 1 is %d\n", b!=1);
    printf("Therefore, (a == 1) && (b != 1) is %d\n",
(a==1)&&(b!=1));
}
```

The program results display like this:

```
Beginning values:
a = 1
b = 2
Tests:
a == 1 is 1
b != 1 is 1
Therefore, (a == 1) && (b != 1) is 1
```

The program starts by assigning two variables (a and b) beginning values. It then displays the result of two simple statements. Finally, it combines the simple statements into a complex one and shows the result.

Logical expressions are important to the way computers are used. Internally, the microprocessor uses only logical tests. Luckily, we do not always need to use them. However, C provides them to enable you to have close interaction with the internals of the microprocessor.

We have covered several important operators in this chapter. Before we end, we must cover one more important topic for discussions about operators: operator precedence.

Operator Precedence

Earlier, when working with arithmetic operators, we used parentheses to force the compiler to evaluate math operations in a specific order. It is a good question then, to ask "How does the compiler evaluate operators?"

The compiler must determine the order in which operators are applied. This is specified by operators' *precedence.* Table 6.7 summarizes operator precedence. Operators with highest precedence (or those that are applied first) are at the top of the list.

Table 6.7. Operator precedence in C.

Operator Type	*Operators*	*Associativity*
Unary	- - ++	Right to left
Logical NOT	!	Right to left
Multiplication	* / %	Left to right
Addition	+ -	Left to right
Relational	< <= > >=	Left to right
Relational (Equality)	== !=	Left to right
Logical AND	&&	Left to right
Logical OR	¦ ¦	Left to right
Assignment	=	Right to left

Each group of operators in the table has a certain associativity. *Associativity* refers to how the compiler performs operations starting with an operator on the right or an operator on the left. If a group of operators has right associativity, the compiler performs the operation on the right side of the expression first, then works its way to the left. The operators are either evaluated from left to right or right to left. The only time this table is used is when you mix operators of different types; otherwise, expressions are evaluated in simple left-to-right or right-to-left order. As you saw earlier, using parentheses we can override the precedence of any of the operators.

What You Have Learned

In this chapter you looked at the main operators available in the C programming language. You learned how they work and what they are used for. Although Chapter 12 returns to the subject of operators, what you learned here is a good basis for continuing to learn the important parts of the C programming language. The following topics were covered:

- Operators are words or symbols that cause a program to do something to variables. This chapter looked at assignment operators, arithmetic operators, relational operators, and logical operators.

- Assignment operators are used to assign a value to a variable. When assignment is between two different data types, the compiler will convert between data types through the use of automatic type conversion.

- Several rules dictate how automatic type conversion works. First, an `int` quantity may be changed if it is assigned to a shorter integer identifier. Second, a `float` value may be truncated if it is assigned to an integer identifier. Last, a `double` value may be rounded if assigned to a variable of type `float`.

- There are five arithmetic operators. The four basic math operations (addition, subtraction, multiplication, and division) are included. The other arithmetic operator is the remainder operator, which is used in integer division. It results in the decimal portion of a quotient to be dropped.

- The relational operators compare two values. If the two values compare favorably, the expression is considered a true expression, otherwise it is considered false. A true and false condition is represented by the compiler as an integer with a value of 1 (true) or 0 (false).

- The increment operator (++) adds 1 to its operand, and the decrement operator (- -) subtracts 1. These are the two unary operators we looked at in this chapter.

● The C programming language includes three logical operators: AND, OR, and NOT. AND and OR work on two operands and return a logical result that is the result of testing the two operands. NOT works on a single operand and returns a value opposite to what it operates on.

● Operator precedence determines the order in which expressions are evaluated in C. Operators with high precedence (as listed in Table 6.7) are applied first.

Conditional Statements

Goals

After reading this chapter, you will

- Know what the three major decision-making statements are in the C programming language.

- Recognize how the `if` statement is used to make a decision.

- Know how to use the `if...else` statement as an extension of the `if` statement and what added benefits `if...else` offers.

- Understand how the `switch` statement is used in C and the `switch` statement's relationship to the `break` statement.

● Know how to use the break statement to escape from a block of code.

The essence of any computer program is the decisions it can make and act on. Every day, humans must make decisions based on certain facts and act appropriately. For example, if somebody knocks on my front door, I look to see who it is. If it is a friend, I will ask her in for a cup of coffee. However, if I see the newspaper carrier, I will go fetch my wallet so I can pay my monthly newspaper tab.

The same sort of decision making occurs in computer programs. Certain tests are made and a response is set into motion depending on what the results of the test were. Any computer program must make decisions to be useful. The conditional statements we look at in this chapter allow a program to make decisions and act on them.

The C programming language has three major decision-making statements: the if statement, the if...else statement, and the switch statement. This chapter examines the methods a C program can use to react to program information using these decision-making statements.

The if Statement

In making decisions, the computer decides on the basis of current conditions within your program which statements to execute. The if statement is the basic decision-making statement in C.

Syntax

The general form of the if statement is

```
if (expression)
    statement;
```

The if statement enables your code to test an expression and branch according to how the expression is evaluated. If the expression evaluates to true (1), the computer will execute the statement that follows. However, if the condition evaluates false (0), the statement is not executed. The expression is one of the relational tests we covered in Chapter 6.

If you have used another programming language, such as Pascal or BASIC, you will notice that the `if` statement in C does not use the `then` keyword. If you try to slip it in, the compiler reminds you not to use the term with a friendly message—undefined symbol 'then'. The compiler forces you to remove the undefined symbol before it will compile your program.

For example, consider Listing 7.1, which plays a version of the "guess the number" game. You are prompted to enter a number. The program uses the equality operator (==) to determine whether the players guess matches the constant `secretnumber` declared in the program. If you enter the right number, the program will display the message `You guessed it!`. If you do not enter the correct number, the program displays nothing.

Listing 7.1. Sample `if` statement.

```
/*****************************************************
 IF.C--Sample program to demonstrate the if statement.
 Do It Yourself Turbo C++ by Paul J. Perry
 *****************************************************/

#include <stdio.h>

void main()
{
     const int secretnumber = 24;
     int number;

printf("Enter a number and try to guess the one I am thinking of: \
");
     scanf("%d", &number);

     if(number == secretnumber)
       printf("\nYou guessed it!");

}
```

In the previous program listing, the if statement could actually have been displayed on one line, such as follows:

```
if(number == secretnumber) printf("\nYou guessed it!");
```

The idea for splitting the statement into two lines is to make it easier for humans to read and understand.

When you type the program listing, be careful not to type too many semicolons at the end of the lines. Especially notice line 16, which starts with the if statement. It does not end with a semicolon, as you may have become used to in previous C programs. This is because the line following it is actually part of the statement. If you add an extra semicolon, such as in

```
if(number == secretnumber);
    printf("\nYou guessed it!");
```

the result will cause the printf() function to be executed every time the program is run, regardless of whether number is equal to secretnumber. The terminating semicolon in the if statement tells the compiler that the conditional statement is complete, and the next printf() statement is executed just like a regular statement. This is a common notational convention that causes beginning C programmers to start pulling their hair out when they find it after hunting laboriously through a program for an error.

Using Program Blocks with the **if** Statement

The body of the if statement may consist of a single statement followed by a semicolon (as was demonstrated earlier) or by a number of statements surrounded by braces. The modified form of the if statement that executes a block of statements follows:

```
if (expression)
    {
        statement1;
        statement2;
            .
```

.
.
statementX;

    }

The braces surround the multiple statements that are to be executed if the expression evaluates to true. There is no limit to the number of statements you can include in an if statement.

It is important to include both opening and closing braces. If you forget to include one, the compiler gets confused quickly.

Listing 7.2 is a version of the earlier program, rewritten to display several lines of congratulations to the player who guesses the correct number.

Listing 7.2. Using program blocks in an if statement.

```
/*************************************************************
 IF2.C--Sample program to demonstrate multiple statements
        in an if statement.
 Do It Yourself Turbo C++ by Paul J. Perry
 *************************************************************/

#include <stdio.h>

void main()
{
     const int secretnumber = 24;
     int number;

printf("Enter a number and try to guess the one I am thinking of: \
"); scanf("%d", &number);

     if(number == secretnumber)
         {
         printf("\nYou guessed it!");
printf("\nYou must have extra special intelligence.");
printf("\nCongratulations to you!");
         }
}
```

Each statement in the block terminated with a semicolon. The entire block is surrounded with braces. Using program blocks within an `if` statement allows the complexity of programs to expand. This point leads us to the topic of nested `if` statements.

Nested `if` Statements

A nested `if` statement is an `if` statement that is included inside another `if` statement. The general case follows:

```
if (expression)
  if (another expression)
    statement;
```

The second `if` statement is actually part of the body of the first one. The inner `if` statement will not be executed unless the outer one evaluates to true. The `statement` will not be executed unless both `if` statements evaluate to true.

Listing 7.3 shows how to use nested `if` statements. This is a modification of the original "guess a number" program. This time, if you don't guess the correct number, the program tells you whether you guessed too high or too low.

Listing 7.3. Example of nested `if` statements.

```
/****************************************************
 IF3.C--Sample program showing nested if statements.
 Do It Yourself Turbo C++ by Paul J. Perry
 ****************************************************/

#include <stdio.h>

void main()
{
    const int secretnumber = 24;
    int number;

printf("Enter a number and try to guess the one I am thinking of: \
"); scanf("%d", &number);
```

```
if(number == secretnumber) printf("\nYou guessed it!");

    if(number != secretnumber)
        {
        printf("Sorry, you didn't guess it...\n");

        if (number > secretnumber)
printf("You guessed too high\n");

        if (number < secretnumber)
                printf("You guessed too low\n");
        }

}
```

Line 19 checks whether the number the player guessed is not equal (using the != operator) to secretnumber. If it is not, it checks whether the number is greater than or less than secretnumber. One of two messages is then displayed depending on whether the number is greater than or less than secretnumber.

The **if...else** Statement

The if statement is a powerful part of the C programming language that you can use in your programs to test expressions and take an appropriate action depending on the expression tested. By definition, the if statement executes a single statement or group of statements when an expression evaluates to true. It does not take any action if the expression is false. This is where the if...else statement comes into action.

Syntax

The if...else statement is similar to the if statement. It adds an additional set of instructions, as follows:

```
if (expression)
  statement1;
else
  statement2;
```

The first two lines are the same as our original `if` statement. The `else` keyword signifies the statement that is to be executed if the expression does not evaluate to true. To demonstrate the added power of the `if...else` statement, let's rewrite the number-guessing program, as shown in Listing 7.4.

Listing 7.4. Sample of the `if...else` statement.

```
/*************************************************************
IFELSE.C--Sample program showing the if...else statement.
Do It Yourself Turbo C++ by Paul J. Perry
*************************************************************/

#include <stdio.h>

void main()
{
    const int secretnumber = 24;
    int number;

printf("Enter a number and try to guess the one I am thinking of: \
"); scanf("%d", &number);

if(number == secretnumber) printf("\nYou guessed it!");
    else
        printf("\nSorry, you didn't guess it");

}
```

You can see how the `if...else` statement simplifies the program. It has a single `if...else` group of statements that either displays the message `You guessed it!` if you entered the correct number, or `Sorry, you didn't guess it` if the number you entered was not equal to `secretnumber`.

All along the sample programs have tested different variables. You can also test a function, because functions return values. The following example, Listing 7.5, tests the result of the getche() function and displays a value depending on what the user enters.

Listing 7.5. Program that uses a function as an expression.

```
/***********************************************************
IFELSE2.C--Use a function call instead of an expression
           in the if...else statement.
Do It Yourself Turbo C++ by Paul J. Perry
***********************************************************/

#include <stdio.h>
#include <conio.h>  /* used for getche() function */

void main()
{
    printf("Type a key on the keyboard: ");

    if (getche() == 'y')
        printf("\nYou pressed the y key");
    else
        printf("\nYou did not press the y key");

}
```

This example starts to show some of the power of the C programming language in testing the result of a function within an if...else statement.

Nested **if...else** Statements

The if...else statement can be nested just as the if statement can. However, you need to be careful, because nested if...else statements have the potential for ambiguity. For example, consider the program IFELSE3.C in Listing 7.6.

Listing 7.6. Nested `if...else` statements.

```
/************************************************************
   IFELSE3.C--Sample program that uses nested if...else
              statements.
   Do It Yourself Turbo C++ by Paul J. Perry
 ************************************************************/

#include <stdio.h>

void main()
{
printf("Enter a number and try to guess the one I am thinking of: \
");

    if (getche() == '2')
        if (getche() == '4')
                    printf("\nYou guessed the number!");
        else
printf("\nSorry, you didn't guess it, however you did guess the \
first digit correctly!"); /* goes with second if */
    else
printf("\nSorry, you didn't guess it"); /* goes with first if */
}
```

The program nests two `if...else` statements. It first checks whether the user entered the number 2. If the user did press this key, the code tests whether the number 4 key was pressed. However, if the user did not initially press the number 2, a message is displayed informing the user that he or she didn't guess the correct number. If the first digit is guessed correctly but the second one is not, a message is displayed telling the user so.

The moral of the story is that the C programming language always associates an `else` with the closest preceding `if` statement. In Listing 7.6, the code is formatted to make it obvious what should occur (or at least partially obvious). Don't let the formatting of code mislead you into misinterpreting what a statement does. It might not always have been entered correctly, and formatting the code incorrectly will create a logical error that can be difficult to track down.

The **switch** Statement

We can make some pretty advanced decisions using the if or if...else statements. However, sometimes, the resulting code can be difficult to follow and can confuse even an advanced programmer. The C programming language has a built-in, multiple-branch decision statement, called switch. The switch statement causes a particular group of statements to be chosen from several available groups. The switch statement is similar to the else...if statement but has increased flexibility and a clearer format.

Syntax

The switch statement is similar to the case statement in Pascal or the Select...Case statement in Microsoft QuickBASIC. Neither BASICA nor GWBASIC has an equivalent statement.

The general form of the switch statement is

```
switch (expression)
    {

    case constant1 :
        statement1;
        break;

    case constant2 :
        statement2;
        break;

    case constant3 :
        statement3;
        break;
                    .
                    .
                    .

    case constantX :
        statementX;
        break;
```

```
default :
    default statement;
}
```

In the switch statement, the computer tests a variable consecutively against a list of integer or character constants. After finding a match, the computer executes the statement or block of statements that are associated with the specified constant.

The default statement is executed if the compiler does not find a match in the list of constants. The default statement is optional. If default is not present, no action takes place if all matches fail. When it finds a match, the computer executes the statements associated with the specified case until it reaches the break statement or the end of the switch statement.

Following each of the case keywords is an integer or character constant. This constant is completed with a colon (not a semicolon). There can be one or more statements following each case keyword. The statements are not required to be enclosed in braces. However, the entire body of the switch statement is enclosed in braces.

Listing 7.7 shows how to use the switch statement to process keyboard commands, much as would be used in a menu program. The program displays a menu and prompts the user to enter a value. It then displays a message about what is happening. In a real menu program, you would use a function call that would execute an appropriate command to carry out the request of the user.

Listing 7.7. MENU.C Sample switch statement.

```
/***************************************************************
 MENU.C--Show use of the switch statement.
 . Do It Yourself Turbo C++ by Paul J. Perry
 ***************************************************************/

#include <stdio.h>

void main()
{
    char ch;

    printf(" ***Main Menu***\n");
```

```
printf("1. Word Processor\n");
printf("2. Spreadsheet\n");
printf("3. Database\n");
printf("...else\n");
printf("   Press any other key to skip the menu \
           selection\n\n");
printf("Your Choice: ");

ch = getche();  /* Get the selection from the keyboard */

switch (ch)
{
    case '1' :
             printf("\nExecuting Word processor\n");
             break;

    case '2' :
             printf("\nExecuting Spreadsheet\n");
             break;

    case '3' :
             printf("\nExecuting Database\n");
             break;

    default :
             printf("\nNo menu selection made!\n");
}

}
```

Notice the use of the break statement at the end of each case. If you do not use the break statement, program flow continues to the next case. Sometimes this can be very helpful when several conditions use the same piece of code. Most of the time, this is not what you want. Sometimes, the ability of the cases to run together when no break statement is present enables you to write efficient code by avoiding duplication of code.

Listing 7.8 demonstrates how to use more then one case statement with a set of instructions.

Listing 7.8. Program showing other uses of the switch statement.

```
/
**************************************************************************
 SWITCH.C--Sample program showing other uses for the switch state-
ment.
 Do It Yourself Turbo C++ by Paul J. Perry
**************************************************************************/

#include <stdio.h>

void main()
{
    char ch;

    printf("Do you wish to continue program execution (Y/N) ? ");

    ch = getche();   /* Get the selection from the keyboard */

    switch (ch)
    {
        case 'y' :
        case 'Y' :
                printf("\nThe answer was YES\n");
                break;

        case 'n' :
        case 'N' :
                printf("\nThe answer was NO\n");
                break;

        default :
                printf("\nWrong answer.\n");
    }

}
```

The program shows a common case (no pun intended) in which you need to respond to a letter selection from the user (Y for yes or N for no). However, you don't want to force the user to type the letter in either upper- or lowercase. The SWITCH.C program uses the same code to process the key, no matter whether the user entered the value in upper- or lowercase.

As you progress in your study of the C language, you will learn other ways to work with letters and methods that we can use to convert them from upper- to lowercase and vice versa. For now, the previous program gives a good example of the switch statement.

Nested **switch** Statements

As with the if and if...else statements, the switch statement can be nested. When you nest it, the switch statement is part of the statement sequence of an outer switch. Even if the case constant of the inner switch and the outer switch contain common values, no conflicts will arise.

The general form of the nested switch statement is

```
switch (expression)
    {

    case constant1 :
        switch (another expression)
            {
                        case constant1 :
                            statement1;
                            break;

                        case constant2 :
                            statement2;
                            break;

                        default :
                            default statement;

            }

    case constant2 :
        statement2;
        break;

    case constant3 :
        statement3;
        break;
```

```
                .
                .
                .
    case constantX :
        statementX;
        break;

    default :
        default statement;
    }
```

This general form probably looks familiar, because it is just a switch statement inside another switch statement. The expression used for each switch statement is usually different.

The switch statement is such a powerful element of the C programming language, it is actually the core statement used in advanced graphical operating environments such as Microsoft Windows. Although programming for this environment is a topic of its own, the core of every program written for Microsoft Windows has a switch statement that is The break Statement

You have seen the break statement used to exit the switch statement. You will see it used in other ways in programs as well. The break statement causes a transfer of control out of the switch statement to the first subsequent statement.

We have looked at the three fundamental decision-making statements in the C programming language. The next chapter takes an equally important look at program flow control statements.

If you have typed in the sample programs in this chapter and feel comfortable with the material presented, let's continue our exploration of the C programming language. Otherwise, go ahead and follow through the sample programs now, take a break, and pick up the book tomorrow, after a well-deserved break.

What You Have Learned

This chapter focused on decision-making statements. You learned the commands used in C to make decisions and act on them. Specifically, the following topics were covered:

● The three decision-making statements in the C programming language are the `if` statement, the `if...else` statement, and the `switch` statement.

● The `if` statement is the fundamental decision-making statement in C. It allows your program to test an expression and execute a statement or group of statements depending on the outcome of the test.

● The `if` statement can be used to execute a block of statements by surrounding the block with braces.

● A program can nest `if` statements, by including an `if` statement inside another `if` statement. This expands your programs' decision-making capabilities.

● The `if...else` statement is an expanded version of the `if` statement that will take action if the expression is true as well as if the expression is not true.

● You can nest the `if...else` statement just like the `if` statement can. When doing so, you must be careful in interpreting which `else` belongs to which `if` statement. The rule to remember is that C always associates an `else` with the nearest preceding `if` statement.

● The `switch` statement is used to cause a particular group of statements to be chosen from among several available groups.

● The `switch` statement can cause several cases to use the same code, resulting in more efficient use of your program's resources.

● Because of C's flexibility, the `switch` statement can be nested, similar to the way the `if` and `if...else` statements can. When this occurs, the `switch` statement is part of the statement sequence of an outer `switch`. Even if the `case` constant of the inner `switch` and the outer `switch` contain common values, no conflicts will arise.

8

Program Flow

Goals

After reading this chapter, you will

- Know the three basic program flow statements available to C programmers and why program flow instructions are used.

- Understand how the for loop is used inside a C program.

- Comprehend how to use a while loop in a program and what situations are favorable for using the while statement. The reader will be presented with several examples demonstrating the use of the while statement.

- Know what the uses are for the do...while statement.

- Know how and when to use the goto statement and why it was included in the C programming language.

The previous chapter introduced the C decision-making statements. Just as important as the decision-making statements you learned about are program flow statements.

By default, C program instructions are usually executed in the order in which they appear in the program listing, from beginning to end. Each instruction is executed once and only once. Programs of this type are limited and not practical, because they do not include any logical control structures.

To increase flexibility in the order of code execution, C provides *program flow statements,* which allow a computer to continuously attack a repetitive task without getting bored or tired. We can tell our programs to repeat a task for any number of times. The computer does not whine, get cranky, or speak back.

Many programs require a group of instructions to be executed repeatedly, until some logical condition has been satisfied. This condition is known as *looping.* Sometimes you won't know the number of repetitions required in advance. You may have a situation in which a loop continues until a logical condition becomes true. All of these operations can be carried out using different types of looping statements in C.

Looping statements are used to control program flow. One of the chief strengths of a computer is its ability to perform repeated tasks rapidly, accurately, and without complaint. You can tell the computer to do the same thing over and over again, millions of times, if necessary.

There are three major program loop statements in the C programming language: the for loop, the while loop, and the do...while loop. Each of them are discussed in this chapter in turn. We will take a look at the different varieties of each type of loop, too.

The **for** Loop

The for loop is the fundamental looping statement in C. Often in C programming, a programmer wants to carry out a task a specific number of times. The `for` loop is the statement you use to carry out the job. The `for` loop is found in almost every programming language available. However, the C `for` statement gives you more power and flexibility (read: more complexity) than do most languages' versions of `for`.

The general form of the `for` statement is

```
for (initialization; condition; increment)
    statement;
```

The parentheses following the keyword `for` contains the necessary elements of the statement. The `initialization` section is used to initialize an index parameter that controls looping action. The `condition` represents a condition that must be satisfied for the loop to continue execution. Finally, `increment` is a value representing how to increment (add to) the index variable.

The body of the `for` loop is located in the `statement` section. You can use braces to enclose multiple statements or to list a single statement (as shown in the syntax).

> A common error is to place a semicolon between the loop expressions and the body of the loop. Don't do it. The resulting code does not create a complex C statement, and therefore will not be compiled.

To get you started, Listing 8.1 gives an example of a simple `for` loop. It displays the numbers from 1 to 100.

Listing 8.1. Loop to count from 1 up to 100.

```
/*************************************************************
 FORLOOP.C--Display the numbers from 1 up to 100.
 Do It Yourself Turbo C++ by Paul J. Perry
 *************************************************************/

#include <stdio.h>

void main()
{
```

continues

Listing 8.1. continued

```
    int x;
    for (x=1; x<=100; x++)
        printf("%d \n", x);


}
```

This program declares an integer index variable called x. The loop initially sets it to 1. The second part of the for statement checks to see if x is less than 100. If it is less than 100, the program calls the printf() function. After the number is displayed, the program increases x by 1 with the increment operator (++). This process repeats until x is greater than 100, at which time the loop terminates and the program ends.

There is no law that says that the loop is required to always run in a positive direction. You can create a program that counts down, by changing the increment operator. For example, Listing 8.2 is a modification of the earlier program, and it displays the numbers from 100 down to 1 on the screen.

Listing 8.2. Loop to count from 100 down to 1.

```
/*************************************************************
 FORLOOP2.C--Display the numbers from 100 down to 1.
 Do It Yourself Turbo C++ by Paul J. Perry
 *************************************************************/

#include <stdio.h>

void main()
{
    int x;
    for (x=100; x>0; x--)
        printf("%d \n", x);


}
```

Listings 8.1 and 8.2 just begin to show the versatility of the for statement. Notice that we use the decrement (--) operator in the second program. We initialize the control variable to 100 at the beginning and compare it to determine whether it's greater than 0. If it is, the loop continues executing. Otherwise, the loop is terminated and the program ends.

C does not restrict you to incrementing or decrementing the value of the control variable by one. You can use any type of assignment operator.

For example, the FORLOOP3.C program in Listing 8.3 displays the numbers 0 to 100, counting by 10.

Listing 8.3. Loop to count by 10 from 0 to 100.

```
/*****************************************************************
 FORLOOP3.C--Display the numbers from 0 up to 100 counting
             by 10.
 Do It Yourself Turbo C++ by Paul J. Perry
 ****************************************************************/


#include <stdio.h>

void main()
{
    int x;
    for (x=0; x<=100; x=x+10)
        printf("%d \n", x);


}
```

The preceding examples have used only a single statement in the body of the loop. Multiple statements can easily be used by enclosing the block of statements in braces. The AVG.C program in Listing 8.4. calculates the average of five numbers entered by the user.

Listing 8.4. Loop to calculate the average of five numbers.

```
/*****************************************************************
 AVG.C--Calculate the average of 5 numbers entered by the user.
 Do It Yourself Turbo C++ by Paul J. Perry
 ****************************************************************/

#include <stdio.h>
```

continues

139

Listing 8.4. continued

```
void main()
{
    int counter;
    const int max = 5;
    float x, average, sum = 0;

    printf("This program will prompt you for five numbers\n");
    printf("It will then display the average of these five \
            numbers \n\n");

    for (counter=1; counter<=max; counter++)
        {
        printf("\nEnter value of number %d : ", counter);
        scanf("%f", &x);
        sum = sum + x;
        }

    average = sum/max;
    printf("\nThe average of the numbers is %f", average);
}
```

The program in Listing 8.4 uses the for statement to prompt the user for five values (because the integer constant max is equal to five). Each time through the loop, the program prompts the user to enter a value and stores it in the variable x. The variable is added to the running total stored in the variable sum. After the loop ends, the program divides the sum by the number of values entered (5). Finally, it displays the results to the user before the program terminates.

The important element of the previous program was the use of braces around the three statements that form the body of the for loop:

```
{
printf("\nEnter value of number %d : ", counter);
scanf("%f", &x);
sum = sum + x;
}
```

The whole group of statements, from brace to brace (rather like from sea to shining sea) is treated as a single statement by the compiler. You will notice that each statement in the block is itself a C statement and requires a final semicolon. However, the entire block is not terminated with a semicolon.

The C programming language allows several variations that increase the power of for loops. One of the more common variations is the ability to use two or more control variables. Listing 8.5 presents the FORLOOP4.C program, which shows how two variables are initialized at one time within the for loop.

Listing 8.5. Sample initialization of several variables in a loop.

```
/************************************************************
 FORLOOP4.C--Show how to initialize several variables.
 Do It Yourself Turbo C++ by Paul J. Perry
 ************************************************************/

#include <stdio.h>

void main()
{
    int counter, total;

    for (counter=0, total=0; counter<=100; counter=counter + 10)
        {
        total = total + 1;
        printf("counter = %d and total = %d\n", counter, total);
        }

}
```

The output of Listing 8.5 is as follows:

```
counter = 0 and total = 1
counter = 10 and total = 2
counter = 20 and total = 3
counter = 30 and total = 4
counter = 40 and total = 5
counter = 50 and total = 6
counter = 60 and total = 7
counter = 70 and total = 8
counter = 80 and total = 9
counter = 90 and total = 10
counter = 100 and total = 11
```

The variables `counter` and `total` were both initialized inside the `for` loop construction. Although the variable `total` was not used as an index variable in the loop, it can still be initialized at the beginning of the loop.

> Initializing variables within loops is one of the nice features of C. It does not force you to use any specific initialization style.

The output of the program displays the value of the counter, as well as the number of times the loop was executed.

Nested **for** Statements

Just as decision-making statements could be nested, so can program flow statements. A nested `for` statement includes one `for` statement within another. To demonstrate this structure, Listing 8.6. presents a short program that displays a multiplication table.

Listing 8.6. Loop to generate a multiplication table.

```
/***********************************************
 TABLE.C--Create a multiplication table.
 Do It Yourself Turbo C++ by Paul J. Perry
 ***********************************************/

#include <stdio.h>

void main()
{
    int column, row;

    for (row=1; row<=10; row++)                    /* main loop */
        {
        for (column=1; column<=10; column++)      /* inner loop */
                printf(" %5d", column * row);
```

```
        printf("\n");
        }
}
```

The program displays a table that looks like the following:

1	2	3	4	5	6	7	8	9	10
2	4	6	8	10	12	14	16	18	20
3	6	9	12	15	18	21	24	27	30
4	8	12	16	20	24	28	32	36	40
5	10	15	20	25	30	35	40	45	50
6	12	18	24	30	36	42	48	54	60
7	14	21	28	35	42	49	56	63	70
8	16	24	32	40	48	56	64	72	80
9	18	27	36	45	54	63	72	81	90
10	20	30	40	50	60	70	80	90	100

The numbers in the left column and top row serve as the labels of the multiplication table. If you go to the intersection point of a row and a column, you find the sum of the two numbers. For example, if you start on the top column at 6 and go down 7 rows to the intersection of 6 and 7, you will see the number 42, because $6 \times 7 = 42$.

Listing 8.6 creates two loops: an inner loop and an outer loop. The inner one steps through 10 columns, from 1 to 10, and the outer loop steps through 10 rows. For each row, the inner loop is cycled through once, then a carriage return is inserted to prepare for the next line of the table.

Each time through the inner loop, at the intersection of each column and row the program multiplies the two numbers and displays it in the table. To ensure that the columns line up correctly, a field-width specifier of 5 is used in the printf() function.

We have examined several different variations of the for loop. You will notice that each for loop requires that you always perform the conditional test at the beginning of the loop. This means that the program may not execute the code inside the loop at all if the condition tested is false.

Next, we will take a look at some program flow structures that grant you more control over when the test is executed.

The **while** Loop

The second type of loop available in the C programming language is the while loop. Its form is

```
while (expression)
    statement;
```

The reserved word while is followed by an expression surrounded by parentheses. The statement can be a single statement followed by a semicolon or a block of statements surrounded by braces.

In the while loop, the body of the loop is executed as long as the expression is true. When the expression becomes false, program control passes to the line that follows the loop.

Listing 8.7 shows a program that gives similar results to Listing 8.1, except it uses the while statement. It counts from 1 to 100 and displays the numbers on the screen.

Listing 8.7. Sample program using the *while* loop.

```
/**************************************************************
 WHILE.C--Example of while statement to count from 1 to 100.
 Do It Yourself Turbo C++ by Paul J. Perry
 **************************************************************/

#include <stdio.h>

void main()
{
    int counter = 1;

    while (counter <100)
        {
```

```
        counter++;
        printf("%d\n", counter);
        }
    }
```

This program has many of the same elements of the simple program that demonstrated the for statement. You will notice how we initialize an index variable (counter, in this case) and increment it within the loop.

The program could have been made more concise as follows:

```
#include <stdio.h>

void main()
{
    int counter = 1;

    while (counter <100)
        printf("%d\n", counter++);
}
```

When executed, this program generates the same output as the first; however, it is three lines shorter. As is usual with C, we can compact our code to do the same thing in fewer instructions. Instead of incrementing the index value as a statement itself, the second example shows it as part of the printf() function call. By doing this, we were able to use a single statement as the target to the while loop.

You can easily argue that one of the two methods (the for statement or the while statement) is easier to use. Each statement has its own time and place. Many times they can be used interchangeably, as you have just seen.

Now take a look at a different type of example. Listing 8.8 (WAIT.C) loops until the user presses a specific key.

Listing 8.8. Loop to wait for user to press P key.

```
/************************************************
 WAIT.C--Wait for user to press the P key.
 Do It Yourself Turbo C++ by Paul J. Perry
 ************************************************/
```

continues

Listing 8.8. continued

```c
#include <stdio.h>

void main()
{
char ch = '\0';  /* initialize variable to 0 */

    printf("\nType the letter P\n");

    while (ch != 'P')
        ch = getche();

    printf("\nYou pressed the letter P");

}
```

First, the program declares a character variable and initializes it to the null (or 0) value. The program displays whatever you type at the keyboard. It only responds when you type the uppercase P. (However, it does display everything you type, because of the `getche()` function.) The `while` loop checks whether `ch` is not equal to P. Each time you press a key, the program tries the test again. After you press the key, the condition becomes false, because `ch` equals the character P, and the loop terminates.

The `while` loop is best used when your loop may be terminated unexpectedly by conditions developing within it. The previous program brought us to the topic. As a more specific example, lets look at a program that counts the number of characters the user types. Listing 8.9 is just what we want to check.

Listing 8.9. Loop to count characters typed by user.

```c
/***********************************************************
 COUNT.C--Count the number of characters typed by the user.
 Do It Yourself Turbo C++ by Paul J. Perry
 ***********************************************************/

#include <stdio.h>
void main()
{
```

```
int count = 0;
char ch = '\n';

printf("Type in a phrase :\n");

while (ch != '\r')
    {
    ch = getche();   /* get keyboard input */
    count++;      /* same as count = count + 1 */
     }

printf("\nYou typed %d characters.", count-1);

}
```

This program is the same as the previous one in structure. It adds a couple of variables to keep track of how many characters the user has entered. You will notice that as we wrote COUNT.C we had no way to know how many characters the user would enter. We could not have written the same program using a for statement.

The last statement in the program displays the number of characters entered by the user. Notice that we subtract one from the count. The reason for this is that we are subtracting the keystroke for the carriage return that was executed at the end of the line. Although we could include the count for it, if the user typed a single letter, it would look strange to always report that there is one more keystroke than it appears there is.

Nested **while** loops

Just as for loops can be nested, so can while loops. By now you know what is meant by the term *nested.* Nested while loops enable us to put a while loop inside another while loop.

The general form of the nested while loop is

```
while (expression1)
    {
    while(expression2)
```

```
        {
        statement;
        }
    }
```

Rather than show you an example of the nested while loop, I will leave it as an exercise for you. Be sure to follow the general form just listed. If you need additional hints, see the examples for other while statements earlier in this chapter.

The do...while Loop

The loop variety in C is the do...while loop. This loop structure is similar to the while loop. Unlike the for and while loops, which test the loop condition at the top of the loop, the do...while loop checks its condition at the end of the loop. This means that a do...while loop will always execute at least once.

The general form of the do...while loop is as follows:

```
do
    {
    statement1;
    statement2;
        .
        .
        .
    statementx;
    } while (expression);
```

The do...while loop, unlike the other loop statements we have examined, has two keywords: do and while. The do keyword marks the beginning of the loop. The while keyword marks the end of the loop and contains the loop expression. Notice that the do...while loop terminates with a semicolon.

The statements enclosed in braces will be executed repeatedly, as long as the value of *expression* is true (not equal to 0). Although the braces are not necessary when a single statement is present, they are usually used to improve the overall readability of the statement. They are required when you are working with a block of statements—and most of the time the do...while loop is used with a block of statements.

Listing 8.10 is the equivalent program to Listing 8.7, which displays the numbers from 1 to 100. It uses the do...while loop.

Listing 8.10. Count from 1 up to 100 with the do...while loop.

```
/**********************************************************
 DOWHILE.C--do...while loop that counts from 1 up
           to 100.
 Do It Yourself Turbo C++ by Paul J. Perry
 **********************************************************/

#include <stdio.h>

void main()
{
    int x = 1;

    do
     {
     printf("%d\n", x++);
     }
    while ( x <= 100);


}
```

The important point to notice about this program is that the body of the loop will always be executed at least once, because the test condition is at the end of the loop. If you are familiar with the Pascal programming language, you may think that the do...while loop is similar to the Pascal repeat...until statements. The difference is that the repeat...until statement loops until the test condition is true, but the C do...while loop continues to loop while the test condition is true.

For most applications, it is more natural to test for continuation of the loop at the beginning rather than at the end of the loop. For this reason, the do...while statement is used less frequently than the other looping statements we have covered.

Labels and the **goto** statement

If you are familiar with programming in any language, you might be surprised to see the "dreaded" goto statement showing up in a language as prestigious as C. The use of the goto statement is looked at by many programmers as a mark of inferior coding style. The reason is that its indiscriminate use leads to poor programs.

However, the designers of the C programming language included the goto statement because, in their own words "there are a few situations where goto may find a place."

The goto statement is used to alter the normal sequence of program execution by transferring control to some other part of the program. In its general form, the goto statement is written as follows:

```
goto label;
```

where *label* is an identifier that names the target statement where control will be transferred. The target statement must be labeled, and the label must be followed by a colon. The target statement appears in the form

```
label:
```

```
    statement;
```

Each statement within the program must have a unique label. No two statements can have the same label. The problem with programs that use the goto statement is that the code is generally harder to understand and to update than code written without goto statements. Its "spaghetti code" tangle of leaps forward and backward through the program is why it is looked down on by many programmers.

Listing 8.11 shows how to use the goto statement.

Program 8.11. Use of the goto statement.

```
/***************************************************
 GOTO.C--Example of the goto statement.
 Do It Yourself Turbo C++ by Paul J. Perry
 ***************************************************/

#include <stdio.h>
```

```
void main()
{
    int counter = 0;

    try_again:
        if (counter > 100) goto stop;
        printf("%d\n", counter);
        ++counter;
        goto try_again;

    stop:
        /* Loop is done executing. */

}
```

Listing 8.11 counts from 0 to 100. If you compare this program to Listings 8.7 and 8.10, you will probably find that the version in Listing 8.10 is not as clear. Execution is not smooth, in that it jumps from location to location.

You should avoid using the goto statement and instead use an appropriate looping statement. In every case, you should be able to find a more elegant method using one of the looping structures you have already studied.

Because the goto statement leads to the creation of unstructured programs, you will not see it used in the rest of this book.

What You Have Learned

In this chapter we focused on program flow statements. You learned the commands used in the C programming language to direct the flow of a program. You learned the three basic program control statements and how they are used. Specifically, the following topics were covered:

● There are three basic program control (looping) statements in the C programming language: for, while, and do...while.

● The for loop is the fundamental looping statement in C. It can consist of a single statement terminated by a semicolon or a block of statements surrounded by braces. You can also nest the for statement.

● The while statement is used in a program when you do not know how many times the program will need to execute the loop when you are writing the program.

● The do...while statement is similar to the while statement, except it makes its logical test at the end of the loop. Therefore, the body of the loop is always executed at least once.

● The goto statement is included in the C language because sometimes it is the only way out of a certain condition. However, the goto statement should not be relied on to change program flow. It results in the creation of unstructured programs.

● Each of the three program control statements can be nested within one or more other loops.

9

Data Structures

Goals

After reading this chapter, you will

- Recognize what a data structure is and understand what it is used for.

- Know what an array is and be able to declare and use both one- and two-dimensional arrays.

- Be able to initialize one- and two-dimensional arrays.

- Understand an important guideline to follow when you are working with arrays.

- Know how to manipulate arrays and how to search as well as sort integer arrays.

● Know how to declare and manipulate C string variables.

● Understand how to create custom data structures in C.

Up to now you have learned the basics of the C programming language. Starting with this chapter, you will learn about topics that build on the concepts you already have learned. Therefore, it is important that you understand the material in previous chapters as you continue on your journey of learning C.

This chapter discusses some of the more advanced data structures available in the C Programming language. A *data structure* is a collection of data organized in a particular way. You already learned about the fundamental data types: `int`, `char`, `double`, `float`, and `long double`. The basic data types involve only a single piece of information. Data structures build on these fundamental data types to organize information regarding groups of data.

The first type of data structure we will examine is the array. You will learn about different types of arrays, including one or more-dimensional arrays. You will also learn how to manipulate arrays. In the process you will learn about string variables. C does not have a specific string data structure, but string variables are closely related to arrays.

Arrays

An *array* is a list (or table) of variables of a related type. The variables in an array have a common name. Each individual item, or element in the array is accessed using an integer number called an *index*. Index values are always positive numbers.

Several rules exist for using and defining arrays. You must specify the size of the array—that is, how many elements it will hold. Arrays can also have one or more dimensions. Therefore, you also must specify the number of dimensions of the array.

The number of dimensions refers to how many index values are used to access variables in the array. A *one dimensional* array has a single index value and is similar to a list of data. A *two-dimensional* array has two index values and can model objects such as graph paper with rows and columns or a spreadsheet.

One-Dimensional Arrays

The simplest type of array is the one-dimensional array. The general form of a single-dimensional array is

```
datatype variablename[size];
```

Where `datatype` declares the type of the array (`int`, `char`, `double`, and so on) of each element and `size` defines how many elements the array will hold. The `variablename` is the identifier given to the array.

For example, the following line declares an integer array named `table` that is four elements long:

```
int table[4];
```

To refer to the elements of the array, we use the *index value.* All array elements are numbered starting at 0. Therefore, if you create an array with 4 elements, the first element is numbered 0, and the highest element is numbered 3. Here are the statements to use in order to access the declared array elements:

```
table[0]
table[1]
table[2]
table[3]
```

The four variables—`table[0]`, `table[1]`, `table[2]`, and `table[3]`—all share a common name. They are distinguished by means of the index value 0, 1, 2, or 3. Each of the four variables may be assigned a value. Figure 9.1 is a visual representation of what a variable looks like in memory.

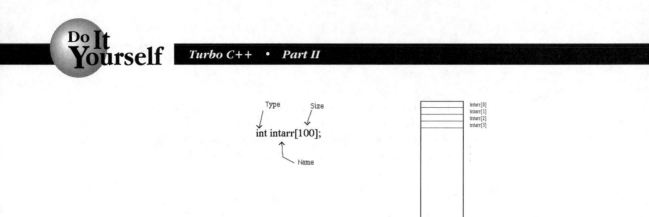

Figure 9.1. *A one-dimensional array.*

Benefits of Arrays

The point at which arrays really appear to shine is when we use them with some of the loop statements. Listing 9.1's program fills an integer array with the numbers 10 down to 1.

Listing 9.1. Program to access array elements.

```
/*****************************************************
 ARRAY.C--Access an array.
 Do It Yourself Turbo C++ by Paul J. Perry
 *****************************************************/

#include <stdio.h>

void main()
{
    const int MAX = 10;

    int arr[10];    /* array declaration */
    int count;

    for (count=0; count<MAX; ++count)
     {
     arr[count] = MAX - count;  /* assignment statement */
     printf("variable count[%d] is equal to %d\n", count,
            arr[count]);
     }

}
```

By accessing the array within the `for` loop, it's easy to access an individual element. The output of the program looks like this:

```
variable count[0] is equal to 10
variable count[1] is equal to 9
variable count[2] is equal to 8
variable count[3] is equal to 7
variable count[4] is equal to 6
variable count[5] is equal to 5
variable count[6] is equal to 4
variable count[7] is equal to 3
variable count[8] is equal to 2
variable count[9] is equal to 1
```

We started from the first element in the array to the last and assigned each element a numeric value using a simple `for` loop.

To learn an important rule about arrays in C, examine this short code excerpt:

```
#include <stdio.h>
int arr[10];        /* 10-element array */
int count;

main()    /* does this program compile? */
    {
    for (count=0; count<100; ++count)
     arr[count] = 100 - count;
    }
```

Do you think the Turbo C++ compiler will accept this short piece of code?

Let's describe the program we just set up. If you have been following along closely, you will notice that a 10-element array is declared at the beginning of the program. The `for` loop counts from 0 to 100 and assigns a value to every array element.

Wait a moment—we only declared an array with 10 elements. This does not appear to be valid code. You would think a compiler would not accept this.

Wrong! The C programming language performs no bounds checking on arrays. That is, there is no test to see whether the index value used in an array exceeds the actual size of the array. Nothing stops you from accessing elements at the end of an array that were not previously declared. If this happens, you will be assigning values to some other variable's memory space. Data entered with too large a subscript will simply be placed in memory outside the array.

As the programmer, your job is to ensure that all arrays are large enough to hold the data the program will put in them. If there is any reason to believe that your program may be accessing array elements outside of the declared array, you should add checks to the code to prevent it.

To answer the question posed earlier, this program will compile. However, *it may crash your system when it is run*. Not a good situation to run into.

> You might be wondering why C does not provide bounds checking. The answer is that C was designed to compile programs that will execute as quickly as possible. Error checking slows the execution of a program. Therefore, it is left to the programmer to prevent array overruns.

Let's look at another sample program. Listing 9.2 finds the average of 10 numbers entered by the user. It uses a floating-point array to store the numbers the user entered. The `for` loop is used to access array elements sequentially.

Listing 9.2. Program to average 10 numbers.

```
/****************************************************************
GETAVG.C--Find the average of 10 numbers entered by user.
Do It Yourself Turbo C++ by Paul J. Perry
****************************************************************/

#include <stdio.h>

void main()
{
    int const SIZE = 10;
    float sum, average, values[10];
    int index;

    printf("Please enter %d numbers\n\n", SIZE);
```

```
for (index=0; index<SIZE; index++)
  {
  printf("Enter number %d : ", index+1);
  scanf("%f", &values[index]);        /* read in numbers */
  }

printf("The values were entered as follows : \n");

for (index=0; index<SIZE; index++)
  printf("%f ", values[index]);
printf("\n");

for (index=0; index<SIZE; index++)   /* add up the numbers */
  sum = sum+values[index];
average = sum/SIZE;                  /* calculate the average
*/

printf("The sum of scores = %f, the average = %f", sum,
average);
}
```

After the user has entered 10 numbers, the program displays them and goes on to report the sum of the numbers as well as the average of the numbers. There are several programming concepts to explore in this program.

Notice line 11, which is the array declaration. C enables us to declare variables and arrays of the same type on the same line—a convenience. Also notice in line 18 that when we ask the user to enter the number, we refer to the index value +1. This is because arrays always start from element 0 and go up, therefore adding 1 to the value we display to the user makes it clear to the user what number we want them to enter.

Initializing One-Dimensional Arrays

Remember how we were able to declare a variable and initialize it to a specific value? We can do the same initialization trick for arrays. To initialize array elements to specific values, we specify initialization values at the time we declare the array. Here is an example:

```
int numbers[5] = { 1, 135, 10, 71, 23 };
```

The list of values is enclosed in braces, and each value is separated from the next by a comma.

Another form of array initialization enables us to omit the number that defines the size of the array, and the compiler will count the number of elements in the initialization list and create an array with the appropriate size. For example:

```
int numbers[] = { 1, 135, 10, 71, 23 };
```

creates the same array as the previous example did and lets the compiler worry about setting the appropriate size for the array.

Two-Dimensional Arrays

The C programming language enables us to use multidimensional arrays to reference more complex information. The simplest form of the multidimensional array is the *two-dimensional array*.

You can think of a two-dimensional array as a list of one-dimensional arrays.

Defining Multidimensional Arrays

Two-dimensional arrays are defined in much the same manner as one-dimensional arrays, except that a separate pair of square brackets is required for each index. Thus, a two-dimensional array requires two pairs of square brackets. A generalized two-dimensional array has the form

```
int twodim[25][50];
```

This declares a two-dimensional integer array named twodim. It can be thought of as a table having 25 rows and 50 columns. A diagram of the format of two-dimensional arrays appears in Figure 9.2.

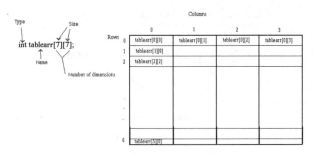

Figure 9.2. *A two-dimensional array.*

The two-dimensional array declaration in C is a little different than in most computer languages. Usually (in Pascal for instance), commas are used to separate the array dimensions. However, C places each dimension in its own set of brackets. Be sure not to try to refer to a two-dimensional array element as `twodim[15,10]`. This will only cause the compiler to issue an error message.

Listing 9.3. is a sample program that records the number of calls technical support representatives answer per week. It could be used at a software company to track the activity of technical support people. It uses a two-dimensional array with 3 rows and 4 columns.

Listing 9.3. Program to use a two-dimensional array.

```
/*********************************************************
 ARRAY2.C--Use a two-dimensional array to store info.
 Do It Yourself Turbo C++ by Paul J. Perry
 *********************************************************/

#include <stdio.h>

const int MAXTECHS = 3;
const int MAXWEEKS = 4;
void main()
{
    int tech, week;
    int calls[3][4];
```

continues

161

Listing 9.3. continued

```
    for(tech=0; tech<MAXTECHS; tech++)
      for(week=0; week<MAXWEEKS; week++)
        {
        printf("Enter number of calls answered for technician # \
              %d "tech+1);
        printf("for week # %d :", week+1);
        scanf("%d", &calls[tech][week]);
        }

    printf("\n\n\n");
    printf("\t\t\t  Week\n");
    printf("\t\t1\t2\t3\t4\n");
    printf("\t\t----------------------\n");

    for (tech=0; tech<MAXTECHS; tech++)
      {
      printf("Tech # %d  - \t", tech+1);
      for (week=0; week<MAXWEEKS; week++)
        printf("%d\t", calls[tech][week]);

      printf("\n");
      }

}
```

When you run Listing 9.3., the output looks something like this:

```
Enter number of calls answered for technician # 1 for week # 1 :175
Enter number of calls answered for technician # 1 for week # 2 :188
Enter number of calls answered for technician # 1 for week # 3 :132
Enter number of calls answered for technician # 1 for week # 4 :166
Enter number of calls answered for technician # 2 for week # 1 :125
Enter number of calls answered for technician # 2 for week # 2 :150
Enter number of calls answered for technician # 2 for week # 3 :160
Enter number of calls answered for technician # 2 for week # 4 :170
Enter number of calls answered for technician # 3 for week # 1 :165
Enter number of calls answered for technician # 3 for week # 2 :185
Enter number of calls answered for technician # 3 for week # 3 :175
Enter number of calls answered for technician # 3 for week # 4 :180
```

	Week			
	1	2	3	4

Tech # 1 -	175	188	132	166
Tech # 2 -	125	150	160	170
Tech # 3 -	165	185	175	180

There are two parts to the program. The first `for` loop gets the data from the user and stores the data in the array. The second part of the program prints out the contents of the array.

The first `for` loop obtains the number of calls answered by each technician. As the loop is carried out, we store the number of calls in the array using the `scanf()` function, as follows:

```
scanf("%d", &calls[tech][week]);
```

The first number is the row, which changes for each technician. The second index value tells for which of four weeks we are getting information. Each index value gets its own set of brackets following the variable name.

The second part of the program is similar to the first, except we create a table and output the information to the screen. Notice the liberal use of the special character constant \t to output a tab to the display. This enables our output to be formatted and to line up nicely.

Initializing Multidimensional Arrays

You learned how to initialize one-dimensional arrays earlier. Two-dimensional arrays can be initialized in a similar manner. For example, to initialize a two-dimensional array, use the following statement:

```
int initarr[3][5] =
    { { 45, 213, 78, 12, 98},
      { 12, 423, 27, 39, 76},
      { 19, 82,  47, 55, 100} };
```

Manipulating Arrays

Often as you program you will need to search or sort information. Arrays are a natural data structure to be manipulated using these techniques.

Searching and sorting routines are used in virtually all types of programs, including database programs, word processors, and compilers. Although searching and sorting arrays is a topic of itself, the next discussion briefly shows you a way to manipulate array values.

Searching Arrays

Finding a specific item in a list of data is a common task. One of the most common types of searches is trying to find a phone number in the phone book. If you were given a phone book and told to find a name, you would probably start at the beginning of the phone book, flip to the page that starts the list of the name's first letter, and continue searching until you found the name. That is because you have a systematic method of searching.

Computers must use a systematic method as well. When you search for a name in the phone book, you have it pretty easy because you are starting with a sorted list. If you were given a list of people that was not in any particular order and told to find a name there, you would probably start at the first name and compare it to the one you are trying to locate. If it was the same name, you would write down the phone number and stop. If it was not the name you were looking for, you would check the next name on the list and continue until you found the correct name. The computer uses a similar method.

Listing 9.4 is an example that prompts you to enter 10 numbers. It then asks you what number you want to find. It finds which array position that number is in and reports it to you.

Listing 9.4. Program to search an array for a number.

```
/****************************************************
 SEARCH.C--Search an integer array for a number.
 Do It Yourself Turbo C++ by Paul J. Perry
 ****************************************************/

#include <stdio.h>
#include <stdlib.h>    /* for exit() function */

void main()
{
    const int MAX = 10;
    int number, count=0, list[10];
```

```
printf("You will be prompted for 10 numbers\n");

do
    {
    printf("Enter Array Position #%d: ", count);
    scanf("%d", &list[count++]);              /* get value */
    }
while ( count < MAX);

printf("\nPlease enter value to find: ");
scanf("%d", &number);

for (count=0; count<MAX; count++)
    if (list[count] == number)
    {
    printf("Value found in array position # %d \n", count);
    exit(0);
    }
printf("\nNumber Not Found\n");

}
```

A sample interaction with the program looks like this:

```
You will be prompted for 10 numbers
Enter Value #0: 23
Enter Value #1: 456
Enter Value #2: 99
Enter Value #3: 83
Enter Value #4: 128
Enter Value #5: 1992
Enter Value #6: 618
Enter Value #7: 98
Enter Value #8: 287
Enter Value #9: 555

Please enter value to find: 618
Value found in array position # 6
```

Instead of using the `for` loop when getting the numbers from the user, this program uses the `do...while` loop—either method could be used.

Notice that the program returns the array position where the number is stored. If the program could not locate the string, it displays the message `Number Not Found`.

You will probably recognize the use of a new function call in the program, that of `exit()`. Its purpose is to quit the program. It does not pass go and cannot collect 200 dollars. It merely leaves the program and returns to DOS or the Integrated Development Environment (IDE). It is useful when you need to exit a specific situation in a program.

The sort algorithm used to find the number is the one that you or I would probably use, similar to the earlier phone book example. You are probably thinking that there must be more efficient ways to search a list. There certainly are. Although I am not going to go into them here, one of the ideas is that if the list is previously sorted in a specific order, we can make our search algorithm look through fewer numbers. This point leads us to the next topic, that of sorting.

Sorting Arrays

There are more methods of sorting than there are of searching. Computer scientists have devised literally dozens of methods, each having trade-offs among three factors: how fast they operate, how much code they require to execute, and the memory required to sort the array.

This discussion involves a simple sort procedure known as a *bubble sort*. Before detailing how it works, enter Listing 9.5 into your computer and execute it.

Listing 9.5. Program to sort an integer array.

```
/****************************************************
 SORT.C--Sort an integer array.
 Do It Yourself Turbo C++ by Paul J. Perry
 ****************************************************/

#include <stdio.h>

void main()
{
```

```
const int MAX = 10;
int i, j, temp, count=0, list[10];

printf("You will be prompted for 10 numbers\n");

do
  {
  printf("Enter Number %d: ", count+1);
  scanf("%d", &list[count++]);
  }
while ( count < MAX);

for (i=0; i<MAX-1; i++)
  for (j=i+1; j<MAX; j++)
    if (list[i] > list[j])
    {
    temp = list[j];
    list [j] = list[i];
    list [i] = temp;
    }

printf("\n\nResults\n");

for (count=0; count<MAX; count++)
  printf("Position %d is now %d\n", count, list[count]);

}
```

Sample program output is as follows:

```
You will be prompted for 10 numbers
Enter Number 1: 234
Enter Number 2: 987
Enter Number 3: 1676
Enter Number 4: 55
Enter Number 5: 11
Enter Number 6: 23
Enter Number 7: 99
Enter Number 8: 66
Enter Number 9: 841
Enter Number 10: 12
```

```
Results
Position 0 is now 11
Position 1 is now 12
Position 2 is now 23
Position 3 is now 55
Position 4 is now 66
Position 5 is now 99
Position 6 is now 234
Position 7 is now 841
Position 8 is now 987
Position 9 is now 1676
```

After the program gets the ten values from the user, it starts the sort routine. The sort algorithm is known as a bubble sort. The algorithm received this name because values tend to float to the top of the list, similar to how bubbles float to the top of water.

Two nested `for` statements are set up to go through the entire list of numbers. The following test is used to determine whether any two elements are out of order:

```
if (list[i] > list[j])
```

If one number is greater than another in the list, the program swaps the position of those two numbers in order to place them in numerical order. It continues this process through the entire list to place the numbers in sorted order. After the sort is complete, the program displays the sorted list of numbers.

Listing 9.5 did an *ascending* sort. That is, the sorted numbers start from the lowest one and go up. The numbers could have been sorted in *descending* order (highest down to lowest) by changing the program as follows :

```
if (list[i] < list[j])
```

Once the test has been completed, we swap the array positions, so that the larger number gets to the top. This swap can only be done by putting the first value into a temporary variable, putting the second value into the first one, and then putting the value stored in the temporary variable into the second one.

The bubble sort is one of the least efficient sort algorithms around. On long lists of data, the sort becomes incredibly slow.

Character Arrays

So far, we have only been dealing with numbers. However, words are the most common forms of communication. A common example of a computer program that works on characters is a word processor. To run a word processor, the computer must have some way to store text.

Many computer languages have a specific data type for strings, usually referred to as *string variables*. C does not have a string data type, per se. What it does have is character arrays, which we will discuss next.

In C, a string is characterized as a number of character values terminated with a null value. A null is specified with the \0 escape sequence. The null terminator is simply an ASCII 0 value. When the compiler runs into this value in a string, the compiler knows it has located the end of the string. It looks like two characters but is treated as one. Because of the null terminator, it is necessary to declare character arrays to be one character longer than the largest number of characters they are to hold.

Defining Character Arrays

The general definition of a character array looks like this:

```
char string[size];
```

Where *size* is the length of the string. Each character occupies one byte of memory. We must always make space for the terminating null character. Therefore, if we know a string will be 10 characters long, we must define it as 11 characters long when it is declared. Figure 9.3 shows a visual representation of a character array in memory.

Listing 9.6 is an example of how a program declares and uses a character array. It asks the user for the current day, then echoes the current day back to the screen.

Listing 9.6. Program to work with string variables.

```
/****************************************************
 STRING.C--Declare and use a string variable.
 Do It Yourself Turbo C++ by Paul J. Perry
 ****************************************************/
```

continues

Listing 9.6. continued

```c
#include <stdio.h>

void main()
{
    char day[26];

    printf("Enter today's day: ");
    gets(day);
    printf("Today is ");
    puts(day);

}
```

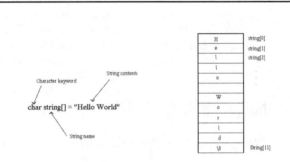

Figure 9.3. Representation of a string variable.

The program uses a new function, `gets()` (which stands for "get string"), to get the current day from the user. We could have used `printf()` with `%s` specifier, as follows:

```c
printf("%s", &day);
```

However, this program introduces two functions for working with strings. The second of the two is the `puts()` function (and it stands for "put string"). As you can imagine, it displays a string on the screen. We could have used `printf()`, as follows:

```c
printf("%s", day);
```

But isn't it worth it to try new techniques as you learn more about C?

Remember that C does not check the bounds of the array when it works with arrays. This is as true for character arrays as it is for numeric arrays. So, if you type a string into Listing 9.6. that is longer than 25 characters (it is declared to 26, but the null character is always added and it takes 1 byte) the characters would start writing over memory locations of other variables. You must be careful as you declare character arrays so that they have enough memory to store the strings you wish to use.

Initializing Strings

Just as numerical arrays can be initialized, so can character arrays. You can specify each character in the string, like this:

```
char name[] = { 'P', 'a', 'u', 'l', '\0'  };
```

However, you can specify the characters as a single string, using quotes, as follows:

```
char name[] = "Paul";
```

Both of the preceding lines are the same to the compiler. Notice that it is easier to type in a full string, rather than each character separated from the next with apostrophes and a comma. When declaring the string at once, we don't need to insert the null character. The string initialization adds the null character automatically.

Structures

Arrays are an excellent way to store data. However they are limited: each element of an array must be of the same data type. Just as in real life, things don't always come bundled in similar packages. C provides a data structure that enables us to combine information on different types of data.

For example, you might decide to computerize your address book. Although there are hundreds of programs on the market available to do this, you decide you would rather write a program to do it yourself, figuring that the knowledge you learn is worth any extra time it may take. In your simplified address book, the data you have for each person includes a name, address, city, state, and phone number.

You can't use a single array to store these values, because they include both numbers and character strings. Structures are the best method you can use to store the data items. Elements of a structure do not need to be of the same type.

Structures are declared using the following general description:

```
struct name
{
    datatype element1;
    datatype element2;
        .
        .
        .
    datatype elementX;
};
```

A *structure* is actually a data type whose format is defined by the programmer. The previous description shows how to define the structure to the compiler. Once the structure is declared, you must create a variable declaration, which associates a symbol name with the structure.

Each element of the array is accessed by using the base name of the variable along with a period and the name of the element, as follows:

```
name.element1
name.element2
name.elementX
```

Listing 9.7. demonstrates the process of defining, declaring, and using structures.

Listing 9.7. Program to use a structure.

```
/*********************************************************
 STRUCT.C--Create custom data types with structures.
 Do It Yourself Turbo C++ by Paul J. Perry
 *********************************************************/

#include <stdio.h>
```

```
void main()
{
    struct astruct                  /* structure definition */
      {
      int number;
      float amount;
      char let;
      };

    struct astruct thisstruct;    /* variable declaration */

    thisstruct.number  = 99;        /* assignment statements */
    thisstruct.amount  = 29.95;
    thisstruct.let     = 'A';

    printf("value thisstruct.number = %d\n", thisstruct.number);
    printf("value thisstruct.amount = %f\n", thisstruct.amount);
    printf("value thisstruct.let    = %c\n", thisstruct.let);

}
```

The first section of the program declares the structure, as follows:

```
struct astruct                  /* structure definition */
  {
  int number;
  float amount;
  char let;
  };
```

This declares a structure with three elements. The first is of type integer (int) and is named number. The second is type floating point (float) and is named amount. Finally, the last element is a character (char) and is named let. The previous lines only declare what the structure will be like. It does not reserve memory for the structure. This is done with the following line:

```
struct astruct thisstruct;    /* variable declaration */
```

Note the use of the keyword struct, which is followed by the structure name, and finally the name of the variable. C enables you to use a shortcut definition of a structure that includes both the definition and variable declaration. For the preceding program, the shortcut would look like this:

```
struct astruct            /* structure definition with variable */
  {                       /* declaration */
  int number;
  float amount;
  char let;
  } thisstruct;
```

This enables the definition and declaration at once.

To access structure elements we use the dot operator, as follows:

```
thisstruct.number  = 99;
thisstruct.amount  = 29.95;
thisstruct.let     = 'A';
```

These are assignment statements. We can access each element in the structure using dot notation. It is a convenient method to access structure elements. When the contents of the elements are displayed on the screen, we use the same dot operator to access each element.

Structures are an extremely convenient method of storing unrelated data. They are used often in large programs.

What You Have Learned

This chapter covered a lot of material. We looked at what a data structure is. We then took a close look at arrays and structures. In between we learned how to manipulate arrays. In particular, the following topics were covered:

● Data structures are used to store a collection of data types. You saw data structures that enable a program to store both related and unrelated types of information.

● An array is a list of variables of a related type. An array must be declared to be a specific size and is limited by memory constraints. Arrays can be declared as either one- or multidimensional.

● Array elements are accessed by an index value that is the relative location within the array of the element.

● C does not perform any test to see whether an index value used in an array exceeds the size of the array. It is up to the programmer to ensure safeguards so a program does not access array elements outside of the declared array.

● Two common forms of manipulating data include searching and sorting. When you search for data, you look for a specific piece of information in an array. When you sort an array, the program rearranges the array into a specific order.

● There is no string variable data type in C. Instead, the programmer uses character arrays to access groups of characters. Special functions are used to get a string from the keyboard or output the string to the user.

● Structures enable you to combine unrelated types of data into a single variable. To use a structure, you must first declare it and then define it as a variable, which allocates the memory for the structure.

● Structure elements are accessed by referring to the base name of the structure, which is separated from the element you want to access by a period.

10

Using Functions

Goals

After reading this chapter, you will

- Understand what a function is and why a C programmer uses functions.
- Know how to use the Turbo C++ library functions.
- Be able to declare a function.
- Know how to return an integer value from a simple function.
- Be able to pass a simple data type to a function.
- Know how to pass arrays and structures to a function.

- Understand how to use the features of C++ to return data from a function by reference.

- Know what visibility and lifetime have to do with functions.

Functions are the core of the C programming language. Through functions the language is extensible and expandable. This chapter examines the syntax, format, and purpose of functions. Most importantly, you will learn how to use functions to convert your programs into logical units that fit together like a puzzle.

The Idea Behind Functions

A *subprogram* is an important concept associated with a high-level programming language. Subprograms, or *functions* as they are called in C, are the basis of all heavy-duty computer programming languages. A *structured program* is one that consists of subprograms that, when combined, create a working program. All programs written today are made up of subprograms. A function is really a means of abbreviating program logic into small parts.

The idea behind a function is to take a section of code that accomplishes a specific task and separate it into its own section and treat it separate from the rest of the program. Then, whenever you need to accomplish the task that the function carries out, you just call the function. A function can be called as many times as required.

A function is given its own name and accessed by that name. Data can be passed to a function, which the function then operates on. From the beginning of this book you have been using functions. The main() function definition of every program is considered a function that the C compiler passes program execution to when a program starts running.

You have also used the built-in *library functions*. These general-purpose functions come with the compiler. Examples of library functions include printf(), scanf(), gets(), and puts(). You probably get the idea.

There are actually about 250 functions in the entire Turbo C++ library. Each function in the library is not part of the C language but rather separate from the C language. Although there are certain conventions for what functions to include within a C Compiler, the definition of the C language does not specify any functions that must be included with a compiler.

Using Library Functions

The Turbo C++ function library provides routines for the most common programming tasks. The functions provide a convenient interface to using the language and relieve you of the task of writing common functions yourself.

The function library is divided into smaller, related groups. For example, the graphics library includes functions for working with high resolution graphics. The standard I/O library includes functions that control input and output on the computer.

In order to use the functions in your own programs, all you need to do is include the appropriate header file in your program. The *header file* contains the declarations of the functions that you can use in your own programs. The statement that includes header files looks like this:

```
#include <stdio.h>
```

The #include statement is a preprocessor directive that tells the compiler to merge the specified header file, here STDIO.H, into your source file during compilation. The included file is referenced when your program is being compiled. The angle brackets surrounding the header filename tell the compiler to look in the standard library directory (which is usually defined as C:\TC\INCLUDE). In this example, the file included is the STDIO.H header file, which is used for standard input and output. You have already used library functions for many tasks in your programs up to this point, so using the function library should not be a new concept to you.

A Simple Function

As you saw earlier, a function is a self-contained program within another program that carries out a specific, well-defined task. A program may contain multiple functions, each of which is considered a separate program.

There are several reasons for using functions:

- They aid in the overall organization of a program.
- They reduce the memory overhead required by the compiler.
- They enable you to create reusable code.

By dividing tasks into logical, well-defined functions, program organization is improved. This aids the programmer working on a team, as well as the one working on a solo project.

Thus, functions are useful for helping you get and stay organized in your coding. The second important aspect of functions is their ability to reduce the memory required in a program. By calling a function instead of repeating the code every time the task is carried out, a program uses less memory. Although computers can now be expanded to 16 megabytes of memory and beyond, creating memory-efficient programs is still a priority for most developers.

Finally, functions enable programmers to reuse code in various applications. Reusability can save you many hours of programming time. To create reusable code, the programmer separates a program into well-defined tasks, places one task into each function (the task can be rather complex, like sorting), then stores the most standard functions in function libraries for use in more than one programming project.

For example, almost every program that uses disk files must have a section of code that asks the user for a filename and checks whether the file is present on the disk. By putting this task into a function and storing it in a library, you don't have to rewrite that piece of code for your next program. As a result, programmers build up large libraries of their favorite routines so they can create new applications quicker.

Declaring the Function

The function carries out its intended action whenever it is accessed (or whenever the function is "called") from another portion of the program. The same function can be accessed from several different places within a program. Once the function has carried out its intended action, control is returned to the point from which the function was accessed.

A function usually contains three parts: the function declaration, the actual function, and the function call.

Just as you can't use a variable without first telling the compiler what it is, you also can't use a function without telling the compiler about it. The function is usually declared at the beginning of the program. The function declaration takes on the following general form:

```
type function_name(type varname1, type varname2, ..., type varnameX);
```

The declaration tells the compiler that at some point in the program you plan on creating a function with the name *function_name*. The first `type` keyword tells the compiler what data type the function will return. Any C data type can be specified. If the function is not to return any value, use the keyword `void`.

The list of types and variable names within parameters are the *arguments* that will be passed to the function. A function may be used without parameters, in which case the parameter list will be empty. However, parentheses are still required for an empty list. The function declaration ends with a semicolon.

It is important to point out that unlike a variable declarations in which many variables can be declared of a common type at once, as in

```
int dollars, cents, total;
```

all function parameters must include both the type and variable name. For example, the following is the correct parameter declaration for the variables when used as arguments to a function:

```
int dollars, int cents, int total
```

The Function Body

The second part of using a function is writing the body of its code. The general form is as follows:

```
type function_name(type varname1, type varname2, ..., type varnameX)
{
    /* body of function */
}
```

The first line of the function is virtually a copy of the function declaration, except that it is not followed by a semicolon. Again, the rule applies that all parameters must include both the type and variable name. The statements that form the body of the function are enclosed in braces.

Calling the Function

Once the function is written, you can use it in your program. Here is an example of how a function is used in a program:

```
void main()
{
    /* other statements */
    function_name(var1, var2, ..., varX);
    /* more statements */
}
```

If you wish to use the value returned by a function, you would put it on the right side of an assignment statement, as follows:

```
value = function_name(var1, var2, ..., varX);
```

Figure 10.1 shows the three steps necessary for using a function.

Step 1:
Declaring
the function

```
type function_name(type varname1, type varname2, ..., type varnameX);
```

Step 2:
Writing
the function
body

```
type function_name(type varname1, type varname2, ..., type varnameX)
{
    /* Body of the function */
}
```

Step 3:
Calling
the function

```
function_name (var1, var2, ... varX);
```

Figure 10.1. *Using a function.*

An example of a program that uses a simple function is given in Listing 10.1.

Listing 10.1. Program that uses a basic function.

```
/*****************************************************
 FUNC1.C--A simple function used in a program.
 Do It Yourself Turbo C++ by Paul J. Perry
 *****************************************************/

#include <stdio.h>

void showdashes();    /* declaration */

void main()
{
     printf("This is to be underlined\n");
     showdashes();   /* function call */
     printf("Hey, do that once again\n");
     showdashes();   /* function call */
}

/**********************/
void showdashes()     /* function body */
{
     printf("-----------------------\n");
}
```

When the program is executed, it displays four lines, as follows:

```
This is to be underlined
-----------------------
Hey, do that once again
-----------------------
```

Notice that the function was called twice, thereby saving the hassle of typing the code twice as well as the memory required to store it twice.

The function just shown, named showdashes(), is the simplest type of function a C program can use. It doesn't return a value and is not passed any values from the main program. Although the simple function may help organize a program, in order for functions to be useful we must be able to receive values from them and to pass values to them.

183

Functions That Return a Value

Some functions, like showdashes(), don't return any data. Other functions can return values by using the return statement.

The return statement actually has two uses. First, it causes an immediate exit from the current function. That is, program flow will return to the statement located after the function call. Second, it is used to return a value to the program.

Program execution in a function usually ends when the compiler finds the closing brace in the function. You can force a function to return to the calling program at a specific point by using the return statement.

To return a value from a function, you must follow the return statement with the value to be returned. For example, the following function returns the absolute value (removes a negative sign) of a number:

```c
int absolute(int number)
{
    int result;
    if (number>1) return number;   /* if number is positive,
                                        return now */

    result = number-number-number; /* make number positive */

    return result;
}
```

Listing 10.2. is a full-blown example of using the function in a program.

Listing 10.2. Program to return absolute value of a number.

```c
/***************************************************
FUNC2.C--Return integer value from a function.
Do It Yourself Turbo C++ by Paul J. Perry
***************************************************/

#include <stdio.h>

int absolute(int number);  /* function declaration */
```

```
void main()
{
    printf("%d\n", absolute(9) );    /* test function */
    printf("%d\n", absolute(-9) );
    printf("%d\n", absolute(0) );
}



/***************************************/
int absolute(int number)   /* body of function */
{
    int result;
    if (number>0) return number;    /* is number positive? */

    result = number - number - number;  /* make it positive */

    return result;     /* return number to main program */
}
```

The main() section of the program feeds a couple of numbers into the function to make sure it works. The output of the program is as follows:

```
9
9
0
```

If it does not come out this way, check that you entered the program correctly.

Each time the function is called, it gets passed an integer value. Inside the function, this value is referred to as the variable *number*. However, because functions are considered separate program modules, you could have a variable with the same name in main() and the compiler would access it as if it were a variable with a different name.

Inside the function, a test is made to see whether the value passed to the function is positive. If it is, the function does not need to do anything and returns to the calling program immediately with the use of the return statement. The calculation then subtracts itself (making 0) and then subtracts itself again (this time, subtracting the negative number is like adding) so the result is the same number without a negative sign.

The result of the calculation is then returned to the main program with the return statement following the value to be passed back (in this case the variable result).

185

Passing Data to a Function

The information to be passed to a function is called *arguments* (also called *parameters*).

Now that you have learned to return data from a function, we must pass data to a function. Listing 10.2 gave you a sneak preview of how it is done. Once you have declared the data types of the argument in the program, you can access them with the specified variable name. Listing 10.3 is an example of a function that is passed two numbers and returns the sum of the numbers.

Listing 10.3. Function to add two numbers passed to a function.

```c
/*********************************************
     FUNC3.C--Pass data to a function with
              argument list.
     Do It Yourself Turbo C++ by Paul J. Perry
*********************************************/

#include <stdio.h>

int add(int num1, int num2);   /* function declaration */

void main()
{
    printf("1 + 2 is %d", add(1, 2) );
}


/*****************************/
int add(int num1, int num2)
{
    int result;  /* local variable */

    result = num1 + num2;    /* actual calculation */
    return result;
}
```

Although this function uses integer parameters, you could rewrite the function to use any of the regular data types. The output of the program is

```
1 + 2 is 3
```

The program shows how multiple variables are used in the function. Notice that the variable declared as `result` is called a *local variable*. What this means is that the variable is used only in the function. If you tried to make access to the variable in `main()` the compiler would report an error. When the function ends, the variable can no longer be accessed. Later, we will learn methods of sharing variables throughout functions and programs.

Passing Different Types of Data Structures

We have seen examples of passing the standard data types to a function. There must be some way to pass a data structure to a function. You guessed right. This section shows how to do it.

Passing Arrays

Here is the bubble sort program from Listing 9.5, rewritten to put the section of code dealing with the sort in a function.

Listing 10.4. Bubble sort routine rewritten to be inside a function.

```
/****************************************************
 SORT2.C--Sort an integer array using a bubble sort.
 Do It Yourself Turbo C++ by Paul J. Perry
 ****************************************************/

#include <stdio.h>

void sort(int list[]);  /* function declaration */
```

continues

Listing 10.4. continued

```c
const int MAX = 10;
void main()
{
    int count=0, list[10];

    printf("You will be prompted for 10 numbers\n");

    do
      {
      printf("Enter Number %d : ", count+1);
      scanf("%d", &list[count++]);
      }
    while ( count < MAX);

    sort(list);

    printf("\n\nResults\n");

    for (count=0; count<MAX; count++)
      printf("Position %d is now %d\n", count, list[count]);

}


/********************************/
void sort(int list[])
{
    int i, j, temp;
    for (i=0; i<MAX-1; i++)
      for (j=i+1; j<MAX; j++)
        if (list[i] > list[j])
        {
        temp = list[j];
        list [j] = list[i];
        list [i] = temp;
        }
}
```

The sorting algorithm is the same, but this time the code has been converted into a function. The function, named sort(), is passed an array of numbers. The function then sorts the list.

However, this program may seem strange after our earlier discussion of returning values. A function can only return a standard data type. You cannot return an array directly. What the program does is take the array as an argument. It then rearranges the array. However, nothing is ever returned.

The reason is that the actual addresses of the array are passed to the function. Passing the array to the function does not create a new copy of the array. Rather, unlike local variables, which are separate between functions, the array is one and the same. When we modify the array in the function, it is actually modifying the original array.

This practice may seem like it could cause trouble. You are right—it may. However, the designers of C decided it was a good idea to pass arrays this way, because creating an entirely new array would use a large portion of memory as well as take a lot of processor time.

Passing Structures

In the same way that a regular data type can be passed to a function, a structure variable can be passed as a parameter to a function. As an example, let's look at an example of a function that uses structures. Examine and run Listing 10.5 now.

Listing 10.5. Function to pass structure variables.

```
/******************************************************************
   STRUCT2.C--Demonstrate the use of structures with functions.
   Do It Yourself Turbo C++ by Paul J. Perry
 ******************************************************************/

#include <stdio.h>

struct aperson                  /* structure declaration */
   {
   char name[25];
   int age;
   };
```

continues

Listing 10.5. continued

```c
struct aperson getdata();          /* function declarations */
void printdata(struct aperson);

void main()
{
  struct aperson me, you;

  printf("Enter information about me\n");
  me = getdata();

  printf("Enter information about you\n");
  you = getdata();

  printf("\n\n");
  printf("I am—\n");
  printdata(me);

  printf("You are—\n");
  printdata(you);
}


/********************/
struct aperson getdata()
{
  struct aperson temp;    /* temporary, local variable */

  printf("Enter first name : ");
  scanf("%s", &temp.name);

  printf("Enter age : ");
  scanf("%d", &temp.age);

  return temp;
}

/********************/
void printdata(struct aperson temp)
{
```

```
    printf("Name is %s \n", temp.name);
    printf("Age is %d \n", temp.age);
}
```

When you run the program, it will look something like this:

```
Enter information about me
Enter first name : Puter
Enter age : 486
Enter information about you
Enter first name : Paul
Enter age : 23


I am--
Name is Puter
Age is 486
You are--
Name is Paul
Age is 23
```

This program includes two functions. One function gets information about a person (or thing) and stores it in a structure, the other function displays the contents of the structure on the screen.

Because both functions and the main program need to know how the structure is declared, the declaration is placed at the beginning of the program. Therefore, the structure is accessible by each function.

The function getdata() is called from the main program to accept information from the user. The function is declared to be of type struct aperson, because it returns a value of this type. It also creates a temporary variable inside which getdata() returns to the main program.

Function printdata() outputs structure information to the screen. Notice that the parameters to the function are of type struct aperson. By passing a structure as an argument, we are able to package several data items into one.

Functions in C++

Everything you have learned so far is applicable to C as well as to C++. However, C++ enables the programmer to declare reference variables. This feature means that you pass the address of the variable, so that instead of working with a copy of the variable, your program works with the actual variable (much like working with arrays). Any changes made to the variable in the function are automatically made to the variable in the rest of the program. The advantage of this is that you can return more than one value to the calling program by modifying the arguments.

Listing 10.6 gives an example of passing variables by reference. You should specify the .CPP file extension to tell the Turbo C++ compiler that you are programming in C++.

Listing 10.6. Function to pass values by reference in C++.

```
/****************************************************
 REFER.CPP--Pass values by reference with C++.
 Do It Yourself Turbo C++ by Paul J. Perry
 ****************************************************/

#include <stdio.h>

void addition(int num1, int num2, int& result);  /* declaration */

void main()
{
    int answer;

    addition(1, 2, answer);
    printf("1 + 2 is %d", answer);

}


/******************/
void addition(int num1, int num2, int& result)
```

```
{
     result = num1 + num2;
}
```

The program is a modification of Listing 10.3, which was used to find the sum of two numbers. This version of the program takes three arguments. The first two are the numbers to add. The third is the result.

You may notice right off that the declaration for the function looks different:

```
void addition(int num1, int num2, int& result);
```

Notice the ampersand (&) symbol after the data type of the third argument. This specifies that the function uses a reference argument.

When the program calls the function, it is passed three values. The first two arguments are constants that are the numbers to add. The third parameter is the result. The value we pass as arguments for this variable does not matter, because it is not used. When the function returns, the answer variable has been modified. This is the result of passing data by reference.

Reference variables are used when you have more than one value you must return from a function. Although C allows a variable to be passed by reference, you won't see how that process works until the discussion of pointers in Chapter 14. For now, remember that reference arguments are indicated by the ampersand (&) following the data type of the argument.

Using Global Variables

We briefly explored the concepts of visibility and lifetime when you were introduced to variables in Chapter 4. Well, functions use variables, so this is an appropriate time to bring this subject up again.

Any variable that is declared inside a function can only be used by statements inside the function. If you declare a variable outside of any functions, it is accessible by all the functions in a program. Functions that can be accessed like this are called *global variables*.

Listing 10.7. Program to show some uses of global variables.

```
/*****************************************************
GLOBAL.C--Demonstrate the use of a global variable.
Do It Yourself Turbo C++ by Paul J. Perry
*****************************************************/

#include <stdio.h>      /* header file */

void functioncall();    /* function declaration */

int number;             /* global variable */

void main()
{
 printf("starting main()\n");
 number = 10;
 printf("number is %d\n", number);
 functioncall();
 printf("number is %d\n", number);

}


void functioncall()
{
 number = 25;
 printf("returning from function\n");
}
```

The output of the program looks like this:

```
starting main()
number is 10
returning from function
number is 25
```

This example creates a global variable, named `number`. It is first assigned the value 10 in `main()`. A function is then declared that assigns 25 to the variable. The value of the variable is displayed several times during execution of the program so you can see how it is changed.

Take care when you declare and use global variables—in fact, you should try to avoid the practice. You can easily start to create functions that rely on certain global variables. The result is the functions cannot be used interchangeably with other programs. Worse, if you have a global variable that inadvertently becomes modified by one function, other functions may react illogically, because they expected the global variable to have a certain value. This can really cause a disaster when you are trying to find out why the program is not working.

Although global variables can be handy, my recommendation is to stay away from defining and using global variables unless they are absolutely necessary.

What You Have Learned

This chapter discussed how to use functions. You learned the syntax, format, and purpose of functions. In particular, the following topics were covered:

- A function is a subprogram, or a program inside a program. Each function has its own variables, which are separate from the rest of the program.

- Functions are used to divide a program into logical units.

- Several reasons to use functions include increased organization of your programs, reduction in their memory size, and reusability of program code.

- Library functions are general-purpose functions that come with the compiler. Although the C definition does not specify any functions that must be included with the compiler, some have become a standard and are available in almost every C compiler available.

- Data can be passed into and out of functions. Arrays and structures can be passed between functions.

- The return statement is used to pass a single value from the function to the line that called the function.

- The variables passed to a function are called arguments or parameters. They provide a means to pass information to the function.

- C++ allows for the declaration of reference parameters. This means that a function can return more than one value to a program. Reference arguments are indicated by the ampersand (&) following the data type of the argument.

- Global variables are variables that are declared outside of any function and can be accessed by all functions in a program.

Part III

Advanced C Topics

11

Working with the Text Screen

Goals

After reading this chapter, you will

- Understand how to access the extended ASCII character set through the use of the `printf()` function.

- Know how to access the special line-drawing characters.

- Be able to set any of the available video modes with Turbo C++ functions.

- Know how to access video memory directly when you are outputting text to the screen.

- Understand the coordinate system used to display text on the screen.

● Know the ways to move the cursor and to find the current cursor location.

● Be able to output text in color to the screen.

● Know how to change the intensity of text displayed on the screen.

One of the handiest features of Turbo C++ (and for that matter, its big brother, Borland C++) is the assortment of functions available for working with the video text display. An extensive library of text functions is available. These library functions enable you to create fancy screens quickly and easily.

This chapter demonstrates how to use the PC's resources to perform different screen operations. You will learn how to display text in color, move the cursor while you take control of the screen, and how to use the special graphics characters available on the PC.

> It is important to remember that the topics covered in this chapter are for the most part *extensions* of the ANSI C language definitions. What this means is that the functions are not available if you are using a compiler other than Turbo C++ on a non-PC-compatible machine.

Using the Video Display

Video monitors have two basic modes of operation: graphics and text mode. You use *graphics mode* to gain absolute control over each pixel on the screen. Graphics mode requires a special video adapter, such as CGA, EGA, or VGA.

Text mode is used with every PC, because it makes use of the built-in character set inherent to the computer. Compared to graphics mode, text mode is easier to program, faster for the computer to process, and a more universal method of outputting information on PCs.

Because graphics-mode programming is a subject of its own, we will tackle it in Chapter 16 (that's right, I want to give you a reason to continue reading this book!). Here we will look at the text mode's way of dealing with graphics.

Special Characters

Text display mode allows for the display of the 256 characters that compose the ASCII character set (see Appendix A). Remember that ASCII stands for the American Standard Code for Information and Interchange, and is a standard way of storing information in the computer. The first 128 characters include numbers, alphabetic letters, and special control codes; collectively they are know as the *standard ASCII character set.* The last 128 characters compose the *extended ASCII character set.* The extended set is only available on PC-compatible machines. Listing 11.1 is an example of a program that uses the extended character set.

Listing 11.1. Program that uses extended ASCII characters in C.

```
/*************************************************
 SPECIAL.C--Use extended character set in C.
 Do It Yourself Turbo C++ by Paul J. Perry
 *************************************************/

#include <stdio.h>

void main()
{
    printf("My PC is multilingual\n\n");
    printf("Habla Espa\xa4ol\n");            /* Spanish */
    printf("Sprechen Sie Deutsch?\n");       /* German */
    printf("Parlez-vous Franc\x85is?\n ") ;  /* French */
    printf("A\xfd + B\xfd = C\xfd\n\n");      /* Mathematics */

}
```

When program SPECIAL.C is executed, its output looks like this:

```
Habla Español
Sprechen Sie Deutsch?
Parlez-vous Francàis?
 A² + B² = C²
```

Although most of the characters are common, you will notice some special characters used in the program that make the program complete.

The first line is translated "Do you speak Spanish?" and is written in Spanish. The second line translates "Do you speak German?". You probably know how the third line translates; however, it is in French. Finally, the last line uses the universal language of mathematics to display the famous relationship of the three sides of a right triangle. (Does the Pythagorean theorem bring back any memories?)

The method we use to access the extended characters is to use the \x specifier with the printf() function. The characters following \x are the hexadecimal (hex) number of the character (as listed in Appendix A).

Hexadecimal Numbering System

If you are unfamiliar with hex numbers, now is a good time for an introduction. Hexadecimal (or hex) is a numbering system unlike the decimal system we normally use. The *decimal system* uses the characters 0 to 9. After using 10 digits (0–9) in the one's column, the ten's column is used to express larger numbers, through 99. Another name for the decimal system is *base 10.* Counting in the decimal system looks like this:

0, 1, 2, 3, 4, 5, 6, 7, 8, 9, 10, 11, 12, 13, 14, 15, 16, 17, and so on

Ten characters are used to represent all numbers in the decimal system.

Hexadecimal is one of the methods of counting that the computer uses. Hexadecimal is a numbering system that uses 16 digits (rather than 10). Because there are only 10 number symbols, letters are used for the remaining digits. So, counting in hex looks like this:

0, 1, 2, 3, 4, 5, 6, 7, 8, 9, a, b, c, d, e, f, 10, 11, 12, and so on

You can count up to F (15 decimal) in the one's column before you shift to the ten's column. This allows the computer to store larger numbers with fewer digits. Here are some numbers in both numbering systems, for comparison:

Decimal Number	Hexadecimal Number
1	1
10	a
15	f

Decimal Number	Hexadecimal Number
16	10
17	11
18	12
25	19
55	37
100	64
255	ff

Although hexadecimal may not be second nature to you (at least not yet), it is a convenient method of representing information inside the computer. We do not have to use it often in C, but it is still good to know how the hexadecimal number system works.

Line-Drawing Characters

Some of the other special characters available on the PC help us to display horizontal and vertical lines on the screen. They were used frequently to create the Turbo C++ Integrated Development Environment (IDE). Listing 11.2 has an example of the line-drawing characters.

Listing 11.2. Program to demonstrate the Turbo C++ line-drawing characters.

```
/***************************************************
 LINEDRAW.C--Show the line-drawing characters in
             Turbo C++.
 Do It Yourself Turbo C++ by Paul J. Perry
 ***************************************************/

#include <stdio.h>

void main()
```

continues

Listing 11.2. continued

```
{
  printf(" Box-Drawing Characters: \n");

  printf(" \xda     \xc2     \xbf\n");
  printf("  da    c2    bf\n");
  printf(" \xc3     \xc5     \xb4\n");
  printf("  c3    c5    b4\n");
  printf(" \xc0     \xc1     \xd9\n");
  printf("  c0    c1    d9\n");

  printf("\n");

  printf(" \xc9     \xcb     \xbb\n");
  printf("  c9    cb    bb\n");
  printf(" \xcc     \xce     \xb9\n");
  printf("  cc    ce    b9\n");
  printf(" \xc8     \xca     \xbc\n");
  printf("  c8    ca    bc\n");

  printf("\n");

}
```

Listing 11.2, LINEDRAW.C, creates a chart of the line-drawing characters, with the hexadecimal code of the character below the character. The output of the program looks like this:

```
Box-Drawing Characters:

  ┌    ┬    ┐
  da   c2   bf
  ├    ┼    ┤
  c3   c5   b4
  └    ┴    ┘
  c0   c1   d9


  ╔    ╦    ╗
  c9   cb   bb
  ╠    ╬    ╣
  cc   ce   b9
  ╚    ╩    ╝
  c8   ca   bc
```

You can create a handy hardcopy output of the chart by viewing the user screen and then pressing the Print Screen key on your computer. The chart should prove to be handy when you use the line-drawing characters.

Another method to enter ASCII characters into the Turbo C++ IDE is available. With this method, you must use the decimal—not hexadecimal—codes of the characters. First, press and hold down the Alt key. Then type the numbers that compose the character you desire *using the numeric keypad* (this trick won't work with the number keys along the top row of the keyboard). Then release the Alt key. The extended character will show up at the current cursor position.

This trick is handy with the extended character codes, however it also works with the regular characters. For example, press and hold down the Alt key and type the number 6 and then 5 on the numeric keypad and release the Alt key. Bingo, the uppercase letter A should appear on the screen.

Video Modes

The information that appears on the screen actually corresponds to an area in your computer's memory. Each location on the screen has a corresponding location in video memory. If there is a character in a video memory location, that character is drawn at the corresponding location on the video display.

Having a memory location for every screen location is known as *memory-mapped screen I/O*. Usually, the printf() function takes care of displaying information, and you don't have to worry about direct access of video memory.

Setting the Text Mode

Most PC computers have several different video text modes, including 80×25, 40×25, and 80×50 columns and rows, respectively. These numbers refer to the number of rows and columns that you can display at one time. The textmode() function is used to set the text mode of the video display, which in turn determines how many characters will be displayed on the screen.

The textmode() function takes one parameter, as listed in Table 11.1, which specifies the mode the screen should be switched to. There are six different text modes. These modes differ in the number of characters displayed on the screen and whether color can be used.

Table 11.1. Text mode constants.

Constant	Value	Description	Size
BW40	0	Black and white	40 columns
C40	1	Color	40 columns
BW80	2	Black and white	80 columns
C80	3	Color	80 columns
MONO	7	Monochrome	80 columns
C4350	64	EGA, VGA	43 lined in EGA, 50 lines in VGA
LASTMODE	−1	Returns to previous text mode	

If you have an EGA or VGA video adapter, you can tell the Turbo C++ IDE to use 43-line or 50-line text mode while you are editing your programs. These extended video display modes enable you to view more text on the screen at a time.

However, they do have their disadvantages, too. By displaying more on the screen at once, each character is smaller. Some people complain that smaller size makes characters unreadable and hard on the eyes.

It's up to you to decide which is better for your purposes—fewer but larger characters, or more but smaller ones. To set the video display mode, choose the Options menu and pick Environment, then choose Preferences. Select the Screen Size radio button for 43/50 lines (as shown in Figure 11.1). When you press Enter to close the dialog box, the change will take effect.

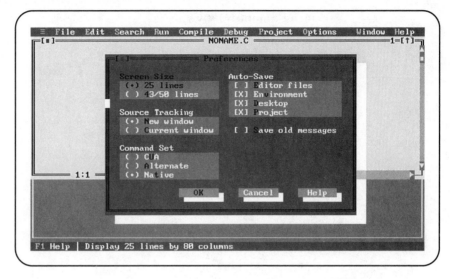

Figure 11.1. *Preferences dialog box accessed through the Options menu.*

To change the text mode, use the `textmode()` function with one of the symbolic constants in Table 11.1. For example:

```
textmode(C4350);
```

will put the computer in 50-line mode (with VGA) or 43-line mode (on EGA). Listing 11.3 (MODES.C) tries every video mode that is available on PC computers.

Listing 11.3. Program to test video modes on your computer.

```
/*******************************************************
 MODES.C--Select different video modes in Turbo C++.
 Do It Yourself Turbo C++ by Paul J. Perry
 *******************************************************/

#include <stdio.h>
#include <conio.h>

char str[] = "Do It Yourself Turbo C++"; /* . . . or type whatever
                                              you like! */
```

continues

207

Listing 11.3. continued

```c
void main(void)
{
  textmode(BW40);
  printf("%s\n", str);
  printf("Mode: BW40");
  getch();

  textmode(C40);
  printf("%s\n", str);
  printf("Mode: C40");
  getch();

  textmode(BW80);
  printf("%s\n", str);
  printf("Mode: BW80");
  getch();

  textmode(C80);
  printf("%s\n", str);
  printf("Mode: C80");
  getch();

  textmode(C4350);
  printf("%s\n", str);
  printf("Mode: C4350");
  getch();

  textmode(MONO);
  printf("%s\n", str);
  printf("Mode: MONO");
  getch();

}
```

Not every video mode works on every combination of display and adapter. For example, if you try to set the display mode to MONO and you have a color monitor with a VGA adapter, *your system may hang!* Therefore, be careful when you run the program.

Using Video Memory Directly

Usually, when the `printf()` function displays information, it sends it out through the PC BIOS. This enables Turbo C++ to create programs that work on the largest number of PCs possible. Displaying information through the BIOS allows for a high degree of compatibility; however, it does slow down the output of the text.

Turbo C++ has a global variable that determines whether the `printf()` function sends through BIOS calls or outputs the data directly to the video RAM area. The variable is available to any program you write in Turbo C++. Outputting through video RAM is quicker, because you bypass the BIOS routines.

The variable that controls the output function is named `directvideo`. If `directvideo` is set to 0, output is processed by the PC's Basic Input/Output System (BIOS) functions. If `directvideo` is 1, all output is sent directly to video memory.

The following statement displays the current value of the directvideo variable:

```
printf("directvideo equals %d", directvideo);
```

The default setting of the variable is 1, which causes output to be sent directly to video RAM. If the computer you are working on is not 100 percent compatible (and how many machines are not these days?) you cannot write directly to video memory.

Coordinate Systems

When you display information with the `printf()` function, the data is printed starting at the current cursor location. The cursor marks the location on the screen where input or output will occur. If the cursor is located on the last row of the screen, the top row is lost, and all text in between is moved up one line, to make space for a new line.

With Turbo C++, we can actually take control of where information will be displayed. The way this is accomplished is by moving the cursor to a new location.

The screen could actually be thought of as a grid. As you know, in regular text mode, the grid extends 80 columns across and 25 lines high. This enables us to display 2,000 characters at any one time (80×25). Each character position on the screen can be referenced by its coordinate location.

The point (1,1) is located in the upper left-hand corner of the screen and the point (80,25) is located in the lower right corner of the screen. You direct the cursor to be relocated with the gotoxy() function. It accepts two integer values, specifying the column and row of where to move the cursor.

Two other functions report the current location of the cursor. The column is returned by wherex() and the row is returned by wherey().

Listing 11.4 is an example that accepts two numbers separated by a space from the user and moves the cursor to the location specified. The current cursor coordinates are displayed in the upper right-hand corner of the screen. If invalid coordinates are entered, the program notifies the user accordingly. To exit the program enter 99 for either the X or the Y coordinate.

Listing 11.4. Program to move the cursor around the screen.

```
/*********************************************************
 MOVE.C--Demonstrate relocating the cursor.
 Do It Yourself Turbo C++ by Paul J. Perry
 *********************************************************/

#include <stdio.h>
#include <conio.h>

void main()
{
  int x, y;

  clrscr();        /* clear screen */

  while ( (x != 99) || (y != 99) )
  {
    printf("Enter an X and Y coordinate : ");
    scanf("%d%d", &x, &y);

    if ( (x>80) || (y>25) )
      printf("Bad coordinate");
```

```
    gotoxy(65,1);
    printf("X=%d, Y=%d", x, y);  /* display current location */

    gotoxy(x, y);
  }
  gotoxy(1, 25);   /* bottom screen line */
  printf("**Program Aborted**");


}
```

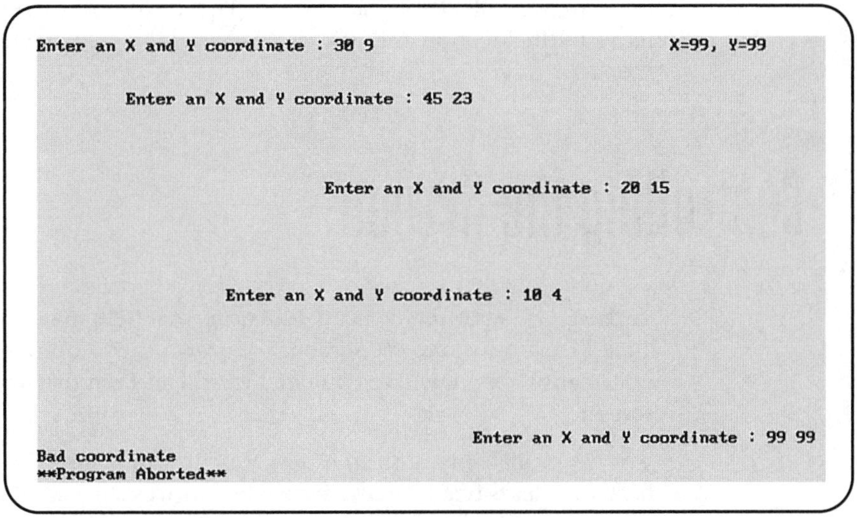

```
Enter an X and Y coordinate : 30 9                                    X=99, Y=99

         Enter an X and Y coordinate : 45 23



                             Enter an X and Y coordinate : 20 15



                 Enter an X and Y coordinate : 10 4




                                         Enter an X and Y coordinate : 99 99
Bad coordinate
**Program Aborted**
```

Figure 11.2. *Sample output of the MOVE.C program.*

Figure 11.2 shows the output of the program. The program sets up a loop that continues until the user enters the values 99 for the X or Y coordinate. The program uses a compound statement:

```
while ( (x != 99) || (y != 99) )
```

This is read "while x is not equal to 99 or y is not equal to 99" and forces our program to continue looping until the user enters 99 for either the X or Y value. It is a good use of some of the operators we have learned about.

Once the loop is set up, the code prompts for the coordinates. We use a scanf() function with two format specifiers:

```
scanf("%d%d", &x, &y);
```

We have used scanf() before; however, we have always requested a single value. By using two format specifiers, the program will ensure that the user enters the two values. The user can either separate the numbers with a space or by pressing Enter after each number.

Once we get the coordinates, we test them to make sure they are valid. In our example, we are using regular 80×25 text mode, so the statement

```
if ( (x>80) || (y>25) )
    printf("Bad coordinate");
```

will be used to make sure the numbers are within boundaries. Although, if they are, we only display a message. The gotoxy() function will still try to move to the location and will wrap around the screen when it tries to use them.

Controlling the Screen

Turbo C++ has built in library functions that help manipulate the appearance of text output to the screen. These routines would be useful in a text editor application, where you need to add and remove lines of text on the screen.

You probably noticed a new function in Listing 11.4. The clrscr() function clears text from the screen and moves the cursor to the upper left corner of the screen. A companion function, clreol(), deletes text starting at the cursor location to the end of the current line.

The delline() function deletes the line containing the cursor and moves all lines below it up one line. The last line of the screen is cleared after you execute this function.

The insline() function inserts an empty line on the screen at the current cursor position. All lines following the new one move down one line, and the bottom line disappears off the bottom of the screen.

Listing 11.5 demonstrates the functions used for controlling the screen discussed in this section.

Listing 11.5. Program to control screen output.

```
/*************************************************************
 MANIP.C--Manipulate video output.
 Do It Yourself Turbo C++ by Paul J. Perry
 *************************************************************/

#include <stdio.h>
#include <conio.h>

void main()
{
  clrscr();

  printf("Half of the next line will be erased\n");
  printf("This part stays; this part goes!\n");
  printf("Nothing happens to this line\n");
  printf("Press any key to continue . . .");
  gotoxy(18,2);    /* move cursor to second line, first column */
  getch();
  clreol();        /* clear to end-of-line */
  getch();

  clrscr();
  printf("The following line will be deleted:\n");
  printf("***remove this line************\n");
  printf("This line will move up one line.\n");
  printf("Press any key to continue . . .");
  gotoxy(1,2);     /* move cursor to second line, first column */
  getch();
  delline();       /* delete the line */
  getch();

  clrscr();
  printf("An empty line will be inserted at the cursor position\n");
  printf("All lines below the empty one\n");
  printf("move down one line.");
  printf("\nPress any key to continue:");
  gotoxy(1, 3);    /* move cursor */
  getch();
```

continues

Listing 11.5. continued

```
insline();      /* insert line */
getch();


}
```

Running the program gives an example of each of the functions, `clreol()`, `delline()`, and `insline()`. The operation of the functions is fairly self-explanatory.

Video Information

To find out the current settings of the video display, use the `gettextinfo()` function. When `gettextinfo()` is called, the function stores information about the current ext mode in a predefined structure (in CONIO.H) called `text_info`, which contains complete information about the video display.

The `text_info` structure is defined in this way:

```
struct text_info {
    unsigned char winleft;          /* left coordinate of screen */
    unsigned char wintop;           /* top coordinate of screen */
    unsigned char winright;         /* right coordinate of screen */
    unsigned char winbottom;        /* bottom coordinate of
                                       screen */

    unsigned char attribute;        /* text attributes */
    unsigned char normattr;         /* normal attributes */
    unsigned char currmode;         /* current video mode  */
    unsigned char screenheight;     /* height of screen */
    unsigned char screenwidth;      /* width of screen /*
    unsigned char curx;             /* current X coordinate of
                                       cursor /*

    unsigned char cury;             /* current y coordinate of
                                       cursor /*
};
```

The following code fragment declares a variable of type `text_info` and displays the X and Y coordinates of the cursor:

```
struct text_info screen_info;

gettextinfo(&screen_info);
printf("The screen is %d characters tall", screen_info.screenheight);
```

Listing 11.6 (TI.C) is a full-blown example of a program that displays information about the video display.

Listing 11.6. Program that displays current information about text.

```
/**********************************************
  TI.C--Display current text information.
  Do It Yourself Turbo C++ by Paul J. Perry
 **********************************************/

#include <stdio.h>
#include <conio.h>

void main(void)
{
    struct text_info ti;     /* declare variable */

    gettextinfo(&ti);
    cprintf("Screen Attribute        %2d\r\n",ti.attribute);
    cprintf("Normal Attribute        %2d\r\n",ti.normattr);
    cprintf("Current Video Mode      %2d\r\n",ti.currmode);
    cprintf("Screen Height           %2d\r\n",ti.screenheight);
    cprintf("Screen Width            %2d\r\n",ti.screenwidth);
    cprintf("Current X               %2d\r\n",ti.curx);
    cprintf("Current Y               %2d\r\n",ti.cury);
    cprintf("Left Window Position     %2d\r\n",ti.winleft);
    cprintf("Right Window Position    %2d\r\n",ti.wintop);
    cprintf("Right Window Position    %2d\r\n",ti.winright);
    cprintf("Bottom Window Position   %2d\r\n",ti.winbottom);

}
```

You should be familiar with most of the information returned by the program. The `gettextinfo()` function requires the address of the structure to be passed to it, hence the use of the & operator:

```
gettextinfo(&ti);
```

We looked at the topic of addresses briefly when you studied the `scanf()` function. We will take up the topic later in more detail. For now, just know that we passed the address of the structure to the function.

The first two values returned by the program may be mysterious. They are the topic of the next section: displaying text with color.

Working with Colors

If you have a color monitor and you are using a color text monitor, you can change the color of the characters displayed on the screen. Remember how the video display is memory mapped? Part of the information that the video memory stores is an attribute. This attribute tells the computer what color to use to display the specified character.

You set background color with the `textbackground()` function, using the following general declaration:

```
textbackground(int b_color);
```

Where *b_color* is an integer number or one of the color constants listed in Table 11.2. You can use one of the symbolic constants as an argument or the corresponding number value. Notice that not all colors can be used as both foreground and background colors.

The header file CONIO.H must be included in your program to use the symbolic constants in Table 11.2, instead of the numerical values of colors. However, if you don't use the symbolic constants, you don't need to include this header file.

Table 11.2. Color constant codes.

Constant	Numerical Value	Background?	Foreground?
BLACK	0	Yes	Yes
BLUE	1	Yes	Yes
GREEN	2	Yes	Yes
CYAN	3	Yes	Yes
RED	4	Yes	Yes
MAGENTA	5	Yes	Yes
BROWN	6	Yes	Yes
LIGHTGRAY	7	Yes	Yes
DARKGRAY	8	No	Yes
LIGHTBLUE	9	No	Yes
LIGHTGREEN	10	No	Yes
LIGHTCYAN	11	No	Yes
LIGHTRED	12	No	Yes
LIGHTMAGENTA	13	No	Yes
YELLOW	14	No	Yes
WHITE	15	No	Yes

For example, to change the background color to red, you can make one of the following calls:

```
textbackground (RED);
```

or

```
textbackground(4);
```

It is usually better to specify a color constant, because the constant is easier to look at and you know instantly what color is being selected when you look at the code.

To set the actual foreground color of the character displayed, use the `textcolor()` function, as follows:

```
textcolor(int t_color);
```

Again, you can use any of the symbolic constants in Table 11.2. An actual call to the textcolor() function looks like this:

```
textcolor (BLUE);
```

This call sets the color of the text to blue.

When you use the previous functions to modify the output colors, you must use different functions to output text: cprintf() and cputs(). They replace the printf() and puts() functions, respectively, when you are using the color modifying functions.

Listing 11.7 is a program that is used to cycle through possible colors and display samples of them on the screen. It does not use the color constants; instead, it uses numbers, because a for loop is used to rotate through all available colors.

Listing 11.7. Program to display samples of color attributes.

```
/***********************************************************
   COLORS1.C--Use colors to enhance video display output.
   Do It Yourself Turbo C++ by Paul J. Perry
 ***********************************************************/

#include <stdio.h>
#include <conio.h>

void main()
{
    int attrib, count;

    clrscr();
    for (attrib=0; attrib<9; attrib++)
    {
        for (count=0; count<80; count++)
            cprintf("O");
        cprintf("\r\n");
        textcolor(attrib+1);
        textbackground(attrib);
    }

}
```

Two nested `for` loops are set up that cycle through color attribute values and display the resulting colors on the screen. It's handy to type in and execute this program, because you can see the result of using different background and text colors and how they each affect contrast and character readability.

Another noteworthy tidbit about these functions is that the `cprintf()` function is a little different in its interpretation of format codes. The `\n` code acts differently with `cprintf()`, in that it only sends a line feed and not a return character. The result is that you must combine it with the `\r` code to achieve a line feed and carriage return sequence (as you have been accustomed to getting from `\n`).

Turbo C++ has several functions that change the intensity of the text characters displayed. The `highvideo()` function causes text to be displayed in high intensity. The `lowvideo()` function causes any following direct video functions to display characters in low intensity. The `normvideo()` function displays characters in the video mode that was used before the program started executing. This function resets the intensity mode as well as the color.

These functions don't require any parameters. The next program, INTENSE.C in Listing 11.8, shows a simple example of how to use the three functions.

Listing 11.8. Program to show examples of different intensities.

```
/********************************************************
 INTENSE.C--Show examples of intensity-modifying
            functions.
 Do It Yourself Turbo C++ by Paul J. Perry
 ********************************************************/

#include <conio.h>

void main()
{
  textcolor(GREEN);
  highvideo();
  cprintf("This is high intensity\n");
  lowvideo();
  cprintf("This is low intensity\n");
```

continues

Listing 11.8. continued

```
normvideo();
cprintf("This is back to normal\n");


}
```

The three functions are used in conjunction with `textcolor()` and `backgroundcolor()` to modify the currently selected color. In effect, the functions extend the selection of colors available to your programs.

What You Have Learned

In this chapter we were able to have some fun and learn about features and functions specific to Turbo C++. The next chapter finishes up the coverage of operators that we started in Chapter 6. Although we were able to experiment with the specific features of Turbo C++ and the PC here, we learned some important information about programming as well.

In particular, the following topics were covered in this chapter:

● The PC uses video memory to store the image that is displayed on the screen.

● There are two basic types of display modes available on a PC: graphics mode and text mode.

● Text display mode is only for character data; graphics mode enables you to access even a single pixel on the screen.

● The characters that make up text display mode include the regular ASCII characters (numbers and letters). The extended ASCII character set includes foreign language characters and line-drawing characters.

● The hexadecimal number system is a method of counting that is based on the number 16. It uses the characters 0–9 followed by A–F to represent the first 16 digits.

● Text mode can be divided into several submodes of operation. There are six different text modes. They differ in the number of characters displayed on the screen and whether color is used.

● The cursor is the location where input or output is going to occur next. Turbo C++ includes functions that enable you to relocate the cursor position, as well as return the current cursor location.

● Text can be displayed in colors. There are really two attributes, or colors related with each character: the background color and the text color.

● The intensity of a character extends the range of colors for displaying text. You can choose high intensity or low intensity. A function is also available that returns the intensity to the state that the IDE was at, at the beginning of the current session.

12

More Operators

Goals

After reading this chapter, you will

- Be able to assign more than one value at a time with a single assignment statement.

- Know how to combine assignment operators with mathematical operators.

- Understand how to count in the binary (base 2) numbering system.

- Know the logical binary operators: AND, OR, and XOR.

- Be familiar with how the left and right shift operators work.

- Know what the conditional operator is and how to use it.

● Understand how to use macros inside a program.

● Be able to apply several rules for using macros in a program.

Chapter 6 covered the basic operators in the C programming language. You probably notice we have constantly been using one or more of the operators in almost every program since then. This chapter takes a look at more operators available in C.

Just to refresh your memory (no pun intended), *operators* are words or symbols that cause a program to do something to variables. Most of the operators you learned about earlier are available in one form or another in most programming languages. The ones we look at in this chapter are a bit more unique, because most of them don't have any equivalent in other programming languages.

So, let's get started. We will cover some new assignment operators, bitwise operators, and conditional operators.

More Assignment Operators

The assignment operator in C is a single equal sign (=). It is used to assign a value to a variable. An example follows:

```
number = 21;
```

This statement assigns the value 21 to the variable named number. You can also use variables to assign values in your program, for example,

```
number1 = number2;
number2 = number3;
```

The first statement assigns the value of number2 to number1. The second assignment statement assigns the value of number3 to number2. The C language enables us to combine the above two statements into one. For example:

```
number1 = number2 = number3;
```

This statement assigns the value of number3 to number2, which is in turn is assigned to number1. A short example is shown in Listing 12.1.

Listing 12.1. Multiple Assignment Statements.

```
/**************************************************************
M_ASSIGN.C--Use multiple assignment statements on one line.
 Do It Yourself Turbo C++ by Paul J. Perry
 **************************************************************/

#include <stdio.h>

void main()
{
  int n1, n2, n3;

  n1=1;
  n2=2;
  n3=3;
  printf("%d, %d, %d\n", n1, n2, n3);
  n1=n2=n3;   /* assignment statement  */
  printf("%d, %d, %d\n", n1, n2, n3);
}
```

The output of the program should look like this:

```
1, 2, 3
3, 3, 3
```

This example shows how to assign several different variables the same value all at once.

Another type of assignment statement uses an arithmetic operator to perform some type of mathematical operation and assign the result to a variable, such as

```
result = 25 + increment;
result = result + 1;
```

By now, you know what is happening with these two statements. Unlike many other computer languages, C allows the assignment operator to be used in expressions that combine an arithmetic operator and the assignment operator.

Take the second statement we just saw. The following two statements are equal:

```
result = result + 1;
result += 1;
```

They both add 1 to the value of the variable named result. The second is C's more compact method of notation. It tells the compiler to assign result to the value of result plus 1. There is a whole list that combines the mathematical and assignment operators in this way, as summarized in Table 12.1.

Table 12.1. Extended assignment operators.

Symbol	Description	Example
+=	Addition	a += b (same as a = a + b)
-=	Subtraction	a -= b (same as a = a - b)
*=	Multiplication	a *= b (same as a = a * b)
/=	Division	a /= b (same as a = a / b)
%=	Modulus Division	a %= b (same as a = a % b)

The next program (A_ASSIGN.C) makes use of the addition assignment operator to give you a complete working example.

Listing 12.2. Program to show uses of addition assignment operator.

```
/**********************************************************
A_ASSIGN.C--Show how to add and assign numbers
at the same time.
Do It Yourself Turbo C++ by Paul J. Perry
**********************************************************/

#include <stdio.h>

void main()
{
  const int increment = 5;
  int total = 0;
  printf("total equals %d\n", total);
  total += increment;
```

```
printf("total equals %d\n", total);
total += increment;

printf("total equals %d\n", total);
total += increment;

}
```

The additional assignment operators in the C programming language add flexibility and enable you to create programs that are shorter and to the point.

Bitwise Operators

The bitwise operators grant you a low level control of program values through C. Because C was designed to take the place of assembly language for many system-level programming tasks, it is important for it to support many operations that are also done in assembly language.

Bitwise operators refer to the testing, setting, or shifting of the actual bits in a number. The bitwise operators in C operate on type char, int, and long data types. Bitwise operators may not be used on float, double, or long double variables, because these data types are stored differently in the computer and can't be manipulated with bitwise operators. Table 12.2 lists the bitwise operators available.

Table 12.2. The bitwise operators.

Operator	Description
&	AND
¦	OR
^	XOR (also called exclusive OR)
~	NOT (also called one's complement)
<<	Shift left
>>	Shift right

Counting by Two

The previous chapter discussed a different numbering system: base 16 (hexadecimal). You are already familiar with base 10 (decimal). Before we continue, we should look at another counting system, called *base 2* or *binary*.

Binary is the simplest method of representing numbers. Its approach is similar to how many common electrical appliances work. For example, a light is either on (1) or off (0).

In the binary system, two symbols represent numbers: 1 and 0. After using the two digits in the one's column, the next column (called the two's column) is used. After two more numbers are counted, the four's column is used, and so on.

Counting from 0 to 7 in binary looks like this:

Binary Number	*Decimal Number*
000	0
001	1
010	2
011	3
100	4
101	5
110	6
111	7

Binary is a natural system of representing numbers inside a computer because the memory used to store numbers can be either of two states: on or off. These two states are represented by the binary values 1 or 0.

Inside the computer, each number can be represented by a byte. A byte is divided into 8 bits. Therefore, the numbers listed above are 3 bits wide. An 8-bit binary number looks like this:

01010101

Using this method, we can store a number from 0 to 255 decimal. This comes from the fact that each bit stores two states and $2^8 = 256$ numbers. To store a larger number, we can use a word value. A *word* (in computer terms) is made up of 2 bytes, which is 16 bits. A word can hold a number from 0 to 65,535 ($2^{16} = 65,536$).

Logical Bitwise Operators

Thus, working with binary numbers and the bitwise operators we can manipulate the bits in a number—a low-level task, usually left to a low-level language. But we are fortunate enough to do it in a high-level language.

The three logical bitwise operators are AND (&), OR (¦), and XOR (^). Each of these operators requires two operands. They are governed by the same truth table as their logical equivalents, except that they work on a bit-by-bit level.

The operations are carried out independently on each pair of corresponding bits within the operands. Thus, the rightmost bit is first compared, then moving to the left, each bit is checked until all the bits have been compared.

The results of these comparisons are

- The bitwise AND operator will return 1 if both bits have a value of 1 (that is, if the first bit and the second bit are true). Otherwise, it will return a value of 0. See Table 12.3.

- The bitwise OR operator will return 1 if one or more of the bits have a value of 1 (if the first bit or the second bit is true). Otherwise, it will return a value of 0. See Table 12.4.

- The XOR expression will return 1 if one of the bits has a value of 1 and the other has a value of 0 (one is true or the other is false). Otherwise, it will return a value of 0. See Table 12.5.

Each of the logical bitwise operators has its own precedence. The bitwise AND (&) operator has the highest precedence, followed by bitwise XOR (^), then OR (¦). The bitwise AND operator follows the equality operators in the table of precedence.

Listing 12.3 is an example of the bitwise operators in action.

Table 12.3. Truth table for the bitwise AND operator.

X	Y	X & Y
1	1	1
1	0	0
0	1	0
0	0	0

Table 12.4. Truth table for the bitwise OR operator.

X	Y	X ¦ Y
1	1	1
1	0	1
0	1	1
0	0	0

Table 12.5. Truth table for the bitwise XOR operator.

X	Y	X ^ Y
1	1	0
1	0	1
0	1	1
0	0	0

Listing 12.3. Program to show use of binary operators.

```
/***************************************************
 BINOPS.C--Demonstrate use of binary operators.
 Do It Yourself Turbo C++ by Paul J. Perry
 ***************************************************/

#include <stdio.h>

void displaybinary(int number);   /* declaration */
```

```
void main()
{
   int value, value2, result;

   clrscr();   /* Clear Screen */

   value = 45;
   printf("value equals:          ");
   displaybinary(value);

   value2= 225;
   printf("value2 equals:          ");
   displaybinary(value2);

   printf("-------------------------------------\n");
             /* separator */

   result = value & value2;   /* AND operator */
   printf("value & value2 equals: ");
   displaybinary(result);

   result = value | value2;   /* OR operator */
   printf("value | value2 equals: ");
   displaybinary(result);

   result = value ^ value2;   /* XOR operator */
   printf("value ^ value2 equals: ");
   displaybinary(result);
}


/*******************************/
void displaybinary(int number)
{
   int temp;

   for (temp=128; temp>0; temp=temp/2)
     if (number & temp) printf("1 ");
     else printf("0 ");
   printf("\n");
}
```

The program sets up several variables and displays the variables in binary. It then displays the result of using the three binary operators. When you run the program, the output should look like this:

```
value equals:         0 0 1 0 1 1 0 1
value2 equals:        1 1 1 0 0 0 0 1
-------------------------------------
value & value2 equals: 0 0 1 0 0 0 0 1
value ¦ value2 equals: 1 1 1 0 1 1 0 1
value ^ value2 equals: 1 1 0 0 1 1 0 0
```

The program includes a handy function, displaybinary(), which displays the binary bits of an integer number passed to it. The function works by testing each bit in the byte, using the AND operator to determine whether the bit is on or off. If the bit is on, the digit "1" is displayed; otherwise, "0" is displayed.

If you are hazy about the results of the program, you should verify that they're correct by comparing bit for bit the results with the truth tables from Tables 12.3 through 12.5. The program should give you a visual feel for how the logical bitwise operators work.

Shift Operators

Besides the previous logical bitwise operators, several bitwise operators that operate on a single variable: the rightshift operator (>>) and the left-shift operator (<<).

The shift operators, represented by two greater-than symbols or two less-than symbols, move all bits in a value to the right or left as specified. The number of places the bits are moved is determined by the number following the operand. What follows is the general form of the shift operators:

```
value >> number of bit positions
```

or

```
value << number of bit positions
```

As bits are shifted off one end, zeros are brought in the other end. Thus, if bits are shifted off one end, they are lost.

Shift operations are extremely useful in decoding external peripheral devices on a computer. Also, the shift operators can be used to perform efficient multiplication and division of integer values. A shift left actually multiplies a number by two, and a shift right actually divides a number by two.

A sample shift operations follows:

```
number >> 4
```

This statement causes all the bits in the number to be shifted right four places. Therefore, if the number was originally 00100000 (which is 32 decimal) the number would be equal to 00000010 (which is 2 decimal) after the shift.

Listing 12.4 shows an example of the left and right bit-shift operators.

Listing 12.4. Program to show bit-shift operators at work.

```c
/***********************************************
 BITSHIFT.C--Give examples of bit shifting.
 Do It Yourself Turbo C++ by Paul J. Perry
 ***********************************************/

#include <stdio.h>

void displaybinary(int number);   /* declaration  */


void main()
{
   int count, number;

   printf("Right Shift Operations\n");
   number = 128;    /* which is 10000000 decimal */
   for (count=0; count<8; count++)
     {
     displaybinary(number);
     number = number >> 1;
     }

   printf("\nLeft Shift Operations\n");
```

continues

Listing 12.4. continued

```
number=1;    /* which is 00000001 decimal  */
for (count=0; count<8; count++)
  {
  displaybinary(number);
  number = number << 1;
  }

}


/*******************************/
void displaybinary(int number)
{
   int temp;

   for (temp=128; temp>0; temp=temp/2)
     if (number & temp) printf("1 ");
     else printf("0 ");
   printf("\n");
}
```

The output of the program looks like this:

```
Right Shift Operations
1 0 0 0 0 0 0 0
0 1 0 0 0 0 0 0
0 0 1 0 0 0 0 0
0 0 0 1 0 0 0 0
0 0 0 0 1 0 0 0
0 0 0 0 0 1 0 0
0 0 0 0 0 0 1 0
0 0 0 0 0 0 0 1

Left Shift Operations
0 0 0 0 0 0 0 1
0 0 0 0 0 0 1 0
0 0 0 0 0 1 0 0
0 0 0 0 1 0 0 0
0 0 0 1 0 0 0 0
0 0 1 0 0 0 0 0
0 1 0 0 0 0 0 0
1 0 0 0 0 0 0 0
```

The program sets up two loops. The first loop right-shifts the number and displays the binary number after each shift. The second loop left-shifts the number, again displaying the binary number after each shift.

The binary operators are extremely useful when you are interfacing closely to the microprocessor. You can use them when you check whether a bit is on or off.

Conditional Operators

Another unique construction in the C programming language is the conditional operator. The conditional operator can be used to replace the `if...else` statement.

The conditional operator consists of both the question mark and the colon. The general form follows:

```
condition ? expression1 : expression2;
```

where condition is a logical expression (which evaluates to true or false) and expression1 and expression2 are values or expressions that evaluate to values. The conditional expression is equivalent to the following if...else statement:

```
if(condition)
  expression1;
else
  expression2;
```

The ? conditional is called a *ternary* operator, because it requires three operands. Here is an expression of how the conditional operator is used:

```
a = b>9 ? 10 : 20;
```

In this example, a will be assigned the value 10 if b is greater than 9. Otherwise, a will be assigned the value 20.

As you may have noticed, the restriction in using the conditional operator is that the target values must both be a single expression, not a statement. That is why constant values are used, 10 and 20 being the numbers used here.

Listing 12.5 gives an example of the conditional operator. It is used to prevent a divide-by-zero error by the compiler.

Listing 12.5. Program to show use of the conditional operator.

```
/******************************************************
   CONDOPS.C--Demonstrate the conditional operator.
   Do It Yourself Turbo C++ by Paul J. Perry
 ****************************************************/

#include <stdio.h>

int errormessage();     /* function declaration */

void main()
{
   int x, y, total;

   printf("Integer Division Calculator\n\n");
   printf("Enter number and number to be divided by : ");
   scanf("%d%d", &x, &y);

   total = y ? x/y : errormessage();
   if(total !=0)
     printf("Answer is %d\n", total);

}


/********************/
int errormessage()
{
   printf("ERROR: Division by zero\n");
   return 0;   /* a value must be returned */
}
```

The important line of the program is the one with the conditional statement, as follows:

```
total = x ? x/y : errormessage();
```

This code evaluates the division statement. If the result is zero, the errormessage() function is executed and the division is not carried out.

Otherwise, the division is carried out and the result is returned in the variable total and then displayed for the user.

Using Macros

Macros are usually associated with a word processor or spreadsheet. You use them to save time in carrying out repetitive tasks. The C programming language includes its own macro facility. Although macros are not operators (as are the elements in the rest of this chapter) this is as good a place as any to discuss how macros can help you.

Macros work similar to functions, but they are not as versatile. Macros are actually part of the C preprocessor. When the preprocessor encounters a macro, the macro name is replaced with a piece of code that performs an action. Macros can be used with arguments or without. You use the following general format to define a macro:

```
#define identifier replacement_string
```

You have already seen the #define statement used to define symbolic constants within a C program. The #define statement can also be used to define single identifiers that are equivalent to expressions.

For example, you could use the #define directive to declare the following identifiers:

```
#define TRUE  1
#define FALSE 0
#define PI 3.1415
#define TAX 8.25
```

You should be familiar with this type of #define example, because it has been used in this book already. The lines tell the compiler to substitute the associated constant each time that the compiler encounters the identifier.

Examples of macro type #define statements follow:

```
#define AREA length * width
#define MESSAGE printf("this is a message")
```

> After you define an expression, you may use it as often as you like. By convention, C programmers use uppercase characters for #define identifiers. This makes it clear in a program that you are referring to a #define identifier rather than a variable name. But, this convention is not required by the compiler.

What Macros Do

The idea behind macros is the same as #define statements we are already familiar with. Whenever the identifier is found in the program by the preprocessor, it is swapped with the replacement string. In the first example, if you use the identifier area in your program, it will be replaced by length * width by the preprocessor. In the second example, if you use the identifier message, it is replaced with the string printf("this is a message").

It is important to understand that macros simply replace an identifier with a string of text. For example, to define a standard error message, you might code something like this:

```
#define MSG "ERROR:  YOU MISSED THE BOAT ON THIS ONE\n"
    .

    .
printf(MSG);
```

This code causes the compiler to substitute the string when it encounters the identifier MSG. Thus the compiler would see the statement as

```
printf("ERROR:  YOU MISSED THE BOAT ON THIS ONE\n");
```

A limitation with macros is that text replacement will not occur if the identifier is found inside a string. For example, the statement

```
printf("MSG");
```

will only print the text MSG rather than the full text associated with the MSG identifier.

Rules for Using Macros

Macro definitions are usually placed at the beginning of a file. The macro definition can be accessed from its point of definition to the end of the file. The following rules apply when you create macros:

- The name of the macro must follow the rules set aside for any other identifier in C. Most importantly, the macro name cannot contain any spaces.

- The macro definition should not be terminated by a semicolon unless you want the semicolon included in your replacement string.

- Macros cannot be used inside quotation marks, as you saw earlier.

- Macro definitions are usually limited to a single line. However, the backslash character (\) can be used at the end of any line except the last to extend the macro definition to more than one line.

Using macros can save you time in a couple of ways. First, macros can save you coding time by making it easy to change constant values. Second, macros make your program easier to read. This is because you can change a meaningless number to read as a useful name.

Listing 12.6 is an example of a program that uses a macro definition. It calculates the area of a rectangle, given the width and height.

Listing 12.6. Program to calculate area by using a macro.

```
/******************************************************
  RECAREA2.C--Calculate area of rectangle using macro.
  Do It Yourself Turbo C++ by Paul J. Perry
  ******************************************************/

#include <stdio.h>

#define area length * width            /* macro definition */

void main()
{
  int length, width;
```

continues

239

Listing 12.6. continued

```
printf("Enter length : ");
scanf("%d", &length);
printf("Enter width : ");
scanf("%d", &width);

printf("\nresulting area is %d\n", area);


}
```

The program (RECAREA.C) contains the macro area, which represents the expression length * width. When the program is compiled, the expression length * width replaces the identifier area within the printf() function. So that the printf() statement becomes

```
printf("\nresulting area is %d\n", length * width);
```

Notice that the string inside quotation marks is unaffected by the program.

Listing 12.7 is an example of a multiline macro. It shows how multiline macros are defined by placing the backslash (\) character at the end of each line in the macro, except the last.

Listing 12.7. Macro containing multiple lines.

```
/**************************************************************
  TRI.C--Use multiline macro to create triangle characters.
  Do It Yourself Turbo C++ by Paul J. Perry
  **************************************************************/

#include <stdio.h>

#define loop for(lines=1; lines<=n; lines++)          \
          {                                            \
          for(count=1; count<=n-lines; count++)    \
             putchar(' ');                             \
          for(count=1; count<=2*lines-1; count++)  \
             putchar('\xb1');                          \
          printf("\n");                                \
           }
```

```
void main()
{
  int count, lines, n;
  clrscr();
  printf("Enter number of lines : ");
  scanf("%d", &n);
  printf("\n");

  loop
}
```

When the program is run, it displays a triangle of squares, whose height is determined by the user. The program looks something like this when you run it:

```
Enter number of lines : 8

       ±
      ±±±
     ±±±±±
    ±±±±±±±
   ±±±±±±±±±
  ±±±±±±±±±±±
 ±±±±±±±±±±±±±
±±±±±±±±±±±±±±±
```

The program demonstrates how you can put almost anything you want in a macro. The entire core loop of the program is in the macro definition.

What You Have Learned

This chapter explored some of the special operators of C that greatly increase its power and flexibility. The following topics were covered:

- Assignment statements can be combined together on one line to assign the value of one variable to several different variables.

- An assignment and mathematical statement can be combined using the extended assignment operators.

● Bitwise operators enable you to perform low-level programming using C.

● The binary numbering system (base 2) uses two symbols to represent numbers. The symbols 1 and 0 represent two logical states in the computer: true and false.

● The logical bitwise operators work independently on each pair of bits within an operand. Truth tables can be used to represent the values that will be returned.

● The shift operators move all bits in a value to the right or left, as specified. As bits are shifted off one end, zeros are brought in on the other end.

● The conditional operator is used as a replacement to the `if...else` statement.

● Macros are used in a program to replace an identifier with a specified string of characters. The replacement of characters is carried out by the C preprocessor, so the actual C compiler does not even know that the replacement is taking place.

● A limitation of using macros is that a macro identifier cannot appear inside a string (within double quotes).

13

Using DOS with C

Goals

After reading this chapter, you will

- Recognize what a command-line argument is and how to access them in a C program.

- Know what is meant by "shelling out to DOS" and which C function to use when doing so from within a program.

- Understand how to access the date and time from within a program.

- Be familiar with some of the data structures and functions used to reference the date and time in a program.

- Know how to access the date and time on a UNIX system and how that method affects using them with Turbo C++.

- Understand what the BIOS is and how to access common BIOS functions from Turbo C++.

- Know how to make simple sounds in a program.

- Have a list of useful BIOS library routines that can be added to your programming toolkit.

Although the C and C++ languages were originally written with a computer based on UNIX in mind, Turbo C++ provides the ability to access functions available only on DOS-based computers. This chapter takes a close look at these functions.

In particular, you will find out what command-line arguments are and how to use them in a program. You will learn how to shell out to DOS, how to query the computer for the current date or time, and how to make some simple sounds using the PC's built-in speaker.

Command-line Arguments

Command-line arguments are parameters that follow the program's name on the DOS command line. For example, you can start Turbo C++ and load a source file at the same time. This is done with the following format for the command entered at the DOS command line:

```
TC filename
```

where `filename` is the name of the file you wish the Turbo C++ Integrated Development Environment (IDE) to load (if no file extension is listed, .CPP is assumed). Many other programs, such as WordPerfect, enable you to do this trick, too. DOS automatically passes any command-line parameters to the program being loaded.

Parameter Passing

Command-line arguments are usually used to pass information to a program when it is run. In a C or C++ program, control starts at the `main()`

function. Command-line parameters are passed to a program as parameters to the main() function.

This is the only time we put into use the parentheses following the main() function (haven't you wondered what they are used for?).

Using **argv[ ]** and **argc**

The general form to use for accessing command-line arguments is

```
void main(int argc, char *argv[])
{
.
.  /* variables are used in body of program  */
.
}
```

Two built-in arguments are used to receive command-line arguments: argc and argv[]. These are the only arguments that main() can have. The argc parameter (short for ARGument Count) is an integer that holds the number of arguments passed on the command line. The argv parameter (short for ARGument Values) is a pointer to an array of character pointers. We have not discussed pointers yet; however, all you need to know about them at this point is that each element in the argv[] array corresponds to a command-line argument.

Listing 13.1 displays the number of command-line parameters passed to the program as well as each command-line parameter. When you are using Turbo C++'s IDE, it may appear that there is no way to specify command-line arguments. However, the Borland designers thought about this ahead of time.

To specify command-line arguments to a program while you are working in the IDE, choose the Run menu and select Arguments. Figure 13.1 shows the dialog box that's displayed for you to specify the program arguments to passed to the program. Each command-line argument is separated from the next with a space.

13

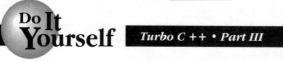

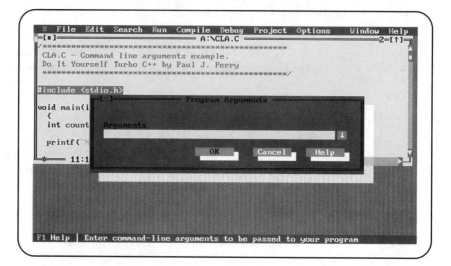

Figure 13.1. *Program Arguments dialog box.*

Listing 13.1 is a sample program that shows how to access command-line arguments.

Listing 13.1. Program to access command-line arguments.

```c
/*****************************************************
CLA.C--Access command-line arguments.
Do It Yourself Turbo C++ by Paul J. Perry
*****************************************************/

#include <stdio.h>

void main(int argc, char *argv[])
  {
  int counter;

  printf("Number of arguments: %d\n", argc);

  for (counter=0; counter<argc; counter++)
  printf("Argument %d is : %s\n", counter, *(argv+counter) );
  }
```

When I run this on my machine by typing

CLA Billy Dusty Frank

from the DOS command line, output looks like this:

```
Number or arguments: 4
Argument 0 is : CLA.EXE
Argument 1 is : Billy
Argument 2 is : Dusty
Argument 3 is : Frank
```

The first array element is always the full pathname of the program itself. Therefore, `argc` will always be the number of command-line elements plus one.

Now that you've been introduced to command-line arguments, we can use them in a program to pass data from the DOS command line. Listing 13.2 is another demonstration program. It displays a line of text in one of three colors, which you choose as command-line parameters.

Listing 13.2. Program to display user-specified colors.

```
/*************************************************************
CTEXT.C--Change colors for text with command-line arguments.
Do It Yourself Turbo C++ by Paul J. Perry
*************************************************************/

#include <stdio.h>
#include <conio.h>      /* for color functions */
#include <stdlib.h>     /* for atoi() function */

void main(int argc, char *argv[])
  {
    if (argc != 3)
      {
      printf("Display text in color be specifying:\n");
      printf("  C>CTEXT COLORNUMBER \"Text to be displayed\"\n");
```

continues

Program Listing 13.2. continued

```
        printf("where COLORNUMBER is either 1=RED, 2=GREEN, or \
                3=BLUE\n");
        }

    switch ( atoi(argv[1]) )    /* convert ASCII character to integer */
    {
      case 1 :
        textcolor(RED);
        break;

      case 2 :
        textcolor(GREEN);
        break;

      case 3 :
        textcolor(BLUE);
        break;

      default :
        textcolor(CYAN); /* if first parameter is not 1, 2, or 3,
                            use cyan */
        break;

    }
    textbackground(BLACK);
    cprintf("%s\r\n", argv[2]);

}
```

The CTEXT.C program first checks to ensure that the user has entered exactly two command-line parameters. We use the comparison

```
if (argc != 3)
```

because we must take into account that argc will always be one more than the number of arguments the user entered. If the user did not enter the correct number of parameters, instructions are given to the user so they know what they should type and they are returned to the DOS prompt.

The first parameter should be a number (1, 2, or 3) relating to a color. The second parameter is the text to be displayed in the selected color. The following are all valid methods of specifying command-line arguments for this program:

```
CTEXT 1 Jennifer
CTEXT 3 "Thomas Edison"
```

Notice, that to include spaces in a parameter, we begin and end the whole string with double quotes. The program then processes the parameter as one parameter, rather than breaking it up into several.

The program selects the video color with the textcolor() function. It does this through the use of a switch statement. The switch argument uses the atoi() function to convert the argument from a character variable to an integer value. An integer value is used for each case of the switch. Finally, the string is displayed using the cprintf() function, discussed in Chapter 11.

> When you design programs that use command-line arguments, the total length of the command-line argument strings, along with the program filename being executed, must not exceed 128 bytes. This is a limitation on the part of DOS, not Turbo C++.

13

Shelling Out to DOS

Another function you may have tried with Turbo C++ (as well as many other applications) is the ability to shell out to—temporarily exit to—DOS. Figure 13.2 shows the shelling out process. In the IDE, the DOS prompt is accessed by choosing the File menu and selecting the DOS shell option.

When you shell out to DOS, you will find yourself at the DOS command line. The program is still resident in memory, waiting for you to return to it. From DOS, you can do just about everything you would usually do at the DOS command line, including renaming files, and executing other programs (as long as there is enough memory).

Using a DOS shell is different from choosing the Exit option on the File menu, because a DOS shell actually loads a copy of DOS into memory while your program remains resident in memory. Furthermore, you can easily return to your program, exactly where you left off by typing EXIT at the DOS command prompt.

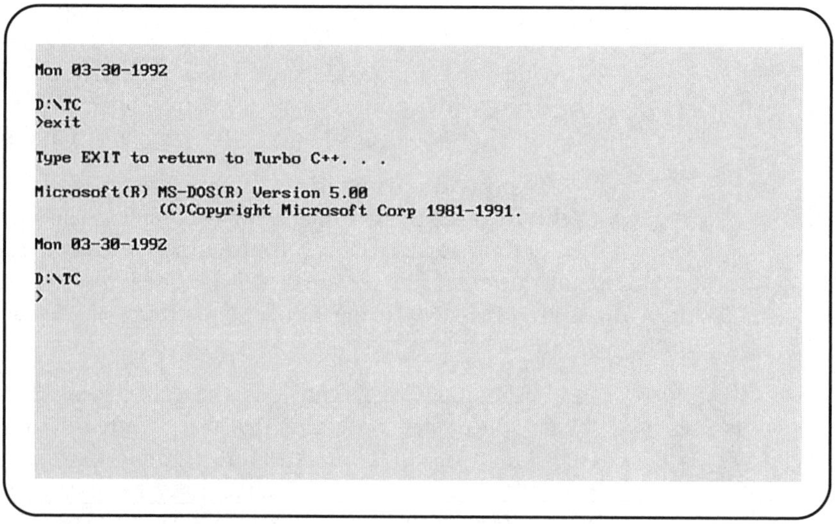

```
Mon 03-30-1992

D:\TC
>exit

Type EXIT to return to Turbo C++. . .

Microsoft(R) MS-DOS(R) Version 5.00
             (C)Copyright Microsoft Corp 1981-1991.

Mon 03-30-1992

D:\TC
>
```

Figure 13.2. *DOS shell in the Turbo C++ IDE.*

You can add the ability to shell out to DOS to your own program through the use of built-in library functions that are included in the Turbo C++ libraries. Although there are about a dozen functions that provide different degrees of control, the one we will use is the spawnl() function.

Listing 13.3 is an example of a program that spawns out to DOS. It is actually an extension of the menu program we saw when the switch statement was introduced. This menu program is designed to be one that you could put into your AUTOEXEC batch file to start up every time your computer is turned on. The program enables you to select an application program from a menu. It then uses the spawnl() function to run that program. Note that because the directories of the files listed in the program may differ on your system, in order for the program to run correctly, you likely will need to change the pathnames so they correspond to the way your system is set up.

Listing 13.3. Program to show use of spawn() function.

```
/****************************************************
 SPAWNIT.C--Use DOS shell to execute programs.
 Do It Yourself Turbo C++ by Paul J. Perry
 ****************************************************/

#include <process.h>
#include <stdio.h>
#include <conio.h>

void spawn_it(char name[]);        /* function declaration */

void main()
{
  int choice='a';   /* anything, as long as it is not 'X' */

  clrscr();
  while (toupper(choice) != 'X')
     {
     printf("\nPlease Choose One:\n\n");
     printf("1 - WordPerfect\n");
     printf("2 - Quattro Pro\n");
     printf("3 - Turbo C++\n");
     printf("X - Exit to DOS\n\n");
     printf("==> ");

     choice = getche();

     switch (choice)
       {
        case '1' :
        spawn_it("C:\\WP51\\WP.EXE");    /* your directories may
                                            differ */
        break;

        case '2' :
        spawn_it("C:\\QPRO\\Q.EXE");
        break;
```

continues

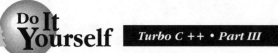

Listing 13.3. continued

```
        case '3' :
        spawn_it("C:\\TC\\TC.EXE");


        }
    }
}

void spawn_it( char name[] )
{
  int result;

  result = spawnl(P_WAIT, name, NULL);
  if (result == -1)
    perror("\nError reported from spawnl function");
}
```

When the program is run, it displays a menu of four selections. The first three will run a selected program. The last selection, X, will exit the program. You will notice an additional header file used in this program:

```
#include <process.h>
```

which contains the declarations for the spawnl() function.

The sharp student of C will notice that the body of this program has a switch statement nested inside a while statement. The while statement checks for the character x (which is first converted to uppercase with the toupper() function) and ends the program if it is pressed. Otherwise, the switch statement responds to the press of a menu selection.

Each case of the switch statement calls a function spawn_it() that calls the appropriate spawnl() function. If an error is returned by the spawnl() function, an error message is displayed. Note that the actual error message is displayed by DOS, not by your program.

One peculiar item you may notice is that the filename for each program includes two backslash characters. Remember, the backslash is used to signify special escape sequences to the printf() function. Therefore, we specify two backslash characters in our call to the function. In that way, it appears as a single backslash to the compiler, and DOS accepts the filename.

The spawn_it() function is passed a character array (actually a string) that in turn is passed on to the spawnl() function. The actual call to the spawnl() function looks like this:

```
result = spawnl(P_WAIT, name, NULL);
```

The function returns an integer value. We store this in the variable result, which we test after the call to the function.

The first parameter to the spanwl() function is a constant that tells DOS to execute the program and to wait for the program to return. The second parameter is the actual filename to execute once DOS is loaded. The final parameter tells the compiler any command-line parameters to pass to the function. We use NULL, which is predefined to mean zero, or no parameters.

We will talk more about NULL when we look at pointers in the next chapter.

Date and Time Functions

Time is a precious commodity. As humans, we never seem to have enough of it in a day. Time is also precious to computers. The computer uses the date and time for a variety of tasks. For example, every time you save a file, the date and time is stored on disk along with the file. Using the DOS DIR (directory) command you can determine the time and date on which any file was last modified.

Word processors, spreadsheets, and databases all use the date and time. You may want to use the date and time in your C program as well. As you may have guessed, Turbo C++ contains routines that give you a chance to get the current system date and time. We will take a look at the most common method of obtaining the date and time in this section.

The date and time functions are declared in the header file TIME.H. In order to understand how Turbo C++ works with the date and time, we must first understand how UNIX keeps track of the time.

In UNIX, the date and time is stored as a number that is the number of seconds elapsed since 00:00:00 hours Greenwich Mean Time (GMT) on January 1, 1970. This is a universal representation of time used throughout the world. Because the time expressed as GMT is not extremely useful to us, most of the functions in Turbo C++ are used to convert values between different date and time formats.

The `time()` function returns the time in UNIX format (which is the number of seconds elapsed since 00:00:00 hours GMT). It fills out the elements in the `tm` structure, which is declared like this:

```
struct tm {
  int tm_sec;    /* seconds */
  int tm_min;    /* minutes */
  int tm_hour;   /* hour (from 0 to 23) */
  int tm_mday;   /* day of month (from 1 to 31) */
  int tm_mon;    /* month (from 0 to 11) */
  int tm_year;   /* year (calendar year minus 1900) */
  int tm_wday;   /* weekday (from 0 to 6, with Sunday = 0) */
  int tm_yday;   /* day of year (from 0 to 365) */
  int tm_isdst;  /* 0 if daylight savings time is not in effect */
};
```

Once the tm structure is filled out, you can use the `localtime()` function to convert the GMT into a format that is easier to use. It takes a value returned from `time()` and converts it to a time usable by Turbo C++, taking into account daylight savings time.

Finally, the `asctime()` function is used to convert the number value returned from `localtime()` into a string, which can then be displayed using the `printf()` function. Listing 13.4. is an example of a program that gets the system date and time and displays it on the screen.

Listing 13.4. Program to retrieve the date and time.

```
/**********************************************
TIME.C--Demonstrate time functions.
Do It Yourself Turbo C++ by Paul J. Perry
**********************************************/
```

```
#include <time.h>    /* for time functions */
#include <stdio.h>

void main(void)
{
    struct tm *curtime;
    time_t    t;

    time(&t);  /* retrieve date and time */

    curtime = localtime(&t);  /* convert time  */

    printf("Current date & time is: %s\n", asctime(curtime) );
}
```

The program displays the current time and date on the screen. Functions that are commonly used to access the date and time are listed in Table 13.1.

Table 13.1. Some of the important time and date functions.

Function	Description
asctime()	Converts time from structure of type tm into a string.
difftime()	Returns the difference between two times.
localtime()	Converts time from type time_t to type tm.
stime()	Sets the system time and date.
time()	Returns the seconds passed since 00:00:00 GMT in time_t.

The time functions can be used in your own programs to record when certain events happen.

Accessing BIOS System Calls

All DOS-based computers come with a basic input/output system (BIOS) built into the read-only memory (ROM). The BIOS includes low-level routines for accessing peripheral devices and reporting on the basic information of the computer.

Turbo-Specific Functions

The Turbo C++ library includes a set of functions to provide access to the BIOS services from within your C program. These calls enable you to access the full power of your PC without having to write in the low-level assembly language of the 8086 microprocessor.

The C routines that access the BIOS are unique to Turbo C++. If you try to compile these programs on a different computer, most likely the functions will not be available and the program won't compile.

The routines used to access the extended BIOS system calls are usually found in the DOS.H or BIOS.H header files. Therefore, these files must be included with the #include directive at the beginning of your program to use them.

Although there are a great number of low-level routines available, the ones we will look at here are primarily ones that return information to a program. There are BIOS functions that can get a character from the keyboard or display characters on the screen, among other things; however, we are already familiar with library functions that do the same function and are more universally used.

When you access BIOS routines, it is important to remember that some machines may not have these functions built in. Because they rely on the ROM built into every computer, there may be subtle differences in the BIOS on different computers that may cause your program to hang the computer. This problem occurred more in the early days of the PC, because the ROM versions were not always 100 percent compatible. You should not encounter any big problem using the BIOS routines on any DOS-based computer today.

Testing for the DOS Version

The information we can query from these routines is interesting; however, you may also need to use them in your program, not just to report information as was done here. For example, you might need to test the version of DOS the user's system is running to ensure that your program is compatible with it. A spreadsheet application should check whether a math coprocessor is available. Many commercial programs that return the information presented here, and more.

Listing 13.5 is an example of code that reports system information about your computer.

Listing 13.5. Program to display system information.

```
/******************************************************
SYSINFO.C--Display system information using
BIOS routines.
Do It Yourself Turbo C++ by Paul J. Perry
******************************************************/

#include <stdio.h>
#include <bios.h>
#include <dos.h>

#define MATH_PROCESSOR_MASK 2

void main()
{

    int memorysize, equipment;

    clrscr();
    printf("System Information\n");
    printf("-----------------\n\n");

    printf("DOS version : %d\n", _version);
    printf("  major version is : %d\n", _osmajor);
    printf("  minor version is : %d\n", _osminor);
```

continues

257

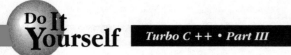

Listing 13.5. continued

```
memorysize = biosmemory();  /* get memory available */
printf("Amount of conventional RAM available : %dK\n",
        memorysize);

equipment = biosequip();  /* get BIOS settings  */
if (equipment & MATH_PROCESSOR_MASK)
   printf("Math coprocessor is installed\n");
else
   printf("No math coprocessor installed\n");
   printf("Number of printer ports : %d \n", equipment >> 14);

}
```

When this program runs on my computer, it looks something like this:

```
System Information
- - - - - - - - - - - - - - - -


DOS version : 5
  major version is : 5
  minor version is : 0
Amount of conventional RAM available : 640K
Math coprocessor is installed
Number of printer ports : 1
```

The program first clears the screen. To access the DOS version number, we access a global variable named _version that is declared as an unsigned integer and contains the DOS version under which the program is currently running. To access the global variable, all we need to do is use #include <dos.h> in our program.

Then we get even more specific and find out the major and minor DOS version numbers. If the overall DOS version number is 5.0, 5 is the major number and 0 is the minor number. To return the major and minor DOS version, we access the _osmajor and _osminor global variables. The DOS version-reporting variables are summarized in Table 13.2.

Table 13.2. DOS version-reporting variables.

Variable	Description
_version	DOS version number
_osmajor	Major DOS version number
_osminor	Minor DOS version number

Next, the program uses the biosmemory() function to return the total amount of conventional memory available to the program.

The BIOS routine that returns the most information is biosequip(). It returns an integer describing the equipment connected to the system. To interpret the number returned by the biosequip() function, we must look at the number bit by bit. Figure 13.3 shows what each bit is used for.

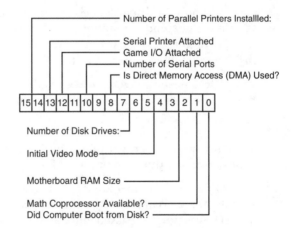

Figure 13.3. *Bit values of number returned by* biosequip() *function.*

To keep the program simple, we only use two of the values returned. We first use the AND (&) operator to compare the value returned with the bit pattern 10. If the value returned is true, a math coprocessor is available. Otherwise, one is not.

We then use the right-shift operator to shift the bits in the 2 leftmost bytes to the right so we have a decimal number relating to how many parallel printers are attached to the system.

Although we only used a couple of the bits returned from the `biosequip()` function, several others are returned. They can be tested with the binary operators to return the information you might need in a program.

Making Sounds

Although the PC comes with a simple, three-inch speaker that is used to create rather simple tones, we need not ignore the subject of sound. Most any program can be extended by adding a couple of blips or bleeps that would emit an audible tone to let the user know if the correct (or incorrect) action was carried out by the user.

Add-on sound boards such as Sound Blaster can be purchased for the PC to greatly extend the sounds that can be created. However, because that product requires extra hardware, we will focus instead on the basic sound making capabilities inherent to the PC.

The easiest way to create a beep is by sending the ASCII code for a bell to the output device using the `printf()` function. For example:

```
printf("\07");
```

sounds a simple beep with little effort from you. However, you have no control over the duration or pitch of the sound created with this function.

Only two routines are really included with Turbo C++ to make sounds. Appropriately enough, they are named `sound()` and `nosound()`. The `sound()` function is passed an integer number corresponding to the frequency of the sound to be created. When you call the routine, the PC's speaker is turned on. To turn the speaker off, use the `nosound()` function.

The two sound functions are usually used in conjunction with the `delay()` function. The `delay()` function suspends execution of a program for a certain number of milliseconds.

Listing 13.6 shows how it is done.

Listing 13.6. Program to create mixed sound.

```
/****************************************************************
 SOUNDS.C--Show use of sound() / nosound() functions.
 Do It Yourself Turbo C++ by Paul J. Perry
 ****************************************************************/

#include <stdio.h>

void beep(void);    /* function declarations */
void siren(void);
void spaceship(void);

void main()
{
  clrscr();
  printf("***Sounds***\n\n");
  printf("Press any key to hear computer beep\n");
  getche();
  beep();

  printf("Press any key to hear siren\n");
  getche();
  siren();

  printf("Press any key to hear spaceship sounds\n");
  getche();
  spaceship();

  printf("That's all, folks...\n");
}

void beep(void)
{
  sound(700);
  delay(200);
  nosound();
}

void siren(void)
{
  int x;
```

continues

Listing 13.6. continued

```c
  for(x=0; x<2000; x++)    /* go up in tone   */
    {
    sound(x);
    delay(x%2);
    }

  for(x=2000; x>0; x--)   /* go down in tone   */
    {
    sound(x);
    delay(x%2);
    }
  nosound();
}
void spaceship(void)
{
  int x;
  for (x=0; x<6; x++)
    {
    sound(800);
    delay(100);
    sound(1000);
    delay(50);
    }
  nosound();
}
```

The program has three separate functions that each create a unique sound: a beep, a siren, or a spaceship sound (whatever that actually sounds like). The program enables you to hear each sound in succession.

The beep() function sounds a simple computer beep by turning on the sound with a frequency 700 Hz. It then delays for 200 milliseconds and turns the sound off. It could be modified to create sounds of different pitches by changing the number passed to the sound() function.

The siren() function sets up two loops. The first loop counts from 0 to 2000, passing the number to the sound() routine. The delay() function is used to wait one half the value of the loop (using integer division). The second loop in the function does about the same thing; however, it counts down from 2000 to 0, therefore causing a lowering of the pitch of the sound. The spaceship() function sets up a loop to create a fluctuating sound.

These routines will get you started. You can experiment with your own. If you are imaginative and creative you can actually create some rather nice sound effects.

The sound() function cannot create every tone of sound that you might try to pass it. For some values, you may not hear anything at all. The reason for this limitations is the hardware. Unfortunately, when IBM originally designed the PC, the company decided to lower costs whenever and wherever possible, which resulted in low-cost speakers being used in the first computers. Unfortunately, 10 years later we are still suffering from that cost cutting. This should all start to change, because third-party vendors are coming up with add-on cards that may become standard on most systems (like the mouse has become). But, only time will tell.

In fact, the multimedia PC (MPC) standard is emerging as a preferred method of incorporating sound and video images into programs. It is exciting to see the upcoming possibilities with this new technology. The way technology moves, this feature should be included in many computers in the near future.

For now, you have the sound(), delay(), and nosound() functions to create your computer sounds on any PC available.

What You Have Learned

This chapter examined some of the methods used to access the features of DOS from a C program. In particular, it looked at the following topics:

- Command-line arguments are characters appearing after a program name at the DOS prompt. They are accessed from a C or C++ program using the argc (for ARGument Count) and argv[] (ARGument Values) variables.

- The first command-line argument returned as argv[0] is always the full pathname of the program. Multiple arguments are separated on the command line with spaces. To include characters separated with spaces, enclose the string in quotes.

● When a program shells out to DOS, a copy of the DOS command interpreter is loaded while the program stays in memory. To return to the program, type EXIT and press Enter. Turbo C++ lets a program shell to DOS by including a family of spawnl() functions in the function library.

● In UNIX, the date and time is stored as a number of seconds elapsed since 00:00:00 hours Greenwich Mean Time (GMT) on January 1, 1970. The time() function is used to return the date in UNIX format.

● The time() function is used to return the date in UNIX format. Use the localtime() function to convert the date and time over to Turbo C++ format. Finally, use the asctime() function to convert the time into a string that can be output with the printf() function.

● All PC-based computers come with a basic input/output system (BIOS). A number of routines are used in Turbo C++ to access these routines and return information about the computer system.

● Turbo C++ includes two routines used to create sounds: sound() and nosound(). They respectively turn on and turn off the speaker of the PC. The delay() function is also used when creating sounds. It suspends execution of the program a certain number of milliseconds.

Pointers

Goals

After reading this chapter, you will

- Understand what a pointer is and what a pointer is used for in C programming.

- Know how to declare a pointer.

- Be able to select which operators to use to work with pointers.

- Recognize the difference between passing data by value and by reference in a function.

- Know how to pass parameters between functions by reference through the use of pointer variables.

● Understand how to access strings with pointers.

● Know another method of accessing one-dimensional array elements with pointers.

The term *pointer* has come up several times in this book so far. Pointer operations in the C language are an area that can cause beginning programmers difficulty. But this is not meant to scare you away. The power you receive from learning pointers is well worth the short-term difficulty required to come up to speed with them.

Although pointers are used in other programming languages, such as BASIC and Pascal, their implementation is hidden from the programmer and is not essential to using the language. However, the understanding and correct use of pointers is critical to the creation of just about every large C program.

Pointer operations are responsible for a great deal of the versatility associated with the C programming language. However, in addition to being one of C's strongest features, pointers can also be one of the most dangerous features. Uninitialized pointers can easily cause a system crash. Also, it is easy to accidentally use pointers incorrectly, causing program errors that are difficult to track down.

About Pointers

A *pointer* is a special type of variable that points to a specific location in memory. A pointer represents the location (rather than the value) of a variable. Most often, the location is the address of another variable in memory, although it can be any memory location. Typically, a pointer points to a part of memory where a value is stored or where one is to be stored.

The reasons for using pointers include

• Pointers provide a method by which functions can modify their calling arguments. Pointers can be used to pass more than one piece of information back and forth between a function and where its calling from.

• Pointers are used to support dynamic memory allocation. You can actually create variables as your program is running.

- Pointer operations provide increased efficiency when they are substituted for accessing arrays. The pointer provides an alternate method to access individual array elements.

Pointers are an important part of the power behind the C programming language.

Declaring Pointers

To declare a pointer, you must use a special *pointer declaration* to tell the compiler that you are about to declare a pointer variable.

Because different data types require different amounts of memory, declaring a pointer must include a specification of the data type to which it refers. This is done by defining a pointer that points to a specific data type. The general syntax for declaring a pointer variable is

```
datatype *name;
```

where `datatype` is any valid C data type (`int`, `char`, `float`, and so on) and `name` is the name of the pointer variable. The data type defines the type of variable the pointer can point to.

The asterisk (*) is called the indirection operator. When following a data type, it is read "pointer to" and indicates that the pointer points to a variable of the indicated type.

The following statements declare pointer variables:

```
char *a;
int *i, *begin;
```

The first statement declares one character pointer and the second declares two integer pointers.

After a pointer is declared but before it has been assigned a value, the pointer contains an unknown value. You should not try to use the pointer before you assign it a value, because you will probably crash your program.

The C language has a convention in which a pointer that is pointing nowhere is set to equal the constant NULL. The NULL constant is a value that signifies to the compiler that the pointer points to nothing. However, just because a pointer is equal to NULL does not mean you cannot use it.

14

The compiler will still let you use it; however, an uninitialized pointer can easily cause your program to crash (not a good thing to have happen).

Pointer Operators

There are two special operators that work with pointers: & and *. The & is the address operator, which evaluates the address of a pointer variable.

For example,

```
address = &ch;
```

places the memory address of the variable ch into the pointer variable address. The variable address represents ch's memory location, not its actual value. The memory location really has nothing to do with the value of the variable. You can think of the job of the & operator as that of returning the address of the variable it prefaces.

The other pointer operator is *, and its job is to return the value of the variable located at an address. For example, if address contains the memory location of the variable ch (as declared above), then the statement:

```
contents = *address;
```

places the value of ch into the variable named contents. If ch originally stored the character Q, then contents will be equal to the character Q because that is the value stored at location &ch. A verbal translation of the * operator is literally "variable pointed to by...."

What makes pointer notation difficult is that the asterisk is used both to declare a variable and to reference the value that a pointer points to. Furthermore, the asterisk is also used for multiplication. However, the compiler can tell when to perform the appropriate action. The notation makes it a little harder for humans to remember. However, after using them a bit the notation begins to be second nature.

Using Pointers

Listing 14.1, VARADDR.C, demonstrates how to return the address of a variable using the & operator.

Listing 14.1. Program to return variable addresses.

```
/****************************************************
 VARADDR.C--Return the addresses of variables.
 Do It Yourself Turbo C++ by Paul J. Perry
 ****************************************************/

#include <stdio.h>

void main()
{
  int var1 = 12;
  int var2 = 13;
  int var3 = 14;

  printf("Address of var1 : %X\n", &var1);
  printf("Address of var2 : %X\n", &var2);
  printf("Address of var3 : %X\n", &var3);

}
```

This simple program defines three integer variables and initializes them to the values 12, 13, and 14. It then prints out the addresses of the variables. Notice that a variable need not be declared as a pointer to use the & operator. The reason is that all variables take up memory, and the & operator returns the memory location where a variable is located.

The actual addresses occupied by the variables in a program depend on many factors, such as the amount of memory available on the computer, the version of DOS, and whether any other programs are currently running in memory. This program is to show you that a memory address is not the same thing as variable contents.

Listing 14.2 is another sample program that illustrates the relationship between two integer variables, their corresponding addresses, and the associated pointers.

Listing 14.2. Program to use pointers.

```
/***********************************************
PTR1.C--Show use of pointer operators.
Do It Yourself Turbo C++ by Paul J. Perry
***********************************************/

#include <stdio.h>

void main()
{
  int a, b;   /* integer variables */
  int *pa;    /* pointer to an integer */
  int *pb;    /* pointer to an integer */

  a = 9;      /* assign 9 to variable a */
  pa = &a;    /* assign address of a to pa */
  b = *pa;    /* assign value of a to b */
  pb = &b;    /* assign address of v to pb */

  printf("Results are:\n\n");

  printf("a=%d   &a=%X   pa=%x   *pa=%d\n", a, &a, pa, *pa);
  printf("b=%d   &b=%X   pb=%x   *pb=%d\n", b, &b, pb, *pb);

}
```

Notice that pa is a pointer to a and pb is a pointer to b. Therefore, pa represents the address of a and pb represents the address of b. The printf() statements illustrate the values of a and b and their associated values *pa and *pb. Notice that a new format specifier is included in printf(): %X. Its purpose is to display a value in hexadecimal (base 16).

Running the program creates the following output:

```
Results are:

a=9   &a=FFF4   pa=fff4   *pa=9
b=9   &b=FFF2   pb=fff2   *pb=9
```

Memory addresses will most likely be different on your computer. In the first line, we see that a represents the value 9, as specified in the declaration. The address of a is determined automatically by the compiler. The pointer pa is assigned this value; therefore, pa also represents the same address. Finally, the value pa points to (*pa) is 9, as would be expected.

Similarly, the second line shows that b also represents the value 9. This is expected, because we assigned the value *pa to b. The address of b, and hence the value of pb are the same. Notice that a and b have different address. Finally, we see that the value to which pb points is 9.

Figure 14.1 shows the relationships between pa and a, and pb and b. Notice that the memory location of the pointer variables are not displayed by the program.

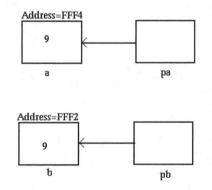

Figure 14.1. *Relationship between variables in PTR1.C.*

Returning Data from Functions

When we discussed functions in Chapter 10, you may remember that we were able to return a single value to the calling program from within a function with the return statement. This transfer of a single piece of information might at times be rather limiting. However, pointers come to the rescue in allowing us to return more than one value from within a function.

Pointers are often passed to a function as arguments. This allows data items in the calling portion of the program to be directly accessed by the function, altered in the function, and then returned to the calling portion of the program in altered form.

The C++ language allows a program to pass parameters by reference. However, the C language does not have a direct method to reference arguments.

Usually, when a parameter or argument is passed to a function, it is passed *by value*. When an argument is passed by value, a copy of the data item is passed to the function. Thus, any alterations made to the arguments inside the function are not returned to the calling program.

However, when an argument is passed *by reference*, the address of a data item is passed to the function. The contents of that address can be accessed and the values stored at the address can be modified within the function and the changes occur in the actual memory location in which the variables are located.

Passing Pointers to Functions

Listing 14.2 is one that illustrates the difference between ordinary arguments, which are passed by value and pointer arguments, which are passed by reference.

Listing 14.3. Program to pass parameters by value and by reference.

```
/***************************************************************
 FUNCTION.C--Show difference between function call by value
 and function call by reference using pointers.
 Do It Yourself Turbo C++ by Paul J. Perry
 ***************************************************************/

#include <stdio.h>

void first_function(int a, int b);        /* function declarations */
void second_function(int *pa, int *pb);

void main()
```

```
{
  int x = 0;
  int y = 0;

  printf("Before calling first_function,   x=%d,  y=%d\n", x, y);
  first_function(x,y);
  printf("After calling first_function,    x=%d,  y=%d\n\n", x, y);

  printf("Before calling second_function,  x=%d,  y=%d\n", x, y);
  second_function(&x, &y);
  printf("After calling second_function,   x=%d,  y=%d\n", x, y);
}

void first_function(int a, int b)
{
  a = 1;
  b = 1;
  printf("Inside first_function,           a=%d   b=%d \n", a,b);
}


void second_function(int *pa, int *pb)
{
  *pa = 2;
  *pb = 2;
  printf("Inside second_function,          *a=%d, *b=%d\n", *pa,
                                           *pb);

}
```

The output of this program should look something like this:

```
Before calling first_function,     x=0,   y=0
Inside first_function,             a=1    b=1
After calling first_function,      x=0,   y=0

Before calling second_function,    x=0,   y=0
Inside second_function,            *a=2,  *b=2
After calling second_function,     x=2,   y=2
```

The program contains two functions. The first receives two integer variables as arguments. These variables are originally assigned the value 0 in the program. The values are then changed to 1 inside the first function.

The values of the original variables are not changed when the program returns to main() because the arguments were passed by value, and any changes made to the arguments in the function are local within the function in which the change occurred.

The second function receives two pointers to integer variables as its arguments. The function is called as follows:

```
second_function(&x, &y);
```

The addresses are provided by the calling program using the & operator. Control is passed to the function along with the addresses of the two variables.

The arguments in the function are identified as pointers with the use of the asterisks that appear in the function argument declaration, as follows:

```
void second_function(int *pa, int *pb)
```

Within the second function, the contents of the pointer addresses are assigned the value of 2. Because the addresses are recognized in both the function and in main(), the values will be changed in the main program as well as inside the function.

Library Functions and Pointers

As you have seen, several Turbo C++ library functions use pointers. The one we have seen so far is scanf(), which is used for getting input from the keyboard, for example,

```
char str[99];
scanf("%s", &str);
```

The & operator passes the address of the first element in the character array str to the scanf() function. The scanf() function gets the keystrokes from the user and returns them in the variable str. The & operator is not necessary when you are using scanf() with strings, because the first element of a string is its address. However, it works either with or without the & operator. You will learn about other functions that pass data between functions through the use of pointers later in this book.

Pointers and Strings

In C, character pointers are used quite often. In fact, character pointers can be thought of as an extension of character arrays. For example, take a look at Listing 14.4.

Listing 14.4. Program to show string and pointer notation.

```
/****************************************************
 PTR2.C--Use pointers with strings.
 Do It Yourself Turbo C++ by Paul J. Perry
 ****************************************************/
#include <stdio.h>

void main()
{
  char *a;

  a = "Hello, World!";

  printf("%s\n", a);
}
```

The program declares a pointer variable. When we declare the pointer variable, it is now available to point to a specific place in memory. To make proper use of it, we assign the string "Hello, World!" to the variable. Turbo C++ automatically adds a terminating \0 character to the string. The constant in quotes is actually written into the program, and when the program is run, the computer allocates a place in memory to store the constant. The pointer a does not equal the string. Rather, a points to the location where the computer has stored the constant.

The output of the program displays the contents of the string. When the printf() function outputs the string, the only way it knows that it has come to the end of the string is the terminating '\0' automatically appended to the string.

To clarify the concept, take a look at a modification to the program, as follows in Listing 14.5.

Listing 14.5. Second pointer and string example.

```
/****************************************************
  PTR3.C--Use pointers with character arrays #2.
  Do It Yourself Turbo C++ by Paul J. Perry
****************************************************/

#include <stdio.h>

void main()
{
  char *a;

  a = "Hello, World!";

  printf("%s\n", a);
  printf("%c\n", *a);

}
```

This program shows some of the notation used with pointers and character arrays. The first printf() function displays the full string; the second printf() function displays the single character H.

The pointer is declared and points to the beginning of the word "Hello, World!" in memory. The first printf() function call prints the string pointed to by a. The second printf() function call displays the letter H, the initial character pointed to by *a.

When a pointer is used with the * operator, it indicates that the memory contents of one element in the string are to be read. The *a uses the asterisk as the indirection operator to return the single character that a points to.

Character Arrays

You remember from Chapter 9 that C has no specific string data type. Instead, you define and use character arrays to represent groups of characters. You are probably thinking that there must be some method of accessing these character arrays using pointers. You are right. Listing 14.6 is an example program that shows how to access character arrays with pointers.

Listing 14.6. Program to use character arrays and pointers.

```
/****************************************************
 PTR4.C--Use pointers with strings.
 Do It Yourself Turbo C++ by Paul J. Perry
 ****************************************************/

#include <stdio.h>

void main()
{
  char *a, *c;
  char b[99] = "Do it yourself!";
  a = "Hello, World!";
  c = b;

  printf("a is : %s\n", a);
  printf("b is : %s\n", b);
  printf("c is : %s\n", c);

  c = a;
  printf("c is now: %s\n", c);

}
```

This program creates two character pointers, *a and *c, and a character array, b. The output of the program looks like this:

```
a is : Hello, World!
b is : Do it yourself
c is : Do it yourself
c is now: Hello, World!
```

The character array is declared to be 99 elements long (to give us breathing space) and it is assigned the string, "Do it yourself!". We then assign a to point to the beginning of the second string. Next, we assign c to point to the beginning of b.

We then display the contents of what each variable points to. We let c equal a with the simple assignment statement:

```
c = a;
```

Next we display what c points to, and you can tell that it is equal to the first string constant.

You can quickly see the relationship between character pointers and character arrays.

Moving Through Memory

Although we cannot do any sort of regular arithmetic operations with pointers, we can use the increment and decrement arithmetic operators with pointers. These operators allow us to cycle through each element in an array.

Listing 14.7. Program to cycle through memory with pointers.

```
/**************************************************
PTR5.C--Cycle through memory.
Do It Yourself Turbo C++ by Paul J. Perry
**************************************************/

#include <stdio.h>

void main()
{
  char *a;

  a = "Just do it";

  while (*a != '\0')
    {
    printf("%c\n", *a);
    a++;
    }

}
```

This example actually counts through each element of a character array. Remember that the statement *a points to the first character in the array. By using the statement

```
a++
```

the code actually moves the pointer to point to the second element in the string. Another a++ counts to the third element, and we continue until we reach the end of the string.

The result of the program prints this:

```
J
u
s
t

d
o

i
t
```

on the display screen. Each character in the string is accessed individually, displayed and then followed by a line feed. The loop continues until the end of the string (\0) is located.

> Each time a pointer is incremented, it points to the memory location of the next element of the data type of the pointer. Each time it is decremented, it will point to the location of the previous element.

In the previous case of the pointer to a character array, the pointer is incremented by one byte each time. However, all other pointers will increase or decrease by the length of the data type they point to. For example let's look at the difference between 1-byte characters and 2-byte integers. When a character pointer is incremented, it is increased by one. However, when an integer pointer is incremented it is actually increased by two (because an integer is stored in two bytes).

You can also add or subtract integer values with pointers. For example, the expressions

```
a++;
a = a+1;
```

are the same. They both increment the location a points to by one. You could increase the location a points to by 5 with the statement:

```
a = a+5;
```

Pointers and One-Dimensional Arrays

As you have seen, there is a close relationship between pointers and arrays. An array name is really a pointer to the first element in the array. Therefore, if we have the declaration:

```
arr[99];
```

the address of the first array element can be expressed as either

```
arr
```

or

```
&arr[0];
```

The address of the second array element can be written as either

```
&arr[1]
```

or

```
(arr+1)
```

As a result, there are actually two different ways to refer to the address of an array element, as follows:

- We can write the actual array element, preceded by an ampersand.

- We can write an expression in which the subscript is added to the array name.

Listing 14.8 Shows the methods you can use for accessing the array elements.

Listing 14.8. Program to access array elements with pointers.

```
/*****************************************************
 PTR6.C--Demonstrate pointers and array elements.
 Do It Yourself Turbo C++ by Paul J. Perry
 *****************************************************/

#include <stdio.h>

void main()
{
 int arr[3] = {11, 22, 33};

 printf("address of first array element (arr) %d\n", arr);
 printf("address of first array element (&arr[0]) %d\n", &arr[0]);

 printf("address of second array element (arr+1) %d\n", (arr + 1) );
 printf("address of second array element (&arr[1])  %d\n", &arr[1]);

 printf("contents of arr[0] is %d\n", arr[0]);
 printf("contents of arr[1] is %d\n", arr[1]);
}
```

Output of the program might be similar to this:

```
address of first array element (arr) -16
address of first array element (&arr[0]) -16
address of second array element (arr+1) -14
address of second array element (&arr[1]) -14
contents of arr[0] is 11
contents of arr[1] is 22
```

The program demonstrates the two methods of accessing the addresses of an array.

An alternate form of specifying the first array element is

```
*(arr + 1)
```

This is equivalent to

```
(arr+1)
```

and the two terms are interchangeable. The choice depends on your own preference. Listing 14.9 illustrates the relationship between array elements and their addresses.

Listing 14.9. Program to access arrays with pointers and different methods.

```
/**************************************************
 ARRPTR.C--Show array and pointer notation.
 Do It Yourself Turbo C++ by Paul J. Perry
 **************************************************/

#include <stdio.h>

void main()
{
  int arr[10] = { 11, 22, 33, 44, 55, 66, 77, 88, 99, 111 };
  int index;

  for (index=0; index<10; index++)
    printf("index= %d, arr[index]= %d, \
*(arr+index)= %d, &arr[index]= %d, \
arr+index= %d\n", index, arr[index], *(arr+index), &arr[index],
arr+index);

}
```

The program will display a table showing how to access array elements with pointers. The ability to access array elements through pointer notation definitely grants us great flexibility in our work in C.

What You Have Learned

This chapter introduced the concept of pointers and covered some of the ways that pointers can be used. In particular, the following topics were covered:

- A pointer is a special type of variable that points to a specific location in memory. The pointer represents a memory location, rather than a value.

- Pointers are used to (1) provide a method by which functions can pass data, (2) allow dynamic data allocation, and (3) allow increased efficiency when accessing array elements.

- A pointer's declaration consists of a base data type, an asterisk (*), and the variable name.

- Two special pointer operators are included with the C programming language: & and *. The & operator returns the memory address of its operand. The * operator is the complement of the & operator and it returns the value of the variable located at an address.

- When parameters are passed to a function, the parameters are passed by value. When data is passed by value, a copy of the data item is passed to the function. By passing pointers between functions, the parameter are passed by reference, where the actual parameters passed to the function can be accessed and changed.

- Strings can be accessed with pointers by using the & and * operator.

- Array elements can be accessed using two different methods. If x is declared a one-dimensional array, the first element of the array can be accessed as either &x[0] or simply as x. The address of the second array element can be written as either &x[1] or as x+1.

14

Advanced Pointers

Goals

After reading this chapter, you will

- Know uses for pointers in addition to those covered in the Chapter 14.

- Understand what dynamic memory allocation means.

- Know how to dynamically allocate memory using the `malloc()` and `calloc()` functions. They will know the difference between the two functions in what they do and how they are used.

- Understand what the `free()` function is used for.

● Be able to access dynamically allocated memory through the use of pointers.

● Know how to access multidimensional arrays by using pointers.

Chapter 14 introduced the subject of pointers. This chapter takes a deeper look at the use of pointers. You will learn how to dynamically allocate memory and access it through the use of pointers. You will also see how to access multidimensional arrays using pointers.

This chapter is purposefully a little shorter, which will enable you to understand the material presented about pointers. So let's get started with the first topic, dynamic memory allocation.

Dynamic Memory Allocation

All of the data structures we have examined so far have been *static* data structures. This means that the Turbo C++ compiler allocates memory for the variables when they are declared. The variables then occupy memory space throughout the execution of the program.

Static memory allocation is simple to manage but is somewhat inflexible. For example, when creating an array, you must tell C how large it should be when you declare it. This is required in order that the correct amount of memory will be made available to your program when it is executed. If you allocate an array of too little space and access elements beyond the maximum size of the array, your program will crash. If you use fewer array elements than the number declared, a certain amount of memory is left unused and therefore wasted.

The opposite of static data structures are *dynamic* data structures. The memory for these data structures are allocated as the program is executed. The size of a dynamic data structure can grow as needed. Furthermore, if after allocating the memory space you find you don't need it any longer, the size of the dynamic data structure can shrink, thereby releasing memory for use by other data.

At first glance, it may seem awkward to refer to a variable through the use of a pointer. However, by using pointers you can achieve incredible power in programming, because pointers enable you to create variables while a program is executing. In fact, with the malloc() and calloc() functions you can define a variable that is not part of any variable declaration. To put it another way, the functions help you to create variables and destroy them during the execution of your program. Using pointers, you can create dynamic data structures that can grow or shrink as your program is executed.

The **malloc()** and **calloc()** functions

Pointers can be made to point to any area of memory. Usually, pointers are aimed at portions of memory that already have data set aside in them. C provides functions that allow a pointer to point to an area of memory that is set aside specifically for storage of new data.

We can tell the system to set aside a certain area of memory that can later be accessed with a pointer. When this is done, we specify how many bytes of storage space is required, and the compiler takes care of where the data is to be stored.

The standard functions that form Turbo C++'s dynamic memory allocation system include malloc() and calloc(). These functions are a part of the standard C language function library and are usually supported by every C or C++ compiler. To use them, you must include the header file named ALLOC.H at the beginning of your program, with a line like this one:

```
#include <alloc.h>
```

The malloc() function allocates a block of memory. The calloc() function does about the same thing but first clears each memory location to 0. You would use the calloc() function in place of malloc() if it is necessary to first initialize the memory space to zero before you use it.

Both functions take a single integer parameter that declares how much memory you would like to allocate. The function returns a pointer to the first byte of memory that was allocated. If not enough memory is currently available, the functions return NULL.

For example, to create an integer variable, you use the following statement:

```
p = (int *)malloc (sizeof (int)));  /* pointer to an int */
```

This is a complicated-looking function, so let's take a look at each separate part. First notice the sizeof(int) expression. This is the parameter passed to the malloc() function. The malloc() function will allocate this much space and return a pointer to the memory. The sizeof() function is used to return the amount of bytes required for an integer.

We then use the expression (int *) in front of the malloc() function. This is called a *type cast* and tells the computer that we want to interpret the return address of malloc() as a pointer to an integer. The malloc() function does not have any specific declaration that its return value is a certain data type. Thus, we must tell the compiler what data type we are using. Finally, we assign the address of the new integer to the pointer p.

Once you have used the malloc() statement as just described, you can use *p just like any other integer variable. For example, you can assign it a value, or return a value to it from another function, such as

```
*p = 1995;
scanf("%d", &p);
```

During the execution of your program, you can create as many variables as you may need using this method. Some other examples include

```
pd = (double *)malloc (sizeof (double));  /* pointer to a double */
pc = (char *)malloc (sizeof (char));      /* pointer to a char */
```

To access the variables you would use the following statement:

```
*pd = 3.14;
*pc = 'P';
```

to refer to the variables.

The **free()** function

The opposite of the malloc() and calloc() functions is the free() function. It returns previously allocated memory to the system. The free() function attempts to free a block of allocated memory, thereby making it available for other purposes. The general form of the function is

```
free(p);
```

where *p* is the pointer to a previously allocated block of memory. The compiler actually keeps an internal list of the actual location of where the memory was allocated. Therefore, it will free the location you refer to with the pointer you pass to the function.

It is important to call the free() function with a valid argument, because passing invalid arguments cause the computer to scramble the memory block list.

Listing 15.1 is an example of dynamic memory allocation.

Listing 15.1. Program to illustrate dynamic memory allocation.

```
/********************************************************
 MEMALLOC.C--Show dynamic memory allocation in a
             C program.
 Do It Yourself Turbo C++ by Paul J. Perry
 ********************************************************/

#include <stdio.h>
#include <alloc.h>

void main()
{
  int counter, number, temp;
  int *arr;

  printf("How many numbers do you want to store?");
  scanf("%d", &number);

  arr = (int *) malloc(number * sizeof(int)); /* allocate memory */
```

continues

Listing 15.1. continued

```
printf("Enter numbers\n");
for (counter=0; counter<number; counter++)
  {
  printf("  Enter number %d : ", counter+1);
  scanf("%d", &temp);
  arr[counter] = temp;
  }

printf("\nNumbers are: \n");
for (counter=0; counter<number; counter++)    /* display
*/                                              numbers
  printf("  Number %d is %d\n", counter+1, arr[counter]);
  free(arr);


}
```

The program asks the user how many numbers should be stored. The program then allocates the memory space and prompts the user for each number. Finally, it displays the numbers on the screen and frees the memory so it can be used for other purposes.

A sample interaction with the program looks like this:

```
How many numbers do you want to store?4
Enter numbers
  Enter number 1 : 44
  Enter number 2 : 33
  Enter number 3 : 22
  Enter number 4 : 11

Numbers are:
  Number 1 is 44
  Number 2 is 33
  Number 3 is 22
  Number 4 is 11
```

The following statement performs the memory allocation:

```
arr = (int *) malloc(number * sizeof(int));
```

The `malloc()` function is passed the number of bytes to create, and a type cast is used to set `arr` to point to the memory returned by the function.

A loop is created that prompts for each number. The number is first stored in the variable temp. The allocated memory can be accessed just like an array, and the element in the array is assigned the value that was stored in the temporary variable. The expression arr still points to the first element in the array. The swap between the temporary variable and the dynamic memory locations is made with the following statements:

```
scanf("%d", &temp);
arr[counter] = temp;
```

After the elements are displayed back on the screen, the free() function is used so the memory can be used for another purpose. In this program, it is not necessary to use free(), because once the program is terminated, memory is reallocated back to the system anyway. But it is always good practice to use the free() function to return memory to the system.

Another program is presented in Listing 15.2 that demonstrates the use of the calloc() memory allocation function.

Listing 15.2. Program to allocate memory with calloc().

```
/*********************************************************
 MEM2.C--Show dynamic memory allocation using calloc().
 Do It Yourself Turbo C++ by Paul J. Perry
 *********************************************************/

#include <stdio.h>
#include <alloc.h>

void main()
{
  int counter, number;
  int *arr;

  printf("How many numbers do you want to store?");
  scanf("%d", &number);

  arr = (int *) calloc(number, sizeof(int)); /* allocate memory */

  printf("\nNumbers are: \n");
```

continues

Listing 15.2. continued

```
for (counter=0; counter<number; counter++)    /* display numbers */
  printf("  Number %d is %d\n", counter+1, arr[counter]);

free(arr);


}
```

Listing 15.2 is similar to the previous program; however, MEM2.C only asks the user how many numbers you want to store, allocates the memory, and displays the numbers. When the program is run, notice that each number is 0, because calloc() initializes the memory location to 0 before returning the pointer.

The other difference is the call to the calloc() function. It looks like this:

```
arr = (int *) calloc(number, sizeof(int)); /* Allocate memory */
```

The calloc() function takes two arguments. Internally, the two numbers are multiplied together to return the number of bytes to allocate. The first argument is the number of elements of storage the user requests the program to store. The second argument is the size of an integer, as returned by the sizeof() function.

Pointers and Multidimensional Arrays

Because a one-dimensional array can be accessed with pointers, it is reasonable to expect that multidimensional arrays can also be represented with pointer notation. This is certainly true.

Two-Dimensional Array Declarations

For example, a two-dimensional array is actually a collection of one-dimensional arrays. Therefore we can define a two-dimensional array as a pointer to a group of one-dimensional arrays. The general form of a two-dimensional array can be written as follows:

```
datatype *pointername[expression1][expression2];
```

instead of

```
datatype arrayname[expression1][expression2];
```

Where *datatype* refers to the data type of the array, *pointername* is the name of the pointer variable, *arrayname* is the corresponding array name, and *expression1* and *expression2* are positive integer expressions that indicate the maximum number of array elements associated with the array.

For example, to declare a two-dimensional array with 5 rows and 10 columns, use one of the following equivalent statements:

```
int arr[5][10];
int (*arr)[10];
```

The first statement declares arr to be a two-dimensional array with 5 rows and 10 columns. The second statement declares arr to be a pointer to a group of one-dimensional, 10-element arrays. Therefore arr points to the first 10-element array, which is actually the first row (row 0) of the original two-dimensional array. Then, (arr+1) points to the second 10-element array, and so on.

Multidimensional Array Declarations

The general form of a multidimensional array declared through pointer notation is

```
datatype (*pointername)[expression1][expression2]...[expressionN];
```

An individual array element within a multidimensional array can be accessed by repeatedly using the indirection operator. Usually, however, this procedure is more awkward than the regular method of accessing array elements.

What You Have Learned

This chapter finished our discussion of pointers. The following topics were covered:

- Static data structures are ones you define when you write your program and remain available throughout the execution of your program.

- Dynamic data structures are variables that can be allocated as the program is executed. The size of a dynamic data structure can grow as required by your program. When the variable is not needed any longer, the memory it occupies can be released for use by other variables.

- The `malloc()` and `calloc()` functions are used to allocate memory and return a pointer to the memory location. The big difference between the two functions is that `calloc()` first clears the allocated memory to zeros before returning a pointer to the memory.

- The `free()` function returns memory previously allocated with the `malloc()` or `calloc()` functions back to the system.

- Memory that is dynamically allocated is accessed through the use of brackets, similar to the means of accessing an array.

- Multidimensional arrays can be accessed with pointers in the same way one-dimensional arrays can be accessed with pointers.

16

The Borland Graphics Interface

Goals

After reading this chapter, you will

- Know what the Borland Graphics Interface is and how to use it.

- Understand what a device driver is used for and which ones are available for use with Turbo C++ programs.

- Be able to initialize the graphics system.

- Know how to draw a single pixel on the screen.

- Be familiar with several ways to draw lines on the screen and how to modify the line styles.

- Know what the current position (CP) is and how to use it to draw lines.

● Understand how to select colors for graphical output.

● Know how to draw graphical shapes with the Borland Graphics Interface and how to select different fill patterns for the shapes.

● Be able to select different fonts for displaying text in graphics mode.

Graphic-based user interfaces are quickly becoming an important, if not expected, part of many PC-based applications. Turbo C++ includes an extensive library of functions designed specifically for working with the high-resolution graphics available on your computers. Appropriately enough, the library is named the *Borland Graphics Interface,* or simply *BGI.*

This chapter introduces the basic routines in the Borland Graphics Interface library. It shows how to use them and gives many sample programs to help you create sharp-looking graphics displays. There are more than 70 functions in the BGI library. You will experiment with and learn how to use the most important functions in this chapter.

The Graphics Screen

In regular text mode you are used to a screen that is composed of 25 rows by 80 columns of characters. However, if you look closely you will notice that each character is actually made up of a group of even smaller dots. Each individual dot is referred to as a *pixel* (short for picture element). The pixel is the smallest screen element that can be accessed.

In text mode, you are limited to referencing a character that is composed of 9 pixels across by 14 pixels high; you cannot access a single pixel at a time. When you switch the display to graphics mode with BGI routines, each pixel can be accessed individually. In effect, you can control each pixel directly from your program.

However, with this added control comes added complexity. No longer can you output a string of ASCII characters or use the printf() function to display text. Special functions are used to access the graphics mode. The Borland Graphics Interface is the set of functions and drivers that are necessary to access graphics mode in Turbo C++.

The Borland Graphics Interface

In order to use the Borland Graphics Interface you must include the following line at the beginning of your program:

```
#include <graphics.h>
```

This code declares and prototypes the graphics functions. You must also ensure that you turn on the graphics library by choosing the Options menu, selecting Linker, selecting Libraries, and checking the box labeled Graphics library, as shown in Figure 16.1. The designers of Turbo C++ figured that most of your programs would not use graphics mode, and, by making it an option to include the graphics library, the compiler runs faster in the majority of situations that don't require the graphics library.

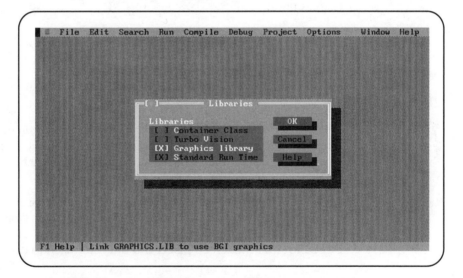

Figure 16.1. The Linker Libraries dialog box.

Furthermore, to use graphics mode, a BGI graphics driver file must be present when your program is executed. Later, you will see how you specify the location of the driver files. You will notice that Borland includes display drivers for a wide range of display adapters, as summarized in Table 16.1. They are found in the \TC\BGI directory of the drive on which you installed Turbo C++.

Table 16.1. Graphics adapter device driver filenames.

Display Adapter type	Driver Filename
Hercules Monochrome Adapter	HERC.BGI
Color Graphics Adapter	CGA.BGI
AT&T 400 Line Graphics	ATT.BGI
IBM PC 3270 Graphics Adapter	PC3270.BGI
IBM 8514 Graphics Adapter	IBM8514.BGI
EGA or VGA Adapter	EGAVGA.BGI

Through the licensing arrangement of Turbo C++, you may distribute these graphic device driver files with your program, free of royalty charges to Borland.

Graphics Resolution and Modes

The number of pixels that can be displayed on the screen determines the screen *resolution*. The greater the resolution (the more pixels on the screen), the sharper the image is. At the same time, the higher resolution you have, the fewer colors can be used at one time.

The reason behind this is that your computer needs memory in order to store the image that is being displayed on the screen. Graphics screens, because of their higher detail, require a large amount of memory. Memory is used to store the screen pixels and the color used to display them.

Initializing Graphics Mode

You start graphics mode with a call to the initgraph() function, which is declared as follows:

```
void initgraph(int *graphdriver, int *graphmode, char *pathtodriver);
```

The `initgraph()` function initializes the graphics system by loading a specific graphics driver from disk and putting the system into a unique graphics mode. You specify the graphics driver, mode, and path to the subdirectory that contains the graphics drivers.

When you call the function, you can tell it to autodetect the type of graphics adapter connected to the system, or you can specify a specific driver. If you tell it to autodetect the graphics adapter type, you must ensure that all the graphics files for all possible modes are available at runtime.

Table 16.2 lists the constants you can pass as the *graphdriver* parameter. Notice that certain adapters share graphics drivers. For example, both EGA and VGA share the EGAVGA.BGI device driver. However the graphics routines take care of loading the appropriate driver for the mode you specify. Usually, it is easiest to specify autodetect mode.

Table 16.2. Graphics driver constants.

Constant	Description	Value
DETECT	Autodetect	0
CGA	Color Graphics Adapter	1
MCGA	MultiColor Graphics Array	2
EGA	Enhanced Graphics Adapter	3
EGA64	EGA with 64K memory	4
EGAMONO	EGA in Monochrome mode	5
IBM8514	IBM 8514 Graphics Adapter	6
HERCMONO	Hercules Monochrome Adapter	7
ATT400	AT&T 400 Line Graphics	8
VGA	Video Graphics Array	9
PC3270	IBM PC 3270 Graphics Adapter	10

Because the `initgraph()` function requires pointers to variables, you cannot pass the constant directly. Instead you must specify the variables, set them to the appropriate values, and then call the function. Here is an example:

```
int graphdriver, mode;

graphdriver = DETECT;
initgraph(&graphdriver, &mode, "C:\\TC\\BGI");
```

This tells the graphics system to autodetect what type of adapter is connected to the system and look for the driver in the C:\TC\BGI subdirectory (remember that we use double backslashes because C uses the backslash character to interpret escape codes). The appropriate driver is automatically loaded by the graphics functions.

> The examples in this chapter assume that the graphics files reside in the C:\TC\BGI subdirectory. If you changed the location for your files, you need to modify the program listings. Furthermore, I will assume you are using an EGA or VGA adapter. They provide the best resolution with the most colors available and come standard on most computer systems today.

Once you have used the `initgraph()` function to initialize the graphics system, you are ready to begin drawing images on the screen using Turbo C++ functions. However, first we are going to learn how to handle error conditions.

Handling Graphics Errors

Before drawing anything on the screen, we should take a look at how Turbo C++ handles graphics errors. When a graphics error occurs, the compiler does not let the program end. Instead, a function fails to perform and an internal variable is set to a value that indicates the nature of the error.

The function used to return the internal error code is `graphresult()`. It does not take any parameters and returns a number that can be compared to a predefined constant. The function is usually used in conjunction with the `grapherrormsg()` function that takes a numeric value—usually returned from the `graphresult()` function—and displays a verbose message about why the graphics operation was not carried out.

An example of handling errors might be

```
int errorcode;
errorcode = graphresult();
if (errorcode = != grOk)
  {
  printf("BGI graphics error: %s\n", grapherrormsg(errorcode));
  exit(1);
  }
```

16

With this example, if an error occurs during initialization, a message is displayed about the cause of the error and the program is terminated.

Drawing on the Screen

The Turbo C++ graphics library includes a variety of functions for displaying graphics. This section examines what functions are used and how to use them.

Making a Point

The simplest graphics operation we can conduct is displaying a single pixel on the screen. The graphics library provides the putpixel() and getpixel() functions for that purpose. They are defined as follows:

```
void putpixel(int x, int y, int color);
unsigned getpixel(int x, int y);
```

The putpixel() function displays the single pixel located at (x,y) with the color specified by the *color* parameter. The getpixel() function returns the color of the pixel located at (x,y).

The upper left corner of the screen is referred to as (0,0). The x coordinate moves from left to right, and the y coordinate moves up and down. The largest number you can have is the lower right-hand corner, which is defined as (639,479) in VGA mode.

The *color* parameter is usually specified through the use of a pre-defined color constant, as listed in Table 16.3. These constants are similar to the ones used to display text in color.

Table 16.3. Predefined color constants.

Color	Constant	Value
Black	BLACK	0
Blue	BLUE	1
Green	GREEN	2
Cyan	CYAN	3
Red	RED	4
Magenta	MAGENTA	5
Brown	BROWN	6
Light Gray	LIGHTGRAY	7
Dark Gray	DARKGRAY	8
Light Blue	LIGHTBLUE	9
Light Green	LIGHTGREEN	10
Light Cyan	LIGHTCYAN	11
Light Red	LIGHTRED	12
Light Magenta	LIGHTMAGENTA	13
Yellow	YELLOW	14
White	WHITE	15

The putpixel() function is demonstrated in Listing 16.1, TWIST.C.

Listing 16.1. Program to show how pixels are set in graphics mode.

```
/*********************************************************
 TWIST.C--Demonstrate setting pixels in graphics mode.
 Do It Yourself Turbo C++ by Paul J. Perry
 *********************************************************/

#include <graphics.h>
#include <conio.h>
#include <math.h>
```

```
#include <stido.h>
#include <stdlib.h>

const int pi = 3.1415927;

void main()
{
  int graphdriver, graphmode, errorcode, i;
  double swing, width, crest, ypos;

  graphdriver = DETECT;
  initgraph( &graphdriver, &graphmode, "C:\\TC\\BGI" );
  errorcode = graphresult();
  if (errorcode != grOk)
    {
    printf(" Graphics System Error: %s\n", grapherrormsg
          (errorcode ) );
    exit( 1 );
    }

  ypos = getmaxy() / 2;
  crest = getmaxy() / 4;
  width = getmaxx();

  for (i=0; i<width; i++)
    {
    swing = crest*sin(10*pi*i/width);
    putpixel(i, ypos+swing, RED);
    putpixel(i, ypos-swing, BLUE);
    }

  getch();          /* wait for user keystroke  */
  closegraph();

}
```

Output of the program is shown in Figure 16.2. The program displays a typical mathematical sine wave. When the program executes, it first initializes the graphics system and checks for any errors that may have been detected (for example, the BGI files not being present at runtime). If an error occurred, a message is displayed and the program is terminated.

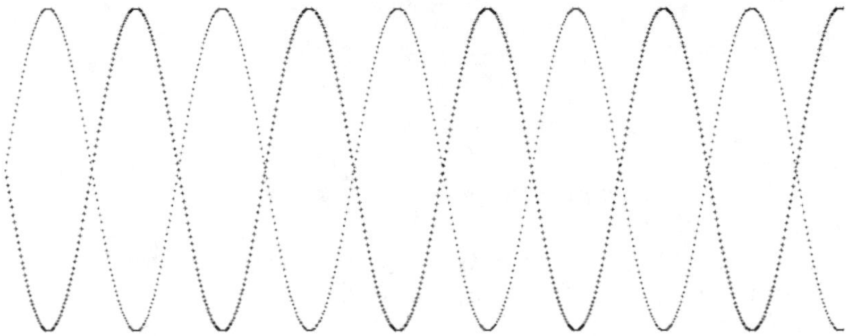

Figure 16.2. *Output of the TWIST.C program.*

Next, you will notice that several variables are set, as follows:

```
ypos = getmaxy() / 2;
crest = getmaxy() / 4;
width = getmaxx();
```

The `getmaxx()` and `getmaxy()` functions return the number of the pixel in the far right column and the bottom row of the screen. We check for these values rather than assume certain preset ones because the BGI routines are meant to be run on different display adapters, each of which has different resolutions. For example, a typical VGA adapter has a resolution of 640 × 480 pixels. In this case, the `getmaxx()` function returns 639, and `getmaxy()` returns 479.

Finally, the program uses the `putpixel()` function to display a group of pixels in the shape of a sine wave. As the sine wave is displayed across the screen, a second `putpixel()` call displays an inverse image of the first sine wave in a different color.

Drawing Lines

Drawing a straight line is the next most common task to displaying points when you use graphics. The `line()` function is used for this process and is declared as follows:

```
void line(int x1, int y1, int x2, int y2);
```

The `line()` function draws a line between two points. It starts at (*x1*, *y1*) and goes to (*x2*, *y2*). Listing 16.2 (LINES.C) shows how the line-drawing functions operate.

Listing 16.2. Program to show line drawing.

```c
/***********************************************************
 LINE.C--Display a 3D box using line-drawing functions.
 Do It Yourself Turbo C++ by Paul J. Perry
 ***********************************************************/

#include <graphics.h>
#include <conio.h>
#include <stio.h>
#include <stdlib.h>
void main()
{
  int graphdriver, mode, errorcode;

  graphdriver = DETECT;
  initgraph(&graphdriver, &mode, "C:\\TC\\BGI");
  errorcode = graphresult();
  if(errorcode != grOk)
    {
    printf("BGI graphics error : %s\n", grapherrormsg(errorcode));
    exit(1);
    }

  setcolor(BLUE);

  line(100, 100, 250, 100);  /* display first box */
  line(250, 100, 250, 250);
  line(250, 250, 100, 250);
  line(100, 250, 100, 100);

  line(150, 150, 300, 150);  /* display second box */
  line(300, 150, 300, 300);
  line(300, 300, 150, 300);
  line(150, 300, 150, 150);

  line(100, 100, 150, 150);  /* connect boxes */
  line(250, 250, 300,300);
  line(250, 100, 300, 150);
  line(100, 250, 150, 300);
```

continues

Listing 16.2. continued

```
getch();
closegraph();
}
```

When the program is executed, it creates the image of a three-dimensional cube, as shown in Figure 16.3. Notice the use of the setcolor() function. It sets the color to be used for subsequent output operations using graphics functions. The function takes a single argument, which can be one of the color constants listed in Table 16.3.

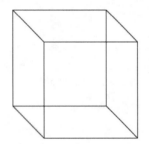

Figure 16.3. *Output produced by the LINES.C program.*

Notice that every time we draw a line we must specify its beginning and ending points. For example, to draw the first box, we use the following statements:

```
line(100, 100, 250, 100);
line(250, 100, 250, 250);
line(250, 250, 100, 250);
line(100, 250, 100, 100);
```

Notice that the second set of points (*x2* and *y2*) in the first statement is referred to as the first set of points in the next call to the line() function. Rather than repeating these points every time, there must be an easier way of drawing lines. There is: the CP value.

The Current Position

In text mode programs, we use the cursor to keep track of where input will occur next. In graphics mode, there is a similar type of pointer, the *current position (CP)*. The current position is a single pixel location that the graphics system keeps track of. Unlike the text cursor, the current position does not flash or give the user any type of visual reference about its location.

Once the line() function is executed, it sets the current position to the point it last drew, which is (*x2, y2*). So instead of specifying redundant points, the Borland Graphics Interface includes additional functions that use the current position. The lineto() function does just that, and is declared as follows:

```
void lineto(int x, int y);
```

it draws a straight line from the current position to the pixel at (*x,y*) and resets the current position to (*x,y*). Therefore, the earlier example can be rewritten as follows:

```
line(100, 100, 250, 100);
lineto(250, 250);
lineto(100, 250);
lineto(100, 100);
```

You can change the current position at any time with the moveto() function, which is declared like this:

```
void moveto(int x, int y);
```

The function has no visible impact on the screen; however, it changes the current position to (*x,y*). To return the coordinates of the current position, use the getx() and gety() functions. They return an integer value specifying the location of the CP.

Line Styles

So far, the lines we have drawn have all been solid lines. Having a choice of line styles and thickness is useful when you want to identify a certain feature in a drawing. To change the type of line that is drawn with the line-drawing functions, use the setlinestyle() function, which is declared like this:

```
void setlinestyle(int linestyle, unsigned upattern, int thickness);
```

The function enables you to modify both the width and style of lines that are drawn. The *linestyle* parameter is set to one of the constants listed in Table 16.4. The names of the constants imply what type of line is to be drawn. The *thickness* parameter can be one of two values, either

NORM_WIDTH or THICK_WIDTH. The *upattern* refers to a user defined pattern, and is set to 0 when you use one of the predefined pattern values.

To create a user-defined pattern, set the *linestyle* parameter to USERBIT_LINE and pass a bit image pattern with the *upattern* parameter. For example, you could create the pattern in binary and convert it to a decimal and then pass it to the function as the *upattern* parameter.

Table 16.4. Line-drawing styles.

Name	Description	Value
SOLID_LINE	Solid line	0
DOTTED_LINE	Dotted line	1
CENTER_LINE	Centered line	2
DASHED_LINE	Dashed line	3
USERBIT_LINE	User-defined line	4

Listing 16.3 shows the types of predefined line styles and widths that are available using a number of different colors.

Listing 16.3. Program to illustrate line styles.

```
/******************************************************
 STYLES.C--Show examples of available line styles.
 Do It Yourself Turbo C++ by Paul J. Perry
 ******************************************************/

#include <stdio.h>
#include <stdlib.h>
#include <graphics.h>
#include <conio.h>

void main()
{
  int graphdriver, mode, errorcode;

  graphdriver = DETECT;
  initgraph(&graphdriver, &mode, "C:\\TC\\BGI");
```

```
errorcode = graphresult();
if(errorcode != grOk)
  {
  printf("BGI graphics error : %s\n", grapherrormsg(errorcode));
  exit(1);
  }

setcolor(RED);
setlinestyle(SOLID_LINE, 0, NORM_WIDTH);
line(100, 50, 100, 150);

setcolor(GREEN);
setlinestyle(DOTTED_LINE, 0, NORM_WIDTH);
line(210, 50, 210, 150);

setcolor(BLUE);
setlinestyle(CENTER_LINE, 0, NORM_WIDTH);
line(320, 50, 320, 150);

setcolor(WHITE);
setlinestyle(DASHED_LINE, 0, NORM_WIDTH);
line(430, 50, 430, 150);

setcolor(LIGHTMAGENTA);
setlinestyle(SOLID_LINE, 0, THICK_WIDTH);
line(100, 200, 100, 300);

setcolor(CYAN);
setlinestyle(DOTTED_LINE, 0, THICK_WIDTH);
line(210, 200, 210, 300);

setcolor(LIGHTRED);
setlinestyle(CENTER_LINE, 0, THICK_WIDTH);
line(320, 200, 320, 300);

setcolor(BROWN);
setlinestyle(DASHED_LINE, 0, THICK_WIDTH);
line(430, 200, 430, 300);

getch();  /* wait for user */

}
```

The program goes through the predefined line styles and widths as shown in Figure 16.4. The process is rather self-explanatory: setting a color, setting a line style, and then displaying the line.

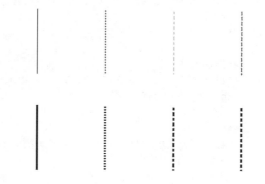

Figure 16.4. Output produced by STYLES.C program.

Drawing Shapes

A useful shape to start with in learning to draw geometric shapes is the square. A square is actually a rectangle with equal sides. The `rectangle()` function is used to draw a rectangle on the screen. It is declared as follows:

```
void rectangle(int left, int top, int right, int bottom);
```

and draws a rectangle (or square) when you specify the upper left-hand corner as (`left,top`) and the lower right-hand corner as (`right,bottom`). The following program listing 16.4 demonstrates the usage of this function.

Listing 16.4. Program to use rectangles.

```
/*************************************************************
 BOXES.C--Demonstrate drawing rectangles on the screen.
 Do It Yourself Turbo C++ by Paul J. Perry
 *************************************************************/

#include <graphics.h>
#include <stdio.h>
```

```
#include <stdlib.h>
#include <conio.h>

void main()
{
  int graphdriver, graphmode, errorcode, x;

  graphdriver = DETECT;
  initgraph( &graphdriver, &graphmode, "c:\\TC\\BGI" );
  errorcode = graphresult();
  if (errorcode != grOk)
    {
    printf(" Graphics System Error: %s\n", grapherrormsg
           (errorcode ) );
    exit( 1 );
    }

  for (x=1; x<(getmaxy()/2); x+=25)
    {
    setcolor(x);
    rectangle(x,x, getmaxx()-x, getmaxy()-x);
    }

  getch();          /* wait for user keystroke  */
  closegraph();

}
```

The program runs through a loop that displays a large rectangle and consecutively smaller rectangles in different colors. Figure 16.5 shows the output of the program.

Displaying Bars

The rectangle() function we just looked at draws a hollow figure. The BGI actually provides several other functions for displaying rectangular figures:

```
void bar(int left, int top, int right, int bottom);
void bar3d(int left, int top, int right, int bottom, int depth,
           int topflag);
```

The bar() function draws a bar using the current fill style (more on that in a moment). The bar3d() function draws a three-dimensional bar. The *depth* parameter specifies the perceived depth of the bar. The *topflag* parameter is a value that determines whether the bar has a top. A nonzero value is used to display a top; otherwise, the function passes 0 and no top is displayed. You usually use 0 if you want to stack another bar on top of the current one.

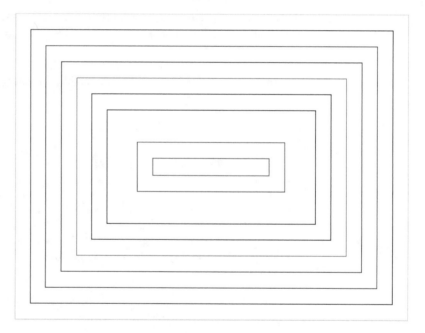

Figure 16.5. *Output produced by the BOXES.C program.*

When displaying a filled shape, you can choose one fill style and color from a large range available by using the setfillstyle() function. It is declared as follows:

```
void far setfillstyle(int pattern, int color);
```

The function takes two parameters. The *color* parameter we have already looked at and is one of those listed in Table 16.3. The *pattern* parameter is one of the constants listed in Table 16.5.

Table 16.5. Predefined fill style constants.

Constant Name	Value	Description
EMPTY_FILL	0	Background color
SOLID_FILL	1	Solid fill
LINE_FILL	2	Straight lines (—)
LTSLASH_FILL	3	Thin slashes (///)
SLASH_FILL	4	Thick slashes (///)
BKSLASH_FILL	5	Thick backslashes (\\\\)
LTBKSLASH_FILL	6	Thin backslashes (\\\\)
HATCH_FILL	7	Light hatch
XHATCH_FILL	8	Heavy crosshatch
INTERLEAVE_FILL	9	Interleaving lines
WIDE_DOT_FILL	10	Widely spaced dots
CLOSE_DOT_FILL	11	Closely spaced dots
USER_FILL	12	User-defined fill pattern

Listing 16.5 is a sample program that cycles through the 13 fill styles and shows you what each one looks like.

Listing 16.5. Program to view predefined styles.

```
/****************************************************
FILLPAT.C--Display different fill patterns.
Do It Yourself Turbo C++ by Paul J. Perry
****************************************************/

#include <graphics.h>
#include <stdlib.h>
#include <string.h>
#include <stdio.h>
#include <conio.h>
```

continues

Listing 16.5. continued

```
char *fname[] = { "EMPTY_FILL",     "SOLID_FILL",
             "LINE_FILL",           "LTSLASH_FILL",
             "SLASH_FILL",          "BKSLASH_FILL",
             "LTBKSLASH_FILL",      "HATCH_FILL",
             "XHATCH_FILL",         "INTERLEAVE_FILL",
             "WIDE_DOT_FILL",       "CLOSE_DOT_FILL",
             "USER_FILL"   };

void main()
{

  int graphdriver, graphmode, errorcode, style, midx, midy;
  char stylestr[40];

  graphdriver = DETECT;
  initgraph( &graphdriver, &graphmode, "c:\\TC\\BGI" );
  errorcode = graphresult();
  if (errorcode != grOk)
  {
    printf(" Graphics System Error: %s\n", grapherrormsg
           (errorcode ) );
    exit( 1 );
  }

  midx = getmaxx() / 2;
  midy = getmaxy() / 2;

  for (style = EMPTY_FILL; style < USER_FILL; style++)
  {
    setfillstyle(style, getmaxcolor());
    strcpy(stylestr, fname[style]);
    bar3d(0, 0, midx-10, midy, 0, 0);
    outtextxy(midx, midy, stylestr);

    cleardevice();
  }

  closegraph();

}
```

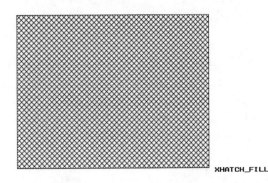

XHATCH_FILL

Figure 16.6. Output produced by the FILLPAT.C program.

The program displays a bar with a specific fill pattern and then waits for the user to press a key. FILLPAT.C then continues through each fill pattern. Figure 16.6 shows an example of how the output of the FILLPAT.C program looks.

Displaying Circles

To draw a circle you must know the center coordinates and radius of the circle. The function used to draw a circle is

```
void circle(int x, int y, int radius);
```

The `circle()` function draws a complete circle centered at (x,y) with a radius of `radius`. The inside of the circle is not drawn.

A circle is a perfectly round shape. Because of its flexibility, the BGI routines have another type of round shape: an ellipse. An ellipse is an oval shape whose width and height can be different. The `ellipse()` function is declared like this:

```
void ellipse(int x, int y, int stangle, int endangle, int xradius,
             int yradius);
```

The function draws an elliptical arc, centered at (x,y), from the starting angle, *stangle*, to the ending angle, *endangle*. The *xradius* and *yradius* parameters are the horizontal and vertical axes.

Just as with the `circle()` function, the `ellipse()` function draws on the outside of the figure. The center of the figure is not changed.

To draw a filled circle or ellipse use the `fillellipse()` function, as follows:

```
void fillellipse(int x, int y, int xradius, int yradius);
```

The function draws an ellipse centered at (`x`,`y`), and the `xradius` and `yradius` parameters are the horizontal and vertical axes. The figure is filled with the current fill style, which you can change with the `setfillstyle()` function (as demonstrated earlier).

Displaying Text

Normally, in our use of the text display mode, we employed the good old `printf()` function to display text. Unfortunately, in graphics mode you cannot use this function. The Borland Graphics Interface provides its own means of displaying text, with these functions:

```
void outtext(char *textstring);
void outtextxy(int x, int y, char *textstring);
```

The `outtext()` function displays a string on the screen, beginning at the current position. After `outtext()` is finished displaying the string, the current position is moved to the first position after the last character displayed. The `outtextxy()` function gives you more control over the placement of text by allowing you to specify a beginning coordinate as (`x`,`y`). It does not change the value of the current position.

Bit-mapped Versus Stroked Fonts

One of the benefits of working with the graphics functions is that when you output text, you can change the size, style, and font of the characters being displayed. The graphics system has a default font but also includes several other font files on disk that you can use in your programs.

The default graphics character set is called a *bit-mapped* font. This means that the shape of each character in the character set is stored in an 8×8 matrix, each matrix element referring to a pixel.

Other typefaces are available in the Borland Graphics Interface that use a different type of font. The other type of font is called a *stroked font,* because each character is defined by a set of instructions that tell how the character is to be drawn.

A stroked font usually looks clearer than a bitmap font, especially if you enlarge the size of the characters.

Controlling BGI Text Fonts

You select the font you want to use for displaying output with the settextstyle() function:

```
void settextstyle(int font, int direction, int charsize);
```

This function controls not only the text font but also the direction (horizontal or vertical) in which the text should be displayed and the size of the characters.

You select the font by specifying a predefined constant, as listed in Table 16.6. If you use any font other than the default font, you must make sure the related font file is available in the same directory as the one you specified when you called the initgraph() function.

The first constant name, DEFAULT_FONT, is the default font, which, as I mentioned is built in as an 8×8 bit-mapped font. All other fonts are stroked fonts. Each font is stored in a separate file with a .CHR extension.

The *direction* parameter enables you to choose between displaying text horizontally (left to right) or vertically (bottom to top). You can use one of two predefined constants, as follows:

```
HORIZ_DIR   0
VERT_DIR    1
```

The *charsize* parameter of settextstyle() is a value containing the multiplication factor in which the font should be enlarged. A value of 1 indicates normal size, 2 indicates twice normal size, and so on. Listing 16.6 (TEXT.C) shows how to display text in your graphics programs.

Table 16.6. BGI text fonts available.

Constant Name	Value	Description	Filename
DEFAULT_FONT	0	Bit-mapped font—built into BGI system	
TRIPLEX_FONT	1	Stroked triplex font	TRIP.CHR
SMALL_FONT	2	Stroked small font	LITT.CHR
SANS_SERIF_FONT	3	Stroked sans-serif font	SANS.CHR
GOTHIC_FONT	4	Stroked gothic font	GOTH.CHR
SCRIPT_FONT	5	Stroked script font	SCRI.CHR
SIMPLEX_FONT	6	Stroked simplex font	SIMP.CHR
TRIPLEX_SCR_FONT	7	Stroked triplex script font	TSCR.CHR
COMPLEX_FONT	8	Stroked complex font	LCOM.CHR
EUROPEAN_FONT	9	Stroked European font	EURO.CHR
BOLD_FONT	10	Stroked bold font	BOLD.CHR

Listing 16.6. Program to use fonts in your text.

```
/***************************************************
 TEXT.C--Display text with different fonts.
 Do It Yourself Turbo C++ by Paul J. Perry
 ***************************************************/

#include <graphics.h>
#include <stdlib.h>
#include <stdio.h>
#include <conio.h>

void main()
{
  int graphdriver, graphmode, errorcode, ;

  graphdriver = DETECT;
  initgraph( &graphdriver, &graphmode, "c:\\TC\\BGI" );
  errorcode = graphresult();
  if (errorcode != grOk)
```

```
    {
    printf(" Graphics System Error: %s\n", grapherrormsg
            (errorcode ) );
    exit( 1 );
    }

setcolor(BLUE);

outtextxy(1, 10,"The default font");

settextstyle(TRIPLEX_FONT, HORIZ_DIR, 1);
outtextxy(1, 20, "The triplex font");

settextstyle(GOTHIC_FONT, HORIZ_DIR, 1);
outtextxy(1, 40, "The gothic font");

settextstyle(COMPLEX_FONT, HORIZ_DIR, 1);
outtextxy(1, 60, "The Complex font");

settextstyle(SIMPLEX_FONT, HORIZ_DIR, 1);
outtextxy(1, 80, "The Simplex font");

settextstyle(SIMPLEX_FONT, HORIZ_DIR, 2);
outtextxy(1,100, "The Simplex font at twice the size");

getch();          /* wait for user keystroke  */
closegraph();

}
```

The program makes use of the settextstyle() function to modify the font being displayed and then outputs it using the outtextxy() function. Figure 16.7 shows the output produced by the program.

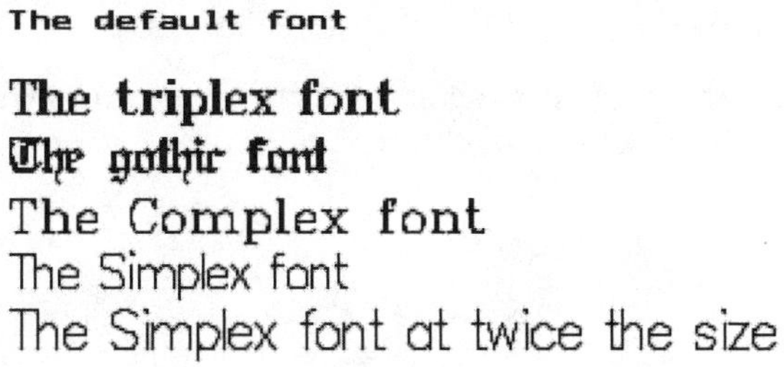

Figure 16.7. Output produced with the TEXT.C program.

What You Have Learned

The Borland Graphics Interface includes the functions and device drivers necessary for displaying high resolution graphics. This chapter looked at how to access the BGI and how to use some of the most important features of the graphics library. In particular, the following topics were covered:

- The high-resolution graphics mode enables you to access each pixel that is on the screen.

- In order to use the Borland Graphics Interface, you must #include the GRAPHICS.H header file in your program and turn the graphics library on.

- When a program relying on the BGI is executed, it requires the presence of certain device drivers, all of which have the file extension .BGI.

- When you initialize the graphics system with the initgraph() function, you specify the type of adapter, the output mode, and the location of the graphics device drivers.

- Individual points can be displayed with the use of the putpixel() function. You can determine the color of an existing point with the getpixel() function.

- The getmaxx() and getmaxy() functions are used to retrieve the coordinates for the maximum resolution of the screen.

- The current position (CP) is the last point that the graphics routines displayed. It can be thought of as the cursor that is used in text display mode. The current position shows where output will occur next.

- When displaying lines, you can choose the line style through the use of the setlinestyle() function. Four predefined line types and one user-defined style are available.

- When displaying text with the Borland Graphics Interface, you must specify the type of font you want to use for output.

17

Sequential File I/O

Goals

After reading this chapter, you will

- Understand what sequential file input and output is.
- Know how to redirect program output into a text file by using features of DOS.
- Be able to send output to a printer using the standard printer output streams.
- Know what the FILE pointer is and what it is used for.
- Understand how to open a file and which modes to use to open one.
- Know how to check for errors when files are opened.

● Be able to read and write characters into and out of a file using character I/O functions.

● Know how to use the string input and output functions to read and write a string of text to a file.

● Understand what formatted input and output is, and how to use the associated functions—fprintf() and fscanf()—during data file accesses.

Disk files are essential to personal computers. File access is used in all important applications (word processors, spreadsheets, and databases) as well as many other types of utilities. Files store programs, documents, data, and information of all kinds. As a programmer, you will need to write programs that create files, write data into files, and read data from files.

Sequential file access refers to the fact that a program must read the contents at the beginning of a file before it can read data at the end of the file. This type of access is often compared to that of listening to music from an audiocassette. That is, you must listen to the songs at the beginning of the tape (assuming there is no fast forward button) before you can listen to the songs at the end. This chapter discusses methods of sequential file access that the C programming language supplies.

In this chapter, you will learn how to process files using Turbo C++'s standard C input and output (I/O) functions. You will learn about I/O modes, character I/O, string I/O, and formatted I/O functions.

About File Input and Output

The simplest method of getting data into a file is through the use of the standard DOS redirection commands. This method is rather limited but simple to implement. By using the greater than sign (>) you can redirect the text which is usually displayed on the video screen into a file. For example, if you type

```
program > myfile
```

at the DOS prompt, your program executes and its output is placed in a file named MYFILE. Notice that this can only be done with programs that use standard output. If you try doing this trick with the Turbo C++ Integrated Development Environment (using: TC > textfile), it will not work, because

Turbo C++ uses direct writes to video memory to improve the screen update rate. A program that makes direct video writes has better performance but cannot be compiled for a different operating system. Most programs for the PC do make direct video writes, because of the almost instantaneous display of characters on the screen.

Using redirection is a rather crude method of creating an output file, because you have little control over what is placed into the file. Furthermore, you cannot display anything simultaneously, because what usually goes to the video display is being directed to the output file.

Accessing data files is another method of input and output within your program. We first looked at input and output back in Chapter 5. At that time we talked about several predefined streams that your program may have access to. They are repeated here in Table 17.1.

Table 17.1. Predefined streams.

Stream Name	Description	Device
stdin	Input stream	Keyboard
stdout	Output stream	Video display
stprn	Printer stream	Printer port
stdaux	Auxiliary output	Serial port
stderr	Error stream	Video display

The C input and output system provides a level of abstraction between the programmer and the device being input from or output to. The abstraction is called a *stream.* The actual device sending or receiving output can be anything from the video display, to a keyboard, printer, or file.

You access every stream in a consistent manner. You first open it, output to it (or input from it), and then close it. However, as shown in the table, the most commonly used streams are already set up to be used by you. Therefore, you don't need to open the standard streams first (opening a stream gets it ready for input and output).

Accessing disk files, however, take a little bit more work. You must first open the file for I/O. Once this is done, you can access the data in the file using several different methods. The file must then be closed before your program terminates.

Sending Output to a Printer

First, let's examine how easy it is to output data to a printer. After all, a printer is just another stream. Beyond that, it is already predefined, so it takes little effort to use the printer. Listing 17.1 is an example of a program that outputs a single line of text to your printer.

Listing 17.1. Program to send output to your printer.

```
/********************************************************
 PRINT.C--Output text to the standard printer device.
 Do It Yourself Turbo C++ by Paul J. Perry
 ********************************************************/

#include <stdio.h>

void main()
{
  char name[55];

  printf("Please enter your name: ");
  scanf("%s",&name);

  fprintf(stdprn, "Hey %s, this is a test!\n", name);
}
```

When you execute the program, it first asks you to enter your name. Then a line is printed on your printer. If you are using a laser printer, remember to press the formfeed button to push the page out of the printer's buffer.

The only new function in this simple program is fprintf(). It is very similar to the printf() function, except it takes a new parameter. It is defined as follows:

```
int fprintf (FILE *stream, const char *format [, argument, ...]);
```

The new parameter is a variable of type FILE. This data type keeps track of important internal information regarding the file. In the case of Listing 17.1, we can use the stdprn stream, because it is predefined by Turbo C++ to output to the printer.

The File Pointer

The FILE data type is commonly referred to as the *file pointer*. It is actually a pointer to the information that defines various things about the file—including its filename, status, and current offset position. The file pointer identifies a specific disk file and is used by the stream associated with it to direct the operation of the input and output functions.

The file pointer is a structure defined in the STDIO.H include file. For your information, the FILE structure is declared as follows:

```
typedef struct {
    short          level;
    unsigned       flags;
    char           fd;
    unsigned char  hold;
    short          bsize;
    unsigned char  *buffer, *curp;
    unsigned       istemp;
    short          token;
} FILE;
```

It is not important to know exactly what every element of the FILE structure is used for; however, knowing what the computer stores internally sometimes makes it easier for you to know what is happening with your program.

To obtain a file pointer variable in your own programs, declare one in a manner similar to this:

```
FILE *fptr;
```

You can now make use of the file I/O functions, which require a file pointer as one of its parameters.

Opening a File

Before we can read or write to a disk file, it must first be opened. Opening a file establishes an understanding between the program and DOS about which file is going to be accessed and how it is going to be accessed.

The fopen() function is used for this purpose. It takes two parameters and returns a variable of type FILE. It is declared as follows:

```
FILE *fopen(const char *filename, const char *mode);
```

where *filename* is a string of characters that make up a DOS filename. It may include a path specification. The *mode* parameter determines how the file will be opened. The mode parameter is a string (and therefore always surrounded by double quotes). Table 17.2 lists acceptable values for the *mode* parameter.

Table 17.2. Legal file mode indicators.

String	*Description*
r	Open file for reading only. File must already exist.
w	Create file for writing. If a file by that name already exists, it will be overwritten.
a	Append, open for writing at end of file, or create for writing if the file does not exist.
r+	Open an existing file for update (both reading and writing). The file must already exist.
w+	Create a new file for update (reading and writing). If a file by that name already exists, it will be overwritten.
a+	Open for append, open for update at the end of the file, or create if the file does not exist.

As mentioned earlier, the fopen() function returns a file pointer. If an error occurs when you try to open the file, the fopen() function returns a NULL pointer.

Your program should not alter the values within the FILE structure directly. If you want to open a file to obtain information from it, you would use statements similar to this:

```
FILE *fptr;

fptr = fopen("C:\\TEST.DAT", "w");
```

However, you will probably want to test the return value to make sure the file was opened correctly. To do this, you would use the following code segment:

```
FILE *fptr;

if ((fptr = fopen("C:\\TEST.DAT", "r")) == NULL)
  {
  printf("Error: Cannot open input file\n");
  exit(0);
  }
```

By using this method, you detect any errors that may occur when you open the file.

Using Character File I/O

Once you have opened a file, you are ready to write data to it or read data from it. Probably the simplest way this can be done is with the fgetc() and putc() functions. They work very much like the functions getchar() and putchar(). The difference is that you must tell them which file to use. You specify the file by passing the file pointer that we received from the fopen() function.

Reading Characters

Listing 17.2, TYPER.C, is a program that mimics the DOS TYPE command. The program's function is to prompt you for a file (it is a little bit more user friendly than TYPE) and then display the contents of the file on the screen.

If the amount of characters in the file is longer than what will display in a single screen full of information, the text is scrolled off the top of the screen so that you can view the entire file. The program works best when you view an ASCII file.

Listing 17.2. Utility to display file contents.

```c
/***************************************************************
   TYPER.C--Send file character-by-character to the display.
   Do It Yourself Turbo C++ by Paul J. Perry
 ***************************************************************/

#include <stdio.h>
include <stdlib.h>
#include <conio.h>

void main()
{
  char ch, filename[85];
  FILE *fileptr;

  printf("\nEnter filename: ");
  gets(filename);

  if ((fileptr = fopen(filename, "r")) == NULL)
     {
     printf("Error: Cannot open input file\n");
     exit(0);
     }

  printf("\n\n***Listing of: %s***\n", filename);
  while (!feof(fileptr))
     {
     ch = fgetc(fileptr);      /* get next character from file */
     putchar(ch);              /* display character */
     }

  fclose(fileptr);

}
```

The logic behind the program is rather simple. It starts out by getting the filename from the user that you wish to display. It then tries to open the file. If there is an error, the user is notified, and the program aborts.

Otherwise, the program enters a `while` loop. It gets the next character from the file with the `fgetc()` function, and displays that character on the screen with the `putchar()` function.

You will notice a few new twists in this program. First, the `while` loop depends on a function called `feof()`, as follows:

```
while (!feof(fileptr))
  {
  ch = fgetc(fileptr);      /* get next character from file */
  putchar(ch);              /* display character */
  }
```

The `feof()` function checks for the end-of-file (EOF) marker. The end-of-file marker is a special character that DOS places at the end of each file that tells DOS that the file is at its end. Therefore, in this program we can continue reading characters until the end-of-file marker is read in from disk. When the `feof()` function is true, we exit out of the `while` loop and close the file.

The last function call in the program is `fclose()`. The `fclose()` function closes the file identified by the file pointer passed to it. The function returns a value identifying whether it was able to close the file. In this simple program we did not check for it. In most cases there is not going to be a problem closing a file.

Writing Characters

The `putc()` function writes a single character to the file. This function is the complement to the `fgetc()` function. Listing 17.3 is a sample program that writes to a file.

Listing 17.3. Program to write characters to a file.

```
/********************************************************
 WRITER.C--Send typed characters to a text file.
 Do It Yourself Turbo C++ by Paul J. Perry
 ********************************************************/
```

continues

Listing 17.3. continued

```c
#include <stdio.h>
#include <stdlib.h>
#include <conio.h>

void main()
{
  char ch, filename[85];
  FILE *fileptr;

  printf("\nEnter filename: ");
  gets(filename);

if ((fileptr = fopen(filename, "w")) == NULL)
   {
   printf("Error: Cannot open input file\n");
   exit(0);
   }

  while ( (ch=getche()) != '\r')
    {
    putc(ch, fileptr);                  /* display character */
    }

  fclose(fileptr);

}
```

This program sits in a loop and records every character you type into the file until you press the Enter key. At this point, the file is closed and the program ends. What is important in this program is the use of the `fclose()` function that writes any data in the file I/O buffers to disk.

You might like to experiment with the previous two programs by using WRITER to create an ASCII text file, then using TYPER to display the contents of the file.

You will notice that your disk is not accessed each time you type a
character. What happens is that the keystrokes you type are stored
into a buffer. The buffer is not written to disk until it fills up or until
you use the fclose() function to close the file. If you don't call the
fclose() function when you are writing data to a file, you may lose
some of the data.

Using String I/O Functions

It may seem like an awful hassle to read in one character at a time from a
file. Luckily, the C library has functions that will read in or write out an
entire line of text at a time. Reading and writing strings of characters from
and to files is just about as easy as reading and writing individual characters.

The fputs() function writes a string of characters, and the fgets()
function reads a string of characters.

Reading Strings

Listing 17.4 is a program whose purpose is similar to the earlier TYPER
program. However, it reads in lines of text from a file (rather than single
characters) and displays the lines. It also keeps track of how many lines it
has read in and tells the user how many lines of text are in the file.

Listing 17.4. Reads in file text as a string.

```
/****************************************************************
 STRREAD.C--Read lines in from a file as strings and
             return a count of how many lines are in a file.
 Do It Yourself Turbo C++ by Paul J. Perry
 ****************************************************************/

#include <stdio.h>
#include <stdlib.h>
#include <conio.h>
```

continues

Listing 17.4. continued

```c
#define MAXLINELEN 125

void main()
{
  char filename[85], strline[MAXLINELEN];
  int line = 0;
  FILE *fileptr;

  printf("\nEnter filename: ");
  gets(filename);

  if ((fileptr = fopen(filename, "r")) == NULL)
     {
     printf("Error: Cannot open input file\n");
     exit(0);
     }

  while (!feof(fileptr))
     {
     fgets(strline, MAXLINELEN, fileptr);
     printf("%s",strline);
     line++;
     }
  fclose(fileptr);
  printf("\n***There were %d lines in that file\n", line);
}
```

The new function in this program is fgets(). It is used in the following context:

```c
fgets(strline, MAXLINELEN, fileptr);
```

The fgets() function takes three parameters. The first is the character array where the string is to be stored. The second is the maximum length of characters to read into the string; this parameter prevents the fgets() function from reading in too long of a string and accessing beyond the bounds of the array. The third parameter is the file pointer, which tells the function which file to access.

This program used a maximum input length of 125 characters. However, you can use any string length that you may need in your own programs.

Writing Strings

Just as easily as we were able to write characters, we can write an entire string at once. Listing 17.5 shows a program that prompts for a string and then writes it out to a file.

Listing 17.5. Program to store typed characters in a file.

```
/***********************************************************
STRWRITE.C--Write strings typed at keyboard to a file.
Do It Yourself Turbo C++ by Paul J. Perry
***********************************************************/

#include <stdio.h>
#include <stdlib.h>
#include <conio.h>
#include <string.h>

#define MAXLINELEN 125
void main()
{
  char filename[85], strline[MAXLINELEN];
  FILE *fileptr;

  printf("\nEnter filename to write to: ");
  gets(filename);

  if ((fileptr = fopen(filename, "w")) == NULL)
     {
     printf("Error: Cannot open input file\n");
     exit(0);
     }

  while (strlen(gets(strline)) > 0 )
```

continues

Listing 17.5. continued

```
    {
    fputs(strline, fileptr);
    fputs("\n", fileptr);      /* output a carriage return */
    }

  fclose(fileptr);

}
```

The user is first prompted for a filename to write the text out to. The user than types a series of lines. Each line is terminated by pressing the Enter key. To exit the program, the user presses Enter as the first character in the line. The file is then written to disk.

The main loop of the program checks the length of the string using the strlen() function. If the length of the string is zero (which means Enter was pressed as the first key on a line) the loop aborts. Otherwise, the fputs() function outputs the string to the open file.

The fputs() function does not automatically output a carriage return, so we use a second fputs("\n") line to output a carriage return into the file.

Formatted Input/Output

So far, we have looked solely at getting or writing ASCII text. First, we looked at character I/O and then string I/O. The designers of C were smart enough to know that there are other types of data out there that you might want to write to or read from a file.

That obvious choice of data is numerical data. What the designers of C put into the language is called *formatted file input and output,* and it enables us to deal with numerical (and string) data very nicely. With formatted input and output we treat a file as if we were prompting for or writing output, similar to using printf() and scanf().

In fact, the functions work almost exactly like printf() and scanf() except they operate with disk files, and take a FILE pointer as their first parameter. By now you probably can guess what the names of the files are (most of the functions that operate on files are prefixed with the character f). These two functions are declared as follows:

```
int fprintf (FILE *stream, const char *format [, argument, ...]);
```

and

```
int fscanf (FILE *stream, const char *format [, address, ...]);
```

Basically, you specify a file pointer and the C functions do all the work. The functions use the same format specifiers as you have already learned about.

The `fprintf()` Function

Listing 17.6 is an example of formatted I/O using the fprintf() function. It creates a data file that contains two pieces of information for each record: a person's name and age.

Listing 17.6. Program to create data file for names and ages.

```
/************************************************************
 FORMAT.C--Use formatted file I/O to create data file.
 Do It Yourself Turbo C++ by Paul J. Perry
 ************************************************************/

#include <stdio.h>
#include <stdlib.h>
#include <conio.h>
#include <string.h>

void main()
{
  char name[25];
  int age;
  FILE *fileptr;

  clrscr();
  if ((fileptr = fopen("NAMES.DAT", "w")) == NULL)
    {
```

continues

Listing 17.6. continued

```
    printf("Error: Cannot open input file\n");
    exit(0);
    }

  do
    {
    printf("Enter Name: \n");
    scanf("%s", name);
    printf("Enter Age: \n");
    scanf("%i", &age);
    fprintf(fileptr, "%s %d\n", name, age);
    }
  while ( (strlen(name) < 1) ¦¦ (age != 0) );

  fclose(fileptr);

}
```

The program creates a data file that would be similar to one used in a database. The program enters a loop in which you can enter as many names and ages as you want. To exit the loop, enter the number zero for the age.

The core of the program is the fprintf() function. It takes one more parameter than the printf() function which we are very used to using (now that we have seen it since chapter 1). The extra parameter is the file pointer that refers to the file we want to write to.

The **fscanf()** Function

Once we have written formatted data out to a file, we need to read the data in from that file. The fscanf() function does just that. It reads the specified data from a file into your program. Listing 17.7 demonstrates how this can be done. Listing 17.8 is an example of a data file you might use with the program.

Listing 17.7. Program to use formatted I/O to display data.

```c
/****************************************************************
 FORMAT2.C--Use formatted file I/O to display file contents.
 Do It Yourself Turbo C++ by Paul J. Perry
 ****************************************************************/

#include <stdio.h>
#include <stdlib.h>
#include <conio.h>

void main()
{
  char buffer[25];
  int number;
  FILE *fileptr;

  clrscr();
  if ((fileptr = fopen("NAMES.DAT", "r")) == NULL)
     {
     printf("Error: Cannot open input file\n");
     exit(0);
     }

  while (!feof(fileptr))
    {
    fscanf(fileptr, "%s", buffer);
    printf("Name = %s, ", buffer);

    fscanf(fileptr, "%d", &number);
    printf("Age = %d\n", number);
    }

  fclose(fileptr);

}
```

Listing 17.8. NAMES.DAT Data File.

```
Harry 23
Bob 34
Jim 58
Fred 192
Tracy 99
Art 23
Bambi 6
```

The program loops until the end-of-file marker is detected, getting the name and age for each person in the data file. The fscanf() function reads in the data. It too takes an extra parameter that identifies the file pointer.

> It is important to realize that the formatted I/O functions create data files that are regular ASCII files. The data is not stored in any cryptic notation. This makes it easier to re-create the files, if they become damaged, and you need to make them "by hand." You can use a regular text editor to enter the data.

The next chapter will cover more methods of accessing data files from your C programs.

What You Have Learned

Disk file input and output is an important part of any program. This chapter showed how to access files in a variety of ways. The following topics were covered:

- To send the output of your program to a file with minimal hassle, use the DOS redirection command (>). It sends all of your program's output to an ASCII file.

- Before you can access a file, you must use the fopen() function to gain access to the specific file. In the call to the function you specify the filename and mode that you want to use to access the file.

● The `fclose()` function is used to close a disk file after it has been opened.

● Every file has an end-of-file (EOF) marker attached at the end of it. Your program can use this marker to tell when it has reached the end of the file. The `feof()` function returns a value telling you whether the EOF marker has been reached.

● The file pointer stores essential information about the location and offset of a data file.

● Character file I/O enables you to read or write a single character of information from a disk file at a time.

● The string I/O functions enable you to read or write an entire line of text from your disk files at once.

● The formatted I/O functions enable you to create data files that create both alphabetic characters and numeric text.

18

Random Access File I/O

Goals

After reading this chapter, you will

- Understand what is meant by random-access file input and output and what its benefits are.

- Know which functions are used for random-access file I/O.

- Be able to read data structures from disk and to write data structures to disk.

- Know how to use the same functions as were used for structured I/O to write an array to disk and read an array from disk.

- Understand how to access specific structure records through the use of random-access file I/O.

● Have an example of a large program that demonstrates most of the concepts in this chapter as well as the previous chapters.

Random-access file input and output is another method of accessing disk files. The last chapter examined sequential file input and output. If you recall, sequential file input and output requires that you first read in the beginning of a file before you can access any data at the end of the file. This chapter takes a look at a method of file input/output that most people believe is more flexible than sequential file I/O.

In this chapter you will learn how to use the file I/O routines that deal with random access. You will learn how to read and write arrays and structures. A program listing at the end of the chapter creates the foundation of a simple database program.

About Random-Access I/O

Random-access file I/O grants us access to any part of a file, without having to first read in earlier parts of it. You can actually treat the file like an array and move directly to any particular byte in a file.

If sequential file input and output is similar to finding songs on an audiocassette, you could say that random-access file I/O is similar to finding songs on a compact disc. That is, you can easily skip to any song on the compact disc. You don't need to listen to the first song before you can listen to the second song. Similarly, with random-access file I/O you go directly to any point in the file and start reading data in (or writing data out).

When working with random-access file I/O, a program uses the same `fopen()` and `fclose()` functions as you learned for sequential I/O file opening and closing. You can use the sequential file I/O functions to get data, once you have told the system where in the file to go.

Although random-access file I/O is similar to sequential I/O, there are differences as well. One of the biggest discrepancies is that when files are opened for random-access I/O, they are usually opened in binary format. The difference with this is that the data file that is created is not a plain old ASCII text file and cannot be easily re-created with a text file editor. If you examined any of the data files created by programs in Chapter 17 such as Listing 17.3, you noticed that they were all ASCII text files. Remember, how we were able to include the data file from Listing 17.8?

Storing data in binary format is quicker for the computer. It also makes it easier for the C routines to read and write the data. Another advantage of storing data in binary format is that the file requires less disk space.

Suppose we need to store the number 20 to disk. If we store the number using text format (as we did in Chapter 17), that number will require 2 bytes (1 byte for the 2 and another byte for the 0). However, if we store that number in binary format, it only requires 1 byte. This is a storage reduction of 50 percent! In large applications this can be significant.

To see how random-access file I/O works, enter Listing 18.1 and run it. It prompts you for an ASCII text file. It then displays a file backward, in reverse order.

Listing 18.1. Program to display a file backward.

```
/************************************************************
BACKWRDS.C—Display a text file in reverse, starting
            from the end and going to the beginning.
Do It Yourself Turbo C++ by Paul J. Perry
************************************************************/

#include <stdio.h>
#include <stdlib.h>
#include <conio.h>

void main()
{
  char ch, filename[85];
  FILE *fileptr;
  long lastpos;

  printf("\nEnter filename: ");
  gets(filename);

  if ((fileptr = fopen(filename, "r")) == NULL)
     {
     printf("Error: Cannot open input file\n");
```

continues

18

Listing 18.1. continued

```
    exit(0);
    }

fseek(fileptr, 0, SEEK_END);
lastpos = ftell(fileptr);

while ( !feof(fileptr) )
    {
    fseek(fileptr, --lastpos, SEEK_SET);
    ch = fgetc(fileptr);
    putchar(ch);
    }

fclose(fileptr);

}
```

A sample interaction with the program looks like this:

```
Enter filename: c:\temp\quotes.dat

?eerga uoy t'noD
egaugnal etirovaf ym si C_
```

Most of the program statements will look familiar to you. However there are two new functions we need to examine: fseek() and ftell().

The fseek() function lets us move to any location within a file. The function takes three parameters and is declared as follows:

```
int fseek(FILE *stream, long offset, int whence);
```

The first of the three arguments is a FILE pointer to the file being accessed. The file pointer is returned from a call to the fopen() function.

The second argument, offset is of type long and is an offset to move to within the file. This parameter tells how far to move from the starting point. The offset can be positive, in which case we will move forward, or the offset can be negative, in which case we move backward. If the offset is 0, we don't move the file location at all.

The third argument is called whence, and it identifies the starting point from which the offset is calculated from. The STDIO.H header file specifies the following constants which can be used for the whence parameter:

Constant Name	Value	Measure Offset from
SEEK_SET	0	Beginning of file
SEEK_CUR	1	Current position
SEEK_END	2	End of file

The fseek() function returns 0 if successful; otherwise, it returns a nonzero value if there was an error in moving to a specific location.

The ftell() function returns a long data type that is the current file position. It actually returns the number of bytes from the beginning of the file. The first byte is numbered byte 0.

In Listing 18.1, we first use the fseek() function to move to the end of the file (notice we use the SEEK_END constant). We then use the ftell() function to return the current file location. That location is stored in the variable lastpos.

From that point, we set up a while loop, which follows:

```
while ( !feof(fileptr) )
  {
  fseek(fileptr, --lastpos, SEEK_SET);
  ch = fgetc(fileptr);
  putchar(ch);
  }
```

This loop moves backward from the last byte in the file by decrementing the lastpos variable. It then reads in the character at the specified location using the fgetc() function and displays that location on the screen with the putchar() function.

Interestingly enough, when we are reading in reverse mode like this, we can still use the feof() function to check for the beginning of the file. When all the characters in the file have been read, the program exits the loop, and the fclose() function is called to close the file.

At this point, you may be thinking that random-access file I/O sounds useful but may be unaware of its practical uses. After all, although it may be nice to read a file in backward, that is not a common feature of most word processors.

In order to understand how useful random-access file I/O is, take a moment to learn about a couple of other file-reading and -writing

functions. Next you'll see how to read and write entire data structures out to disk, all at one time.

Writing Structures

Remember that structures are groups of uncommon data types. Listing 18.2 uses a simple structure with two data elements. The program continues to ask the user to enter records. When the user is done entering data, the program stores the data in a disk file.

Listing 18.2. Program to write data structures to disk.

```
/****************************************************
 STRUCTW.C--Write data structures to disk.
 Do It Yourself Turbo C++ by Paul J. Perry
 ****************************************************/

#include <stdio.h>
#include <stdlib.h>
#include <conio.h>
#include <ctype.h>

struct inforec
   {
   char name[85];
   int age;
   };

void main()
{
   char ch, filename[85];
   FILE *fileptr;
   struct inforec person;

   printf("\nEnter filename: ");
   gets(filename);

if ((fileptr = fopen(filename, "w")) == NULL)
   {
```

```
    printf("Error: Cannot open input file\n");
    exit(0);
    }

do
  {
  printf("\nEnter Name: ");
  scanf("%s", person.name);

  printf("Enter Age: ");
  scanf("%d", &person.age);

  fwrite(&person, sizeof(person), 1, fileptr);  /* write data to
                                                        disk */

  printf("Care to add another name to database? ");
  ch = getche();
  }
while (toupper(ch) == 'Y');

  fclose(fileptr);
  printf("\n\nFile %s successfully saved to disk\n", filename);

}
```

Here is a sample interaction with the program:

```
Enter filename: c:\temp\club.dat

Enter Name: Bob
Enter Age: 33
Care to add another name to database? y
Enter Name: Tim
Enter Age: 17
Care to add another name to database? n

File c:\temp\club.dat successfully saved to disk
```

You can enter as many data records into the database as your system has memory for. (I think you would probably get bored of entering records before your computer runs out of memory!) The new function in this program is called fwrite().

The fwrite() function is declared as follows:

```
size_t fwrite(const void *ptr, size_t size, size_t n, FILE *stream);
```

The function takes four arguments. The first argument, *ptr* is a buffer location to store data in. The second argument specifies how many bytes to write. The third argument specifies how many records to write. Finally, the last parameter is a FILE pointer that (as you know) was returned from the fopen() function.

The function's purpose is to write out a block of data. In the previous program we told the fwrite() function to write out a block of memory the length of the structure. It was easy to use the sizeof() function and let the compiler do the byte counting. The function returns the number of records written (*not* the number of bytes). Usually, it returns 1. If it returns 0, the write operation was unsuccessful.

Now that we have created this file and stored it on disk, we need some way of reading it back in. That's what we'll do next.

Reading Structures

The counterpart to the fwrite() function is fread(). It reads in a specific number of bytes and stores them in a memory location. This is the declaration for the fread() function:

```
size_t fread(void *ptr, size_t size, size_t n, FILE *stream);
```

The parameters are similar to the fwrite() function. The first is the address of a buffer in which to store the data being read. The second tells how many bytes to read in for each record. The third parameter tells how many records to read in. The last parameter is a FILE pointer to our open file.

Listing 18.3 (STRUCTR.C) is a sample program that reads in a data file that was created in the previous program, STRUCTW.C.

Listing 18.3. Program to read in data structures.

```
/*******************************************************************
  STRUCTR.C--Read a file into a structure and display the contents.
  Do It Yourself Turbo C++ by Paul J. Perry
 *******************************************************************/

#include <stdio.h>
#include <stdlib.h>
#include <conio.h>

struct inforec
   {
   char name[85];
   int age;
   };

void main()
{
   char filename[85];
   FILE *fileptr;
   int recnumb = 1;
   struct inforec person;

   clrscr();
   printf("\nEnter filename: ");
   gets(filename);

   if ((fileptr = fopen(filename, "r")) == NULL)
      {
      printf("Error: Cannot open input file\n");
      exit(0);
      }


   while ( fread(&person, sizeof(person), 1, fileptr) == 1)
      {
      printf("Record # %d\n", recnumb++);
      printf("Name is %s\n", person.name);
      printf("Age is %d\n", person.age);
      printf("Press ENTER to view next record\n\n");
```

continues

Listing 18.3. continued

```
    getche();
    }
    fclose(fileptr);
    printf("***End of file reached***\n");
}
```

Here are a sample entry and the results from the program:

```
Enter filename: c:\temp\club.dat
Record # 1
Name is Bob
Age is 33
Press ENTER to view next record

Record # 2
Name is Tim
Age is 17
Press ENTER to view next record

***End of file reached***
```

Now that we can write data out using the fwrite() function and read it back in with the fread() function, we know exactly where on the disk the data is being saved. This is when our random-access file input and output functions really shine.

Accessing Specific Records

By using a combination of the functions we have been using for writing structures, and for random-access I/O we can see how useful this type of file access can be.

Take a look at the RANDACC.C program in Listing 18.4.

Listing 18.4. Program to access specific structure elements.

```
/*******************************************************
 RANDACC.C--Enable random access to structure items.
 Do It Yourself Turbo C++ by Paul J. Perry
 *******************************************************/

#include <stdio.h>
#include <stdlib.h>
#include <conio.h>

struct inforec
  {
  char name[85];
  int age;
  };

void main()
{
  char filename[85];
  FILE *fileptr;
  long position;
  int recnumb;
  struct inforec person;

  int result;

  clrscr();
  printf("\nEnter filename: ");
  gets(filename);

  if ((fileptr = fopen(filename, "r")) == NULL)
     {
     printf("Error: cannot open input file\n");
     exit(0);
     }

  printf("Enter Record # to access: ");
  scanf("%d", &recnumb);

  position = (recnumb-1) * sizeof(person);
```

continues

Listing 18.4. continued

```
result = fseek(fileptr, position, 0);
if (result != 0 )
   {
   printf("Cannot move to that position");
   exit(0);
   }

fread(&person, sizeof(person), 1, fileptr);
printf("Record # %d\n", recnumb);
printf("Name is %s\n", person.name);
printf("Age is %d\n", person.age);

fclose(fileptr);


}
```

Here is a sample interaction with the program:

```
Enter filename: c:\temp\club.dat
Enter Record # to access: 2
Record # 2
Name is Tim
Age is 17
```

The program asks for the data filename, then asks you which record you would like to access. When you specify a specific record number, the `fseek()` function is used to locate the offset within the file and load the specific record with the `fread()` function.

We calculate the offset within the file by using the following formula:

```
position = (recnumb-1) * sizeof(person);
```

This takes the record number that the user specifies (recnumb) and subtracts one and multiplies it by the length of the data structure. We subtract one because if we are accessing the first record in the data file, we want to return an answer of 0, which happens if we multiply by zero.

We then move to the appropriate location within the file using the following statements:

```
result = fseek(fileptr, position, 0);
```

We test the result to make sure that no errors occurred. Finally, we get the actual data from the file with the following line:

```
fread(&person, sizeof(person), 1, fileptr);
```

This line reads in the one record defined by the length returned from the `sizeof()` function into the structure `person`.

Once it is read in, we display the values on the screen and close the file. The process is rather simple once you understand what is happening.

Reading and Writing Arrays

In the same way that we were able to use the `fread()` or `fwrite()` functions to read in or write a data structure, we can do the same for any data type, including arrays.

Listing 18.5 demonstrates how to load and save arrays. Rather than splitting functionality up between two programs, this single program both writes a data file and then reads it back in.

Listing 18.5. Program to both write and read an array.

```
/*****************************************************
 RWARRAY.C--Show how to write an array to disk and
            then read it back in again.
 Do It Yourself Turbo C++ by Paul J. Perry
 *****************************************************/

#include <stdio.h>
#include <stdlib.h>
#include <conio.h>

#define ITEMS 7

void main()
{
  char filename[85];
  int count;
```

continues

Listing 18.5. continued

```
FILE *fileptr;
int data[ITEMS] = {8, 57, 5, 309, 33, 87, 55 };
int data2[ITEMS];

printf("\nEnter filename: ");
gets(filename);

/* Write array into a file. */
if ((fileptr = fopen(filename, "w")) == NULL)
    {
    printf("Error: Cannot open file\n");
    exit(0);
    }

printf("Writing data items to file %s...\n", filename);
fwrite(data, sizeof(data), 1, fileptr);
fclose(fileptr);           /* close the file */

/* Read file into an array. */
if ((fileptr = fopen(filename, "r")) == NULL)
    {   /* check return value just to make sure */
    printf("Error: Cannot open input file\n");
    exit(0);
    }
printf("Reading data items from file...\n");
fread(&data2, sizeof(data), 1, fileptr);
fclose(fileptr);

printf("The elements of the array are: \n");
for (count=0; count < ITEMS; count++)
    {
    printf("Element %d is %d\n", count, data2[count]);
    }

}
```

Sample interaction and output from the program looks like this:

```
Enter filename: c:\temp\numbers.dat
Writing data items to file c:\temp\numbers.dat...
```

```
Reading data items from file...
The elements of the array are:
Element 0 is 8
Element 1 is 57
Element 2 is 5
Element 3 is 309
Element 4 is 33
Element 5 is 87
Element 6 is 55
```

The program stores an array of seven elements into a user-specified disk file. It then reads them back into a separate file and displays the elements on the screen.

We could have written the data elements one at a time using formatted output (with the fprintf() function); however, writing the whole array out to disk with one statement is more efficient. Not only does it take less space, it is also faster to load and save the array.

The program does not really demonstrate any new functions. But you do learn how to write an array to disk using the functions we have been talking about in this chapter.

A Little Database Example

To integrate what we have been learning in this chapter, I decided to write a small database. It is one of the longer programs you have seen so far in this book and brings together many of the things you have been learning about the C programming language.

The database stores information in a disk file. To keep things simple, this database uses the same structure we have used all along, which includes two data elements: a name and an age.

When you first run the program, it asks for a filename to use for the database. You can specify a file that has already been created, in which case records can be added to the end of the file; or you can specify a new file, in which case the file will be created for you.

After the file has been opened, you are presented with a main menu that lets you choose one of five options, as follows:

(G)et Information
(A)dd Records
(D)isplay All Records
(C)hoose to Display Specific Record
(E)xit

The (G)et Information option displays the filename and number of records in the current database. The (A)dd Records option lets you enter as many new records as you have memory for. The (D)isplay All Records option allows you to list every record that is in the database. The (C)hoose to Display Specific Record menu item lets you enter a record number and display information for that specific record. Finally, the (E)xit option closes the current database and exits the program.

Listing 18.6 is the full source code for the program.

Listing 18.6. Little Database Program.

```
/****************************************************
 LDBASE.CA--Create a little database program.
 Do It Yourself Turbo C++ by Paul J. Perry
 ****************************************************/

/******************** Declarations ********************/
#define FALSE 0
#define TRUE 1

/******************** Include Files ********************/
#include <stdio.h>
#include <stdlib.h>
#include <conio.h>
#include <ctype.h>

/******************** Structure Definition **************/
struct inforec
  {
  char name[85];
  int age;
  };

/******************** Function Prototypes ***************/
void getinformation(void);
void addrecord(void);
```

```
void displayall(void);
void displayspecific(void);
void exitprogram(void);

/******************** Global Variables ******************/
char ch, filename[85];
FILE *fileptr;
long position;
int recnumb, numbread;
struct inforec person;

/******************** Program Entry Point ***************/
void main()
{
  clrscr();
  printf("\nEnter database filename: ");
  gets(filename);

  if ((fileptr = fopen(filename, "a+")) == NULL)
    {
    printf("Error: cannot access input file\n");
    printf("returning to DOS");
    exit(0);
    }

  while (TRUE)    /* endless loop */
    {
    clrscr();
    printf("\n**Little Database Main Menu**\n");
    printf("-----------------------------\n");
    printf("(G)et Information\n");
    printf("(A)dd Records\n");
    printf("(D)isplay All Records\n");
    printf("(C)hoose to Display Specific Record\n");
    printf("(E)xit\n");
    printf("\nChoose One: ");
    ch = getche();
    switch (toupper(ch))
      {
      case 'G' :
       getinformation();
```

continues

Listing 18.6. continued

```c
      break;

       case 'A' :
      addrecord();
      break;

       case 'D' :
      displayall();
      break;

       case 'C' :
      displayspecific();
      break;

       case 'E' :
       exitprogram();
       default :
      printf("\nInvalid selection, please try again\n");
      printf("Press any key to continue\n");
      getch();
       }
    }
}

/******************** Get Information Menu Item **********/
void getinformation()
{
  long bytes;
  int numbrecs;

  printf("\nCurrent filename is: %s\n", filename);

  fseek(fileptr, 0, SEEK_END);      /* go to end of file */
  bytes = ftell(fileptr);
  numbrecs = (int) bytes/ sizeof(person);
  printf("Number of records in database is: %d\n", numbrecs);

  printf("Press ENTER key to return to main menu\n");
  getch();

}
```

```
/******************** Add Record Menu Item **************/
void addrecord()
{
  do
    {
    printf("\nEnter Name: ");
    scanf("%s", person.name);

    printf("Enter Age: ");
    scanf("%d", &person.age);

    fwrite(&person, sizeof(person), 1, fileptr);  /* write data to
                                                      disk */

    printf("Care to add another name to database?");
    ch = getche();
    }
  while (toupper(ch) == 'Y');

}

/******************** Display All Records Menu Item *****/
void displayall()
{
  int record = 1;

  fseek(fileptr, 0, SEEK_SET);    /* go to beginning of file */
  while ( fread(&person, sizeof(person), 1, fileptr) == 1)
    {
    printf("\nRecord # %d\n", record++);
    printf("Name is %s\n", person.name);
    printf("Age is %d\n", person.age);
    printf("Press ENTER to view next record\n\n");
    getche();
    }
}

/******************** Display Specific Record ***********/
void displayspecific()
{
  fseek(fileptr, 0, SEEK_SET);    /* go to beginning of file */
```

continues

Listing 18.6. continued

```
printf("\nEnter Record # to access: ");
scanf("%d", &recnumb);

position = (recnumb-1) * sizeof(person); /* calculate specific
                                                position */

if (fseek(fileptr, position, 0)  != 0 )
  {
  printf("\nCannot move to that position\n");
  printf("Press ENTER to continue");
  getche();
  exit(0);
  }

fread(&person, sizeof(person), 1, fileptr);

printf("\nRecord # %d\n", recnumb);
printf("Name is %s\n", person.name);
printf("Age is %d\n", person.age);

printf("\nPress ENTER to continue\n");
getche();

}

/********************* Close Files and Exit Program *******/
void exitprogram()
{
  fclose(fileptr);
  printf("\nFile %s has been closed\n", filename);
  exit(0);
}
```

The program is divided into functions that carry out each main menu item. Each part of the program is commented to make it easier for you to understand.

Program execution starts at main(), where we prompt the user for the filename. Notice in this program that the file is opened with the "a+" option, in order to open the file for appending and therefore to enable us to add data to the end of the file. If a file already exists, we will add records to the end of it. If the file does not exist, it is created automatically.

The Main menu of the database is then displayed, and users respond to menu items through the use of a switch statement. Notice that we include a default condition. This is used in case the user enters an unexpected item from the Main menu.

The getinformation() function displays the filename of the current database. More useful, it displays the number of records in the database. This is done with the following statements:

```
fseek(fileptr, 0, SEEK_END);    /* go to end of file */
bytes = ftell(fileptr);
numbrecs = bytes / sizeof(person);
```

We first seek to the end of the file and return the total number of bytes in the file with the ftell() function. Finally, to find out how many records are in the database, we divide the number of bytes in the program by the number of bytes in a record. This gives us the number of records in the database.

The addrecord() function works similar to the STRUCTW.C program. Basically, we prompt the user for the name and age data elements. Next we write them out using the fwrite() function. We then ask users whether they want to add another element. If they do, we repeat the process. If they do not, we return to the main menu.

The displayall() function is similar to the STRUCTR.C program. It moves in a loop to load each record, display it on the screen, then repeat the process if the end of file has not been found. One difference with this function and the STRUCTR.C program is that we first seek to the beginning of the file. This ensures that we start at the beginning of the file just in case we have moved to a different location in the program.

The displayspecific() function works like the RANDACC.C program. It prompts the user for the record number to display. It then reads in that record and displays it on the screen.

Finally, the exitprogram() function closes the file, displays an exit message, and quits the program.

What You Have Learned

This chapter finished our discussion of disk file access. We looked at random-access file input and output. We learned the following specific things in this chapter:

● Random-access file input and output enables you to access any byte of information in a file without having to read in any of the previous file contents. The process is similar to that of locating songs on a compact disk. You can instantly go to any location on the disk.

● By storing information in binary format, file I/O becomes more efficient, because memory is conserved and the read and write operations are quicker.

● The two main functions that allow a program to use random-access file I/O are fseek() and ftell(). The fseek() function moves to any specific location within a file. The ftell() function returns the current location in the file.

● A specific number of bytes of data can be written to disk at once with the fwrite() function. It enables us to save an entire data structure or array with a single statement.

● Once we write out a number of bytes to disk with the fwrite() function, we can read that data back in with the fread() function, which reads in a specified number of bytes into a buffer.

19

Pitfalls and Debugging

Goals

After reading this chapter, you will

- Know what a software bug is and what a debugger is used for and what types of bugs it will reveal.

- Be able to use the Integrated Debugger and the Debug menu items, as well as the most commonly used debugger hot keys.

- Know how to single step through a program and recognize the difference between tracing into code and stepping over code.

- Understand what a breakpoint is and how to set one.

- Know what the three methods are for viewing variables during program execution and how to use each method.

- Understand what the call stack is and how to view it.

At this point you have learned about the majority of features of the C programming language. When you start creating programs of your own, you will find that errors in logic start creeping into your code. It is at this point that a debugger can help you enhance your programming projects.

Debugging a program is the process of removing bugs from your program. A *bug* is some part of your program that does not work properly (each part of your program that is not working correctly is thought of as a separate bug).

The term first came into existence in the bad old days of computers when a whole room was required to store a computer. In those days, mechanical relays were used as the computer's main switching devices (today we use integrated circuits). In one such installation, the first time the computer stopped working, the engineer examined the relays and found one in which a moth was smashed between the electrical contacts, or switches of the relay. Appropriately enough, these pioneers in computers called the problem a *bug*. Ever since, programmers have used the pet name to refer to programming errors.

This chapter discusses debugging using the Integrated Debugger that is part of the Turbo C++ Integrated Development Environment. You will learn how to single step through a program, how to set breakpoints, how to examine the contents of variables during execution of your program and you will gain experience with using the integrated Turbo C++ debugger.

About Debugging

Almost all programs contain errors of some type during their development process. In fact, bugs are almost always a part of computer programming. It is rare that a program runs on the first try. Programmers are constantly going back and correcting parts of their program to make them work correctly.

There are three types of errors:

- Compile-time errors
- Runtime errors
- Logical errors

Compiler errors are rather straightforward, because they result from an error in the syntax of your program. Compiler errors are displayed during program compilation and must be corrected before you can even run the program. A debugger is not used to correct compiler errors. They must be eliminated before you can use a debugger (a program must be compiled in order for you to debug it).

Runtime errors cause your program to terminate and produce an error message. This type of error results from incorrect error checking within your program. Sometimes runtime errors occur because a program expected a different type of value than the user entered (for example the user entered a string when an integer value was expected). Another typical runtime error is an uninitialized variable, in which a variable was supposed to be set to a specific value and was not.

A *logical error* is one in which your program is doing something different from what you (as the programmer) expected. The computer always does what it was told. You may have thought you told it one thing and then inadvertently told it something else. When using a debugger, you can find out what your program told the computer to do and find the differences from what you want it to do, then change the program accordingly.

With the integrated debugger you can run your programs a line at a time and view the value of variables as the program executes. By using the special features of the debugger you can examine memory locations and control program flow during execution.

19

Using the Integrated Debugger

Thus, a debugger is really just a tool. Much like using a shovel helps you dig a hole, a debugger helps you locate the problems that are occurring in your program. There are many different types of debuggers available on the market. Some debugger packages combine software and hardware together to really let you get at the core of your program. These debuggers usually require deep technical knowledge and are rather expensive.

Others provide the raw functionality a beginning programmer needs. The Turbo C++ Integrated Development Environment (IDE) has a built-in debugger that makes it easy to edit, compile, and debug your programs in one consistent environment.

Starting the IDE Debugger

To use the debugger, make sure that it is turned on. To do this, choose the Options menu and select the Debugger item. In the Debugger dialog box make sure the radio button for Source Debugging is set to On, as Figure 19.1 shows.

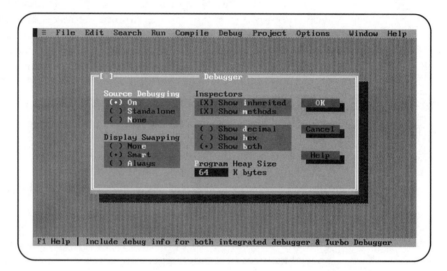

Figure 19.1. Debugger dialog box with Source Debugging on.

Setting the Source Debugging option to On instructs the compiler to include specific information in the executable file of the program that is used for debugging.

With this setting, you will notice that the resulting size of the executable program will increase. For this reason, when you have your program ready to send to a customer or for use with your own purposes, you will probably want to set the Source Debugging option to None and recompile the program.

Notice another radio button option for Source Debugging: Standalone. You set Source Debugging to this mode when you wish to use Turbo Debugger (a stand-alone debugger) to debug your programs. This is usually done when you need more memory for your program (Turbo Debugger requires less memory, because it does not include the editor or the compiler resulting in more memory for your program) or you require added features of Turbo Debugger that we won't go into here.

The Debug Menu

The Debug main menu option in the IDE is used to get to the features of the debugger. Let us briefly review the Debug menu options before we continue:

Inspect...	The Inspect... option opens a window that allows you to examine values of a data element in your program.
Evaluate/modify	The Evaluate/modify menu option enables you to display and possibly alter the contents of a variable.
Call stack...	The Call stack... option opens a box that shows the functions your program has called to reach the location that your program is currently at.
Watches	The Watches option leads to a submenu that lets you view the values of variables in your program.
Toggle breakpoint	The Toggle breakpoint option sets a location in your program in which execution of your program will automatically be halted.
Breakpoints...	The Breakpoints... option opens a dialog box where you can specify information about the breakpoints in your program.

Because many of the options are used frequently, there are hot-key combinations that emulate the menu options. Table 19.1 lists the commonly used debugger hot keys.

Table 19.1. Common debugger hot keys.

Key	Description
F1	Help
F4	Run program to current cursor position

continues

Table 19.1. continued

Key	Description
F7	Trace into program
F8	Step over and execute the next statement in the current function
Alt+F4	Open an inspector window
Ctrl+F2	Reset program.
Ctrl+F3	View call stack
Ctrl+F7	Add watch expression
Ctrl+F8	Toggle breakpoint

As we discuss certain features of the debugger, both their menu options and hot keys will be introduced.

Single Stepping

To learn how to control execution of your program, type in and execute Listing 19.1 (SSTEP.C). It enables us to experiment with some of the features of the debugger.

Listing 19.1. Program for learning about single stepping.

```
/************************************************************
 SSTEP.C--See how to single step a program.
 Do It Yourself Turbo C++ by Paul J. Perry
 ************************************************************/

#include <stdio.h>

void main()
{
```

```
    int i = 123;
    float f = 456.789;
    char ch = 'Q', str[] = "TESTING, TESTING, TESTING\0";

    printf("Welcome to single stepping\n\n");
    printf("the value of i is %d\n", i);
    printf("the value of f is %f\n", f);
    printf("the value of ch is %c\n", ch);
    printf("the value of str is %s\n", str);

}
```

As you have learned to do, you first press F9 (or open the Compile menu and select the Make option) to create the program. To execute programs, you have learned to use Ctrl+F9 (or the Run option from the Run menu). These actions start your program and execute it in its entirety.

At any time you can press Ctrl+Break to exit your program and return to the IDE. This gives you a method for breaking out of a long program loop.

The F4 key (or choosing the Run menu and selecting Go to cursor) proves helpful when you want to execute your program from its beginning until the current cursor location. Try it now by moving the cursor over the second printf() function in the program and pressing F4. You will notice the screen flash, and you will find the cursor positioned over the point in your program you left it along with a large highlighted bar that goes across the entire window (as shown in Figure 19.2).

This shows the currently executing point of the program. You can now press the F8 key (or select the Run menu and choose the Step over option) to single step through your program. At this point, your program is executed one line at a time for each press of the F8 key.

When you are tracking down problems in your programs, single stepping can be extremely useful. If you continue choosing the Step over option, your program eventually executes to the end and the highlight bar disappears. The highlight bar always signifies the current location in the program.

Suppose you are halfway through single stepping your program and you find you need to make a change to the program. You can go and modify the source code to the program. However, when you try to continue through the program you will receive a message saying that the source has been modified and asking whether the program should be rebuilt. Figure 19.3 shows this warning.

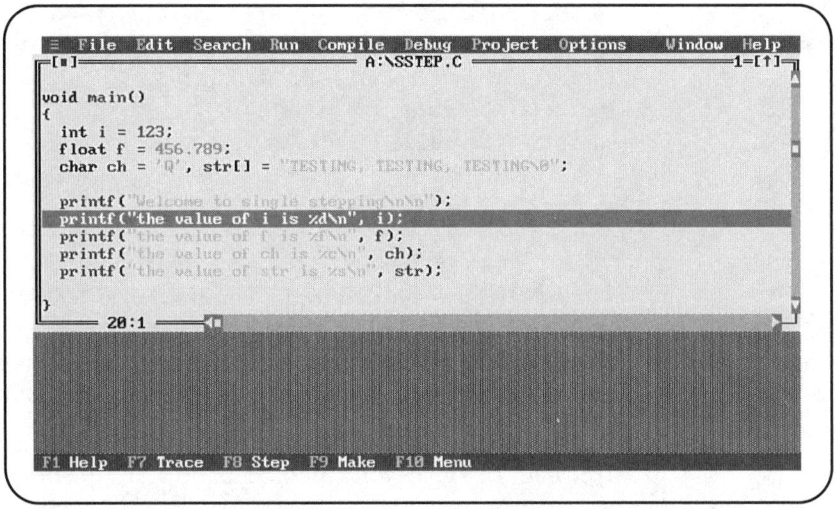

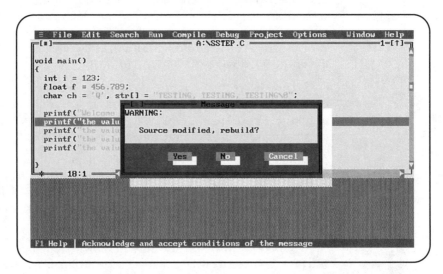

Figure 19.2. Single stepping through a program.

Figure 19.3. Integrated Development Environment warning about modified source code.

Most of the time you will want to respond positively to the question. You can select an option to reset the debugger, so your program will automatically be rebuilt. Pressing Ctrl+F2 or choose the Run menu and select Program reset. Choosing this option removes the highlight bar and restarts the program from the beginning.

Tracing Into

There are actually two methods of stepping through your program line by line. You already saw the Step over option. The other option is Trace into, which you select by pressing F7 or choosing the Run menu and selecting Trace into.

At first glance both options appear to do the same thing. They both execute a program a line at a time. The difference between the two is revealed when you start to move over a call to a user-defined function. The Trace into option will actually move to the statements within a function and let you step through each statement in the function.

The Step over command executes the entire function call as one line of the program and does not permit you to go through the function line by line. Take a look at Listing 19.2 for a sample program to use to try the Step over technique.

Listing 19.2. Program to demonstrate Step over and Trace into single stepping.

```
/*******************************************************
 STEPOVR.C--Run when you are single stepping.
 Do It Yourself Turbo C++ by Paul J. Perry
*******************************************************/

#include <stdio.h>

int double_number(int number);  /* function prototype */

void main()
{
  int i = 123;
```

continues

Listing 19.2. continued

```
printf("This program helps you experiment with /
stepping into and over a function\n\n");
printf("the value of i is first equal to %d\n", i);
i = double_number(i);
printf("the value of i is now %d\n", i);
i = double_number(i);
printf("Finally, the value of i is %d\n", i);
printf("Ending program\n");

}


/**********************************/
int double_number(int number)
{
  printf("\nNow executing inside of function\n");
  printf("About to return to main program\n\n");
  return (number*2);

}
```

Try using the Trace into and Step over debugger commands with Listing 19.2. Press F7 over the first call to the `double_number()` function. You will notice that the highlight bar moves to the beginning of the function, and you can view each line of the function being executed. Press F8 over the function the second time it is called. You will notice that the highlight bar does not move to the function; rather, it moves to the next line in the main program.

There are times when both commands have their place. Sometimes you will want to see every line of code that is being executed. Other times you do not need to see what is happening inside a function, only what it returns. As you gain experience in debugging, you will learn which command to use at what point.

Setting Breakpoints

A *breakpoint* is a line in your program that you set to automatically stop program execution during the debugging phase. When the debugger encounters a line that contains a breakpoint, the program unconditionally stops and displays the highlight bar.

To set a breakpoint, move the cursor to the point in your program that you would like to stop at and press Ctrl+F8 (or choose the Debug menu and select the Toggle breakpoint option). The entire line will be highlighted in red (the universal color for stopping—take a careful look at a stop sign the next time you speed past it) as shown in Figure 19.4.

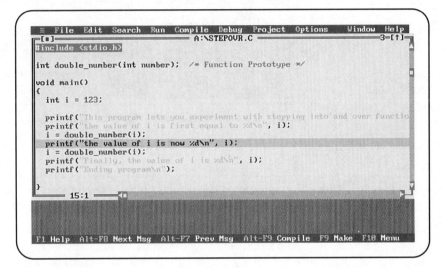

Figure 19.4. A set breakpoint.

Once a breakpoint is set, when you execute your program by pressing Ctrl+F9 (or choosing the Run option from the Run menu) execution of the program will be halted at the location of the breakpoint.

The Ctrl+F8 key works as a toggle. To turn the breakpoint off, move the cursor over a previously set breakpoint and press the same key combination. This time the red highlight disappears.

If you choose the Debug menu and select the Breakpoints option (there is no hot-key combination for this) the Breakpoints dialog box shown in Figure 19.5 displays.

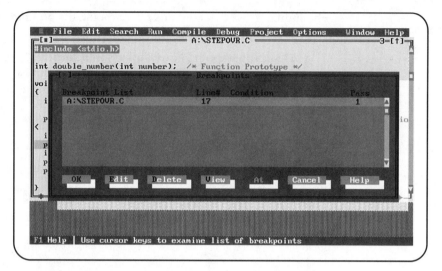

Figure 19.5. Breakpoints dialog box.

The dialog box contains a list of the current breakpoints along with the line number of the source file they are located in. The row along the bottom of the dialog box enables you to choose several options you can carry out.

The Edit button helps you modify how the breakpoint is carried out. Instead of having an unconditional breakpoint (in which case every time the breakpoint is encountered, program execution is halted) you can specify an expression that must be TRUE in order for the breakpoint to take effect. You can also specify a certain number of times that the breakpoint condition must be met before the breakpoint will take effect.

The Delete button removes the breakpoint. The View button returns you to the editor at the location of the current breakpoint. The other buttons are self-explanatory, providing a way to cancel the dialog box and to receive context sensitive help.

The Alt button enables a programmer to specify a breakpoint at a particular function during debugging. This is handy if you want to type a function name and not refer to a specific line number.

Viewing Data

Sometimes it would be nice to find out the value of a variable at a certain point in your program as it is executing. We know how to use the `printf()` function to display variable values to the screen. However, this method is not always practical if you only need to view the values of variables during the debugging phase when you are working on a program.

As you have probably guessed, the debugger provides a way to view the values of variables. In fact, the debugger provides several ways to view variables during runtime. You can create inspectors, watches, and evaluate variables.

Each method of viewing data is different and is used in different cases. Inspectors open a separate window to view the data. Watches combine the values of several variables into a single window. When we evaluate a variable, we actually view the variable and are given a method of changing the value of the variable during program execution.

To give us something to work with, type in Listing 19.3 (WATCHES.C).

Listing 19.3. Program for viewing data.

```
/*********************************************************
WATCHES.C--View data.
Do It Yourself Turbo C++ by Paul J. Perry
*********************************************************/

#include <stdio.h>
#include <string.h>
#include <conio.h>

struct music            /* structure definition */
  {
  int disknumber;
  char diskname[85];
  float price;
  };
```

continues

Listing 19.3. continued

```c
void main()
{
  int i = 321;
  float f = 987.654;
  char ch = 'Q', str[] = "MORE TESTING!\0";
  struct music cd;

  printf("This is the beginning of the program\n");

  i = 222;
  i = i*4;

  strcpy(str,"STILL TESTING");
  cd.disknumber = 9;
  strcpy(cd.diskname, "Beethoven or Bust");
  cd.price = 15.95;

  f = 112.233;
  ch = 'T';
  strcpy(str, "DONE");

  clrscr();
  printf("\ni equals %d, f equals %f, ch equals %c, str equal %s\n",
          i,f,ch,str);
  printf("cd structure elements are equal to:\n");
  printf(" disknumber = %d\n", cd.disknumber);
  printf(" diskname   = %s\n", cd.diskname);
  printf(" price      = %f\n", cd.price);

}
```

By this point, the program is nothing new to you. It declares several variables and then assigns different values to the variables. One statement that is rather new is

```c
strcpy(str,"STILL TESTING");
```

Because string variables are not built into the C language, arrays of characters are used instead. To assign a new value to a string we must use a function: strcpy(). It copies a string constant into a string variable.

Although it would be convenient to include a statement like

```
str = "STILL TESTING");
```

It cannot be done, and we must instead use the `strcpy()` function. It is declared in the STRINGS.H header file. You will find there are other string functions that are used for manipulating strings (or more correctly character arrays).

With that subtlety down, let's examine how to view the contents of variables.

Inspectors

An *inspector* is a window that displays the value of a variable. Although it can be used with any type of variable, an inspector is especially handy for structures, because we can see the value of every element at once.

To display an inspector window, press Alt+F4 or choose the Inspect option from the Debug menu. The Inspect Data dialog box will be displayed, in which you can enter the name of a variable. To see the inspector in action, move to the first `printf()` statement in the `main()` function and press F4. When program execution has halted at that point, open an inspector window and type the variable name, `i`. A window is opened that shows the value of `i`, as Figure 19.6 shows.

The inspector window shows the data type of the variable along with the current value in the window. As you single step through the program you will see the value of the variable change in the window.

To make inspecting variables even easier, you can move the cursor over a variable name in the editor window and press Alt+F4. When you do this, an inspector window is opened for the variable on which the cursor is located.

An inspector window is especially useful when you want to view the contents of a structure. Move the cursor over the `cd` structure variable and press Alt+F4. An inspector window is automatically opened that shows each element of the structure along with its current value. Figure 19.7 shows an example.

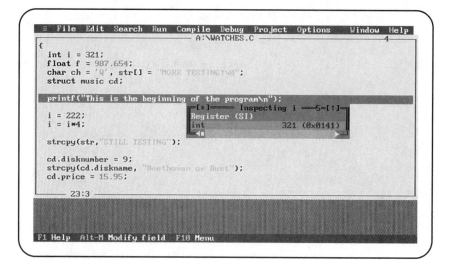

Figure 19.6. *Open inspector window.*

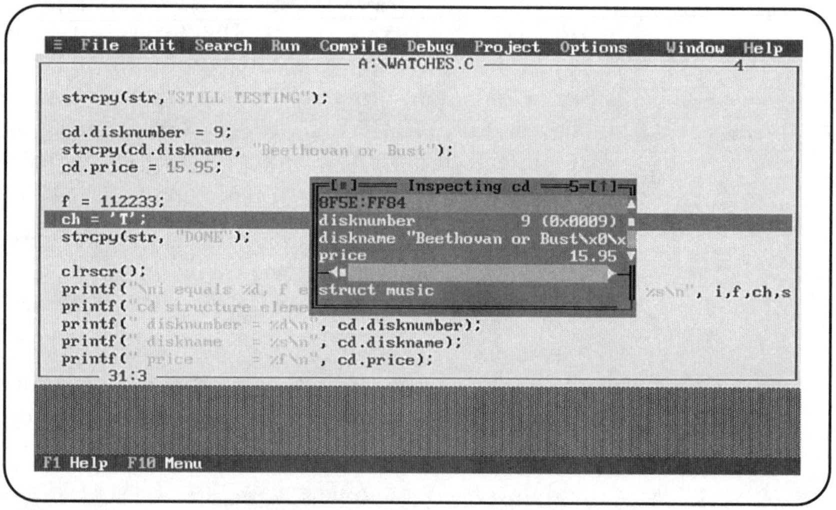

Figure 19.7. *Inspector window for a structure.*

You can open multiple inspector windows at once in which you view different variables. To close an inspector window, press the Esc key.

A limitation with inspector windows is that each window only views one variable. To view multiple variables within a single window, you need to set a Watch window.

Watches

A *Watch window* lets you view multiple variables in the same window. To set a watch variable, press Ctrl+F7 or choose the Watches menu option from the Debug menu and choose Add watch.

The Add Watch dialog box then displays, in which you enter a variable to add to a Watch window. If a Watch window is not already open, one will be opened and the variable will be added to it. Figure 19.8 shows an open Watch window with three variables listed.

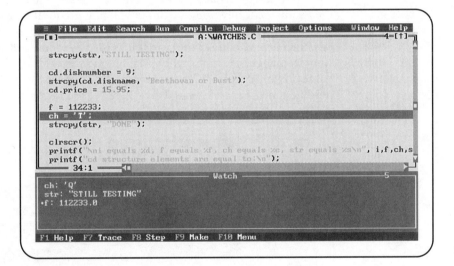

Figure 19.8. *Watch window.*

The variable is displayed in the left of the window, followed by a colon (:) and the value (or contents) of the variable. You can add as many watch variables as you like. If you add more watches than there is room to view at one time, you can resize the window or use the scroll bar on the right side of the window to bring the other watch variables into view.

To delete a watch variable, switch to the Watch window by choosing the Window menu and selecting the Watch option. Move the highlight bar over the variable you want to remove from the window and press the Delete key. You can always close the Watch window by pressing Alt+F3 (or choose the Window menu and select Close).

Evaluate

An *evaluation* lets you view the value of a variable and change it. This feature is handy if you have an idea of what is going wrong in your program and think you know the correct value to supply to a variable. Rather than editing the program, recompiling and testing the program to change the value of a variable, you can quickly do it during the debugging phase. If the change works, you can proceed to change the source code, knowing full well that the problem will be corrected.

To open the Evaluate and Modify dialog box (see Figure 19.9) choose the Evaluate/Modify option from the Debug menu. It provides an expression text box in which you type a variable. As soon as you press the Enter key, the current value of that variable is displayed in the Result box. If you want to change the value of the variable, press the Tab key twice to the New Value box and enter a different number. You can verify that the variable was modified, because the Result box will show the new value of the variable.

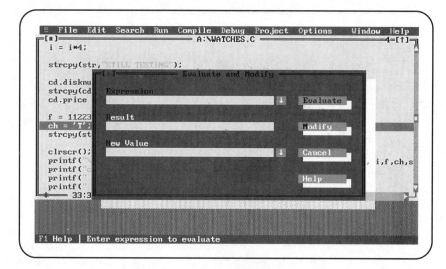

Figure 19.9. *The Evaluate and Modify dialog box.*

Which Viewing Method Is the Best?

Although the integrated debugger provides several ways for viewing the contents of variables, you will soon have a feel for what situations call for each method of viewing the data. In general, a Watch window is the most often used method of viewing program data. Inspector windows are most useful for studying data structures in detail. You use variable evaluation when you need to modify the value of a variable.

Viewing the Call Stack

The call stack shows the sequence of functions your program called in order to reach the function that is now being executed. The Call Stack dialog box is opened by pressing Ctrl+F3 or by choosing the Debug menu and selecting the Call Stack option.

A list box is displayed that shows the functions your program called in order to reach the function now running, along with the values of the parameters passed to each function. The functions are listed in reverse order. That is, the most recently called functions appear at the top of the list. You will always see at least one function call, and that will be that of the main() function. Type in Listing 19.4 for an example.

Listing 19.4. Program to demonstrate Call Stack.

```
/********************************************************
 CALLST.C--Show how Call Stack works.
 Do It Yourself Turbo C++ by Paul J. Perry
 ********************************************************/

#include <stdio.h>   /* include file */

void first_func(void);   /* function prototypes */
void second_func(void);
void third_func(void);
void fourth_func(void);
```

continues

Listing 19.4. continued

```c
void main()              /* main program entry point */
{
  first_func();
  printf("End of program\n");
}

/*********************/
void first_func()
{
  second_func();
}

/*********************/
void second_func()
{
  third_func();
}

/*********************/
void third_func()
{
  fourth_func();
}

/*********************/
void fourth_func()
{
  printf("This is a test—it is only a test\n");
  return;
}
```

Place a breakpoint on the first statement of the fourth_func() function and execute the program. At the time that the breakpoint hits and program execution is halted, press Ctrl+F3 to display the Call Stack dialog box, which appears in Figure 19.10.

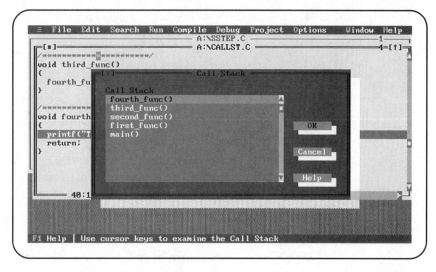

Figure 19.10. Call Stack dialog box.

You will notice that each function that was called to get to the current program location is listed in the dialog box. Moving the cursor over a function name and pressing Enter will move you to the location in your program in which the function was called.

Although the Call Stack is not used all the time, it is sometimes a helpful feature when you want to find out what functions were called to reach the current program location.

What You Have Learned

This chapter introduced the concept of debugging. You learned what a bug is and where the name actually came from. You also learned about the tools that are provided in a debugger. In particular, the following topics were covered:

● There are three types of program errors: Compile-time errors, runtime errors, and errors in logic. Debuggers help a programmer track down errors in program logic.

● The difference between the Trace into (F7 key) option and the Step over (F8 key) option is that Trace into enables you to go through each line of a function, whereas the Step over option executes a function as a single statement.

● A breakpoint is a line in your program that you set to automatically stop execution of your program during debugging. You set a breakpoint by pressing Ctrl+F8 or choosing the Debug menu option and specifying the Toggle breakpoint option.

● There are three methods of viewing program variables during program execution. You can create inspectors, watches, and evaluation windows.

● An inspector is a window that shows the value of a single variable. Inspector windows are best used with structure variables.

● A Watch window enables you to view multiple variables in the same window.

● An evaluate window helps you to view the value of a variable and possibly change it.

● The call stack shows the sequence of functions your program called in order to reach the function that is now being executed.

Part IV

Object-Oriented Programming

20

Introduction to C++

Goals

After reading this chapter, you will

- Recognize the new style of single-line comments found in C++.
- Recall how to pass variables by reference and why you would want to do it.
- Know how input and output operations work in C++.
- Understand `cout` and `cin` and the two operators that work with these standard streams.
- Know how to send output to the display with the `cout` stream.
- Be able to cascade the insertion operator.

- Know what a manipulator is and how to use the two most common ones in your programs.

- Be able to get input with the `cin` stream.

- Know how to declare variables anywhere in a C++ program.

- Understand what function overloading is and how to take advantage of it in a C++ program.

Parts II and III of this book focused on the features C++ has in common with the C programming language. The material we have covered up to this point is fundamental to learning C++ as well. Here in Part IV you will learn about features that are specific to C++.

As has been mentioned before, C++ is really a superset of C. Everything you already know about C is applicable to C++. C++ does offer many features that are not part of C that add great power to the language. The rest of this book examines the C++ programming language, specifically the aspect of object-oriented programming (OOP). You will learn what object-oriented programming is, how to use object classes, what an object hierarchy is, and other important aspects of C++ programming.

However, before we dive into the concepts of object-oriented programming, take a moment to look at the extensions to C++ that are not in the C programming language.

New Comment Style

C++ sports a new type of comment. In C++ comments are defined in two ways. First, you may use C-style comments that begin with /* and end with */.

You can also define a new type of single line comment. Comments start with double slashes (//) and terminate at the end of the line. When you start a comment with //, whatever follows is ignored by the compiler until the end of the line is reached. The comment can start at the beginning of the line or anywhere on a line following a program statement.

Another thing about regular C-style comments is that you can use them anywhere within the text of a program line, such as:

```
void main()
{ /* no statements in here */  }
```

> The new type of comments are most useful when only a single line comment is needed. The regular C-style comments are harder to type (since / is lowercase while * is uppercase) and take up more space on the line. However, they are still used frequently to write multiline comments.

If you tried to use the // style comment in this case, the closing brace would not be visible to the compiler, and the code would not compile correctly.

Listing 20.1 is an example of the new style of comments. If you start using the new comment style in your own work, it will save you time in adding information to your program listings.

Listing 20.1. Program to show new style of comments in C++.

```
/****************************************************
 COMMENTS.CPP--Show example of new comment style.
 Do It Yourself Turbo C++ by Paul J. Perry
 ****************************************************/

void main()

{
 int number;  // declare integer variable
 number = 23; // initialize variable
 number++;    // increment variable

 number = /* a comment! */ number + 5;  // add five to variable

 /* The above line cannot be done with C++ comments. */

}
```

Before we leave the subject of the new style of comments, note that although the ANSI C standard does not include this new style of comments, Turbo C++ enables you to use them in regular C programs as well as C++ programs. Therefore, if you are not planning to use another compiler, you can use the new style of comments in both your C and C++ code with the Turbo C++ compiler.

Passing by Reference

We explored passing function parameters by reference in Chapter 10, when we first discussed functions. They are covered here briefly again, just so you will remember what they are and how they work.

When you pass a function parameter by reference, you pass the *address of a variable,* rather than the *actual contents of the variable.* You saw how this was done with pointers in C. As the people who designed C++ incorporated enhancements to C into the new language, one of the biggest requests they received was a built-in ability to pass variables by reference.

When you pass variables by reference into a function, any changes made to the variable in the function are automatically made to the variable at the calling location in the program. The biggest advantage to this is that it saves memory—especially when you are passing large arrays and data structures. Imagine passing a 64KB array to a function. If it copies that array into a temporary variable, your program requires more memory and won't run as efficiently.

To pass a variable by reference you append an ampersand (&) to the end of the data type of the variable you want to pass by reference. For example:

```
void my_function(int by_value, int& by_reference);
```

This declaration declares two variables. The first, `by_value`, is passed by value. That is, a copy of the variable is passed to the function. However, variable `by_reference` is passed by reference. Only its address is passed to the function, and the function can modify the variable directly.

Listing 20.2 (BYREF.CPP) gives an example of passing variables by reference in a C++ program. You are reminded that you can still use pointers in C++; however, most people find the use of the new pass by reference (&) C++ operator much easier to read and understand.

Listing 20.2. Program to pass variables by reference in C++.

```
/********************************************************
 BYREF.CPP--Pass values by reference with C++.
 Do It Yourself Turbo C++ by Paul J. Perry
 ********************************************************/
```

```
#include <iostream.h>
#include <conio.h>

void addition(int num1, int num2, int& result);  // declaration

void main()
{
  int answer;

  clrscr();                  // clear screen
  addition(1, 2, answer);    // call function to add numbers
  cout << "1 + 2 is ";       // output to screen
  cout << answer;            // display answer

}


/**********************************************/
void addition(int num1, int num2, int& result)
{
  result = num1 + num2;
}
```

The program declares a simple function that adds two numbers together. The main program calls the function. After the function is called, the following statements:

```
cout << "1 + 2 is ";     // Output to screen
cout << answer;          // Display answer
```

display the results of the addition. You will notice some new notation—the use of the keyword cout to output text to the standard output device.

You probably understand by now how to pass variables by reference, because it is not a new concept. So, this brings us to the next topic: input and output in C++.

Input and Output

The statement

```
cout << "This is a test";
```

causes the phrase in quotation marks to be displayed on the screen. The identifier cout (pronounced "C out") is actually an object. It is predefined to correspond to the standard output stream. The standard output stream is usually set to the video display, although it can be redirected to other output devices.

The << operator is called the *insertion operator*. It directs the contents of the variable on its right to the object on its left. In the previous example, it directs the string constant "This is a test" to cout, which sends it to the display.

You probably first recognized the << operator as the left-shift bitwise operator. You may be wondering how it can be used in C++ for something else. In C++, operators can be overloaded—that is they perform different duties depending on their context—and that is what is happening here. We will learn more about operator overloading in chapter 23.

To use the cout stream, we defined a new header file, that of IOSTREAM.H. Although the notation may look obscure at first, using cout is usually easier than using the printf() function. You will see the use of cout and the insertion operator in all pure C++ program examples.

You can display text as well as output the contents of variables through the use of the cout identifier. Strings are always enclosed in quotes, and variables are not. Listing 20.3 shows an example of standard output using cout.

Listing 20.3. Program to demonstrate output with cout.

```
/****************************************************
OUTPUT.CPP--Create standard output in C++.
Do It Yourself Turbo C++ by Paul J. Perry
****************************************************/
```

```
#include <iostream.h>
#include <stdlib.h>

void main()
{
  int value;
  char str[] = "Warning: This string does nothing";

  value = rand();  // Get a random number

  cout << "To err is human; to really foul up requires a computer\n";
  cout << "The number is ";
  cout << value;
  cout << "\n";
  cout << "String variable is... ";
  cout << str;

}
```

The output of this program looks similar to this:

```
To err is human; to really foul up requires a computer
The number is 346
String variable is... Warning: This string does nothing
```

You can get an idea for how the statements work in this program. Notice that we use the \n escape code sequence to generate a line feed. You can use any escape sequences to control the appearance of your text.

Cascading the << Operator

20

To make a program more compact, you can use the insertion operator repeatedly on the same line. This is perfectly legal and saves you retyping the cout keyword. By cascading the insertion operator, notice how much shorter and more compact the previous program becomes, as demonstrated in Listing 20.4.

Listing 20.4. Program to illustrate cascading the insertion operator.

```
/*****************************************************
OUTPUT2.CPP--Show standard output in C++.
Do It Yourself Turbo C++ by Paul J. Perry
*****************************************************/

#include <iostream.h>
#include <stdlib.h>

void main()
{
  int value;
  char str[] = "Warning: This string does nothing";

  value = rand();

  cout << "To err is human; to really foul up requires a computer\n";
  cout << "The number is " << value << "\n";
  cout << "String variable is... " << str;
}
```

Notice that we were able to narrow the number of cout statements down one half from 6 down to 3. Sometimes, by putting more than one cout statement on a single line, the code becomes easier to read.

Manipulators

Manipulators are used with the insertion operator to modify (or manipulate) the way data is output. We will look at the essential manipulators that are provided with Turbo C++.

Although we could display a linefeed character with the cout stream by using an escape sequence, Turbo C++ provides a manipulator that is somewhat clearer. It is the endl manipulator. It works like this:

```
cout << "End of Line" << endl;
```

It is easiest to cascade the endl operator, as shown here. Whenever the standard output stream finds the endl manipulator, a linefeed is sent to the screen. This is easier to read than the escape sequence \n.

Another useful manipulator is setw. It enables you to specify field widths for the names and numbers that follow. The setw manipulator causes the number (or string) that follows it to be displayed within a field a specific number of characters wide. Consider the example in Listing 20.5.

Listing 20.5. Program to show output without a width specifier.

```
/****************************************************
 NOSETW.CPP--Show the need for the setw manipulator.
 Do It Yourself Turbo C++ by Paul J. Perry
 ****************************************************/

#include <iostream.h>

void main()
{
  long pay1, pay2, pay3;
  pay1 = 23239;
  pay2 = 983;
  pay3 = 9283423;

  cout << "Name                 Pay Rate" << endl;
  cout << "Mr. Joe Cool         " << pay1 << endl;
  cout << "Mr. Wish He Had More " << pay2 << endl;
  cout << "Mr. Bigg             " << pay3 << endl;

}
```

The output of this program is:

```
Name                 Pay Rate
Mr. Joe Cool         23239
Mr. Wish He Had More 983
Mr. Bigg             9283423
```

Unfortunately, the output is not ideal. It is rather difficult to read and to compare the numbers presented. Using the setw manipulator we can tell the compiler to insert spaces so that the numbers are right-aligned.

Listing 20.6 is a variation of the program that uses the setw manipulator to line the numbers up correctly.

Listing 20.6. Program to show how to use the setw manipulator.

```
/****************************************************
SETW.CPP--Show the use of the setw manipulator.
Do It Yourself Turbo C++ by Paul J. Perry
****************************************************/

#include <iostream.h>
#include <iomanip.h>  // for setw()

void main()
{
  long pay1, pay2, pay3;
  pay1 = 23239;
  pay2 = 983;
  pay3 = 9283423;

  cout << "Name              Pay Rate" << endl;
  cout << "Mr. Joe Cool    " << setw(9) << pay1 << endl;
  cout << "Mr. Not So Big  " << setw(9) << pay2 << endl;
  cout << "Mr. Bigg        " << setw(9) << pay3 << endl;

}
```

The setw manipulator causes the numbers to be printed in a field the appropriate number of characters that you specify as the width. Here is the output of the second program:

```
Name            Pay Rate
Mr. Joe Cool       23239
Mr. Not So Big       983
Mr. Bigg         9283423
```

You will notice that the output is easier to read and makes more sense.

Input with `cin`

Now that you have seen how output works, let's see how a program accomplishes input. The next sample program (Listing 20.7) asks the user for a temperature in degrees Fahrenheit, converts it to degrees Celsius, and displays the result on the screen.

Listing 20.7. Program to give example of standard input in C++.

```
/***************************************************
 INPUT.CPP--Demonstrate standard input in C++.
 Do It Yourself Turbo C++ by Paul J. Perry
 ***************************************************/

#include <conio.h>
#include <iostream.h>

void main()
{
  int temp, result;

  clrscr();
  cout << "Enter temperature in Fahrenheit: ";
  cin >> temp;

  result = (temp-32) * 5 / 9;

  cout << "Equivalent Celsius temperature is: ";
  cout << result;
  cout << "\n";

}
```

Here is a sample interaction with the program:

```
Enter temperature in Fahrenheit: 85
Equivalent Celsius temperature is: 29
```

20

The statement:

```
cin >> temp;
```

causes the program to wait for the user to type a number. The resulting number is placed in the variable named `temp`.

The keyword `cin` (pronounced "C in") is a predefined object, which corresponds to the standard input stream. In Turbo C++ this stream represents data coming from the keyboard. The >> symbols is the extraction operator. It takes the value from the stream object on the left and places it in the variable on its right.

You can cascade the >> operator `cin` in the same way as you could earlier cascade the << operator with `cout`. This enables the user to enter a group of numbers. However, this capability is rarely used, because it does not give the programmer any way to prompt the user between inputs.

Variable Declarations

When a variable is used in a C program, it is first declared so the compiler can determine what type of data you are working with. Furthermore, you can only declare variables at the beginning of the program, before any executable statements are found.

The C++ language enables you to define variables throughout a program, not just at the beginning. When you define variables where they are used, your program becomes easier to understand, because you don't need to refer to the start of the listing to find a variable declaration.

Listing 20.8 shows an example of this flexible variable definition feature.

Listing 20.8. Program to show how C++ variables are defined as they are used.

```
/
**********************************************************************
VARIABLE.CPP--Declare variables anywhere in program.
Do It Yourself Turbo C++ by Paul J. Perry
**********************************************************************/
```

```
#include <iostream.h>
#include <stdlib.h>

void main()
{
  int count;

  cout << "How high shall I count? " << endl;
  cin >> count;

  for (int temp=0; temp <= count; temp++)
   {
   cout << temp << " ";
   }

  cout << endl << "A random number is: ";
  int result = rand();
  cout << result;

}
```

Notice how the variable `temp` is declared inside the `for` loop. Also the variable `result` is declared when it is first used.

The practice of defining variables at the point of use is handy, however it should be used carefully. Variables that are used in many places in a function are probably better defined at the start of the function anyway. Therefore, they are grouped in one location, and make can make the program easier to read.

Function Overloading

The C programming language requires that every function is passed a specific type of parameter. That is, the program must know what the function declaration is used for. It gives the compiler a method of knowing what sort of variable is passed to the function.

The problem with this is that for certain functions you require a different function name for the same operation. For example, C includes several library functions to return the absolute value of a number (that is the number without a negative sign). Check the following functions and their definitions:

```
abs() gets the absolute value of an integer
cabs() and cabsl() calculate the absolute value of a complex
number
fabs() and fabsl() calculate absolute value of a floating-point
number
labs() calculates the absolute value of a long number
```

In this situation, we have six functions. All the functions do the same thing, except that they work on different data types.

With C++ you can create functions with the same name that are passed different types of parameters. You must include a prototype for each data type that you expect to pass and declare the types of parameters it expects. At runtime the compiler figures out the correct function to call by the values you pass it. The ability for the compiler to notice the same function name with different parameters is known as *function overloading*.

Listing 20.9 gives an example.

Listing 20.9. Program to illustrate function overloading.

```cpp
/*********************************************************
 FUNCOVR.CPP--Show function overloading in C++.
 Do It Yourself Turbo C++ by Paul J. Perry
 *********************************************************/

#include <iostream.h>

int   double_it(int i);      // function prototypes
float double_it(float f);
long  double_it(double d);

void main()
{
```

```
int i1 = 55;
float f1 = 234.56;
double d1 = 918327;

cout << double_it(i1) << endl;
cout << double_it(f1) << endl;
cout << double_it(d1) << endl;

}


/***********************************/
int   double_it(int i)
{
  return(i*2);
}


/***********************************/
float double_it(float f)
{
  return(f*2);
}


/***********************************/
long   double_it(double d)
{
  return(d*2);
}
```

The output of the program looks like this:

```
110
469.119995
1836654
```

If you tried to compile this program as a C program (give it the .C filename extension), it would not compile.

The next chapter starts our examination of the object-oriented features of Turbo C++.

Internally, the compiler uses a process known as *name-mangling* to change the names of the functions (because when it comes down to it, you must have a unique name for each function, despite function overloading). However, this name-mangling is transparent to the user, so you do not need to worry about it unless you are doing some low level operations with machine language.

What You Have Learned

This chapter showed you the nonobject-oriented features of C++ that are not in the C programming language. You saw there are definite improvements to the design of the language of C. The following C++ topics were covered in this chapter:

- The C++ language has a new style of single-line comments that start with a double-slash character (//) and terminates at the end of the line.

- Passing a variable by reference refers to the method that variables are passed to functions. When you pass by reference, only the address of the variable is passed. The function can access and modify the original variable through the use of reference variables.

- Input and output in C++ is handled through the use of the `cin` and `cout` streams. The `cin` stream handles input from the keyboard, and `cout` handles output to the video display.

- Manipulators are used with the insertion operator to modify the way data is output. The `endl` manipulator sends a linefeed character to the stream. The `setw` manipulator enables you to specify field widths for the names and numbers that follow.

- With C++ you can define variables throughout a program, not just at the beginning. This can make a listing easier to understand.

- Through a process known as name-mangling, you can declare functions with the same name that take different parameters. The compiler will automatically call the correct function depending on the type of parameters you pass to it.

21

Using C++ Classes

Goals

After reading this chapter, you will

- Know important milestones in the history of programming and what has led to the development of object-oriented programming.

- Recognize what makes object-oriented programming different from previous programming methods and what some of the benefits are of object-oriented programming.

- Understand what is meant by encapsulation.

- Be able to declare multiple objects in a program.

- Know what the scope resolution operator is and what it helps programmers to accomplish.

● Understand what a class definition is and how it differs from a structure definition.

● Know major uses for a constructor and how to declare one.

● Understand how to create multiple constructors for a single class.

● Know what a destructor is used for.

In this chapter you will learn exactly what object-oriented programming means and how to use object-oriented programming in your own programs.

Object-oriented programming is on the cutting edge of technology. Like other practitioners in finance, accounting, and marketing, software developers have devised a specialized language they use to describe what is being discussed. Object-oriented programming is no exception.

You have probably read or seen some big words associated with C++ and with the concept of object-oriented programming. Object-oriented programming does use some words that may at first glance appear overwhelming. However, the concepts that the words refer to are not difficult. Please don't let the language of object-oriented programming intimidate you. There is a lot to be gained by using objects in your programs.

Evolution of Programming

Before tackling the concept of object-oriented programming, let's review some methods of programming that you are already familiar with.

Programming at the lowest level includes a set of instructions that accomplish very little and allow for simple changes in program flow. This low-level language is known as *machine language.*

Moving up the hierarchy of programming methods are languages such as FORTRAN or BASIC, which are considered *procedural languages.* These are also dubbed *high-level languages,* because you use English-like words to program in these languages. They provide for looping, decision making, and the use of subroutines to simplify programming tasks.

Structured programming is a big step up from procedural languages. You are no doubt familiar with the term, because it was the buzzword of the 1980s. Structured programming expands on procedural languages, in that structured subroutines are *subprograms* (*functions* in C) and are isolated from the main program. Subprograms have their own local variables and are for the most part completely independent from the rest of the program. Structured programming limits program flow to specific blocks and avoids the use of the `goto` statement to change the course of program execution.

With each model of programming we have examined: procedural and structured, each type identifies two important parts of the program: source code and program data. Both elements have been considered separate entities that are treated differently. You write the code and then set up the variables separately.

In *object-oriented programming,* data is part of the code that performs operations on it. With object-oriented programs, your data and code suddenly become one. You don't write functions to operate on data; instead, you write objects that are manipulated by program methods. You can think of *classes* as the combination of code and data:

```
Class = Code + Data
```

A class includes program code and data in one self-contained unit, which fully describes a real-world entity. For the 1990s, you will find that the new buzzword in the industry is object-oriented programming.

The three main characteristics of an object-oriented program are encapsulation, inheritance and polymorphism. *Encapsulation* is the ability to combine data and the code that operates on it. *Inheritance* is the ability for one object to have attributes similar to another object. *Polymorphism* gives code the ability to act on many different objects.

Introduction to Object-Oriented Programming

With all the hype about object-oriented programming, you are probably asking the question "Why bother?". The key breakthrough in object-oriented programming is the ability to simplify programming tasks. The main benefits include:

- **Simplification.** The ability to design a program is easier because objects correspond more closely to real-world entities. With the close association of code and data, object-oriented technology makes programming easier.

- **Reusability.** Because objects are related so closely to the data they operate on, it's possible to reuse old, reliable objects in new programs. This results in a savings of both time and money.

- **Repairability.** When updating programs based on object-oriented technology, objects isolate programs functions from each other, so that a change in one does not change program operations elsewhere. Entire objects can be modified without rewriting the rest of the program.

The result of these benefits is the ability to improve programmer productivity. But, as with all good things, there must be some catch. There are several. Besides having to relearn some basic programming practices, a lot of careful planning is required to create objects. It takes some effort on your part to simplify the programming process with object-oriented programming.

More About Structures

You already know that structures are used to store different types of data in one group. A class definition is similar to that of a structure. To introduce you to classes, let's first look at a version of a program that uses structures. Listing 21.1 is a simple program that uses a structure to store information about a specific point on the screen.

Listing 21.1. Program to display points using structures.

```
/****************************************************
 PTS1.C--Display points on screen using C.
 Do It Yourself Turbo C++ by Paul J. Perry
 ****************************************************/

#include <conio.h>
#include <stdio.h>

// Data Structure
struct point
  {
  char ch;
```

```
  int x, y;
  };
// Function Prototypes
void display(struct point pt);
void erase(struct point pt);

void main()
{
  struct point pt;

  pt.ch = '*';
  pt.x = 40;
  pt.y = 13;

  display(pt);

  getch();

  erase(pt);

}

//*********************
void display(struct point pt)
{
  gotoxy(pt.x, pt.y);
  printf("%c", pt.ch);
}

//*********************
void erase(struct point pt)
{
  gotoxy(pt.x, pt.y);
  printf(" ");
}
```

The program starts out by defining a structure that stores the character to display on the screen, as well as the X and Y coordinates of the screen location to store the character at.

The program's `main()` declares an instance of point and then assigns the data members values. It then calls a function that displays the character

at the specified point on the screen. After the user presses a key, another function is called that erases the point on the screen.

In this C program, notice that the data and code are two separate entities. The data is declared at the beginning of the program. The functions that operate on the data are at the end of the program.

Encapsulation

By combining data and code into one unit, we accomplish *encapsulation* of data, the first tenant of object-oriented programming. Take a look at the next program, Listing 21.2. It is a C++ program that accomplishes the same task as the previous program.

Listing 21.2. C++ program to display a point.

```
/*****************************************************
PTS2.CPP--Display points on screen using C++.
Do It Yourself Turbo C++ by Paul J. Perry
*****************************************************/

#include <iostream.h>
#include <conio.h>

struct point
  {
  char ch;          // data
  int x, y;

  void display()  // code
    {
    gotoxy(x, y);
    cout << ch;
    }

  void erase()
    {
    gotoxy(x, y);
    cout << ' ';
```

```
      }
    };


void main()
{
  point pt;

  pt.ch = '*';
  pt.x = 40;
  pt.y = 13;

  pt.display();

 getch();

  pt.erase();


}
```

Notice that in Listing 21.2 the structure definition includes the three data members as before but also includes the functions to display and erase the point declared right inside of the structure. When functions are declared inside a structure they are referred to as *member functions*. These functions can access structure data members inside their body.

The `main()` section of the program declares a point on the screen. We then assign values to the data elements. To call the functions, we specify the name of the instance of the structure and the name of the function separated by a period, as follows:

```
pt.display();
```

Notice that the data structure no longer needs to be passed to the functions, because the functions can access the data elements as part of the structure.

Just like other variables, you can define multiple instances of a structure. The statement:

```
point pt1, pt2, pt3;
```

defines three instances of the structure `point` called `pt1`, `pt2` and `pt3`. The declaration of the structure does not create any objects of that type. It only describes how they will look when an instance is created.

This is the same as a regular structure declaration that describes how a structure will look but does not create any structure variables. It is the definition that actually creates objects that can be used by the program. Defining an instance of a structure is similar to defining a variable, in that space is set aside for it in memory.

Moving Functions Out

It's handy to be able to put our entire function inside the declaration of the data structure. In our example it works very well. But if your functions become any longer than a couple of lines, the combined declaration of the functions and structure can become rather confusing.

C++ solves this by enabling us to include a short function prototype inside the structure and moving the body of the function out of the structure. It works like you might imagine. Listing 21.3 provides an example.

Listing 21.3. Program to move functions out of the structure definition.

```
/*************************************************************
 PTS3.CPP--Move functions outside of structure definition.
 Do It Yourself Turbo C++ by Paul J. Perry
 *************************************************************/

#include <iostream.h>
#include <conio.h>

struct point
  {
  char ch;        // data
  int x, y;
  void display(); // function prototypes
  void erase();
  };

//***********************
void point::display()   // actual function
```

```
{
   gotoxy(x, y);
   cout << ch;
}

//*********************
void point::erase()
{
   gotoxy(x, y);
   cout << " ";
}

void main()
{
  point pt;

  pt.ch = '*';
  pt.x = 40;
  pt.y = 13;

  pt.display();

  getch();

  pt.erase();
}
```

Notice that the structure definition now only includes the prototypes of the functions. The actual body of the functions are declared separately. The first line of the function body may look strange. The entire function appears as follows:

```
void point::display()
{
   gotoxy(x, y);
   cout << ch;
}
```

The use of the double colon (::) is called the *scope resolution operator.* It is a way of specifying what structure declaration a function is associated with. The first line in this example lists what type of value the function returns. Next, the structure that the function is associated with is listed, followed by the two colons and then the actual name of the function. Any variables passed to the function would be listed inside the parentheses to the function.

Both of the functions in the example use the scope resolution operator. You will get used to seeing this notation used frequently in object-oriented programs.

Introducing the Class

Although we can create objects and use the concepts of object-oriented programming with the structure definition, C++ provides a separate keyword with which you tell the compiler that you are working with an object class. Listing 21.4 is very similar to the previous example, except it uses the new class definition.

Listing 21.4. Program to use a class definition.

```
/***********************************************
 PTS4.CPP--Use a class definition.
 Do It Yourself Turbo C++ by Paul J. Perry
 ***********************************************/

#include <iostream.h>
#include <conio.h>

class point
  {
  public :
    char ch;
    int x, y;
    void display();
    void erase();
  };

//*********************
void point::display()
{
   gotoxy(x, y);
```

```
    cout << ch;
}

//********************
void point::erase()
{
    gotoxy(x, y);
    cout << " ";
}

void main()
{
  point pt;

  pt.ch = '*';
  pt.x = 40;
  pt.y = 13;

  pt.display();

  getch();

  pt.erase();

}
```

The program has the same functionality as the ones we have seen all along, except that this one shows how to declare a class. The declaration of our new object looks like this:

```
class point
  {
  public :
    char ch;
    int x, y;
    void display();
    void erase();
  };
```

Basically, all that we did was change the word struct to class. At the same time you will notice the use of the public keyword, which has to do with how data elements are accessed inside the class. The counterpart of

the `public` keyword is the `private` keyword. In order to keep the definition the same as the previous structure definition, we had to add the public keyword.

The important difference between a `struct` definition and a `class` is that by default, every element in a structure is public, whereas every element in a class is by default private by default. That is why the `public` keyword had to be added to the `class` to give it the same functionality as the structure declaration in the previous programs.

The way in which data is accessed inside a class becomes important next, as we examine constructors and destructors inside a class.

Constructors

In each of the previous programs we have been explicitly giving values to the data elements of the class at the beginning of the program. It is often convenient if an object can initialize itself when it's first created, without the need to assign each data element a value separately. Besides that, it is commonly considered poor form to allow data members of a class to be explicitly modified inside a program.

The initialization of object data is carried out using a special function called a *constructor*. A constructor is a member function that is executed automatically whenever an object is created.

To show how constructors work, take a look at Listing 21.5. It is an expanded version of the program we have been working with which includes the use of constructors.

Listing 21.5. Program to use a constructor in a class.

```
/****************************************************
PTS5.CPP--Display points on screen with
         constructors.
Do It Yourself Turbo C++ by Paul J. Perry
****************************************************/

#include <iostream.h>
#include <conio.h>
```

```
class point
  {
  private :
    char ch;
    int x, y;
  public :
    point(char ch1, int x1, int y1);
    void display();
    void erase();
  };

//********************
point::point(char ch1, int x1, int y1)  // constructor
{
  ch = ch1;
  x = x1;
  y = y1;
}

//********************
void point::display()
{
   gotoxy(x, y);
   cout << ch;
}

//********************
void point::erase()
{
   gotoxy(x, y);
   cout << ' ';
}


void main()
{
  point pt('*', 40, 13);  // constructor call

  pt.display();            // display point

  getch();                 // wait for keypress
```

continues

415

Listing 21.5. continued

```
  pt.erase();                    // erase point


}
```

The first thing you will notice in the class definition is that the data elements are marked `private` and the functions are declared `public`. Usually the data within a class is private and the functions are public. The data is hidden so it will be safe from accidental manipulation. The functions that operate on the data are declared `public` so they can be accessed from outside the class within your program.

The new version of the program can no longer assign values to the data elements using the statements:

```
pt.ch = '*';  // These statements are now illegal
pt.x = 40;    //  with private data members.
pt.y = 13;    //  The compiler won't let you do them.
```

It is usually considered poor form in object-oriented programming to allow data items within a class definition to be changed. The reasons concern the fact that functions should be used to modify data elements. This keeps program bugs out of your code, by not allowing data members to be modified when they shouldn't be.

The constructor function has been added to the program to allow data elements to be declared at the time instances of the class are declared. The constructor must have the same name as the class name. This is how the compiler knows that it is a constructor function. In the previous program, the constructor declaration looks like this:

```
point(char ch1, int x1, int y1);
```

Notice that constructors don't have any return type. This is another way that the compiler knows which function is the constructor. The compiler needs to know which function the constructor is because the constructor is automatically called by the system, at the time the instance of the class is declared. Because the compiler makes the call to the constructor, there is no place that a value can be returned to.

The constructor uses the same scope resolution operator as other functions do. Therefore a constructor always repeats the name of the class twice. The body of the constructor looks like this:

```
point::point(char ch1, int x1, int y1)  // constructor
{
  ch = ch1;
  x = x1;
  y = y1;
}
```

This constructor takes three parameters: a character and two integers. They correspond to the data elements within the class that need to be initialized. The body of the function assigns the class data elements to the parameters passed to the constructor.

The `main()` section of the program declares the object by passing the parameters to the constructor similar to a function call. It combines the call to the constructor with the initialization of memory for data members. In the previous program, class objects are declared like this:

```
point pt('*', 40, 13);
```

This statement declares one instance (called `pt`) of the class `point` and passes the three parameters to the constructor. This enables us to initialize the data elements, the class, and declaration of the class at one time.

When you declare several instances of a class, new memory is put aside for the data elements of each instance of the class. However, each instance of a class shares the same code. This provides for the best use of memory in the program.

Multiple Constructors

Because of the flexibility of C++ classes, you can create multiple constructors. Listing 21.6 shows how this is done.

Listing 21.6. Program to use multiple constructors.

```
/***********************************************************
 PTS6.CPP--Use multiple constructors in a class.
 Do It Yourself Turbo C++ by Paul J. Perry
 ***********************************************************/
```

continues

Listing 21.6. continued

```cpp
#include <iostream.h>
#include <conio.h>

class point
  {
  private :
    char ch;
    int x, y;
  public :
    point();                             // constructor #1
    point(char ch1, int x1, int y1); // constructor #2
    void display();
    void erase();
  };
//*********************
point::point()   // constructor #1
{
  ch = '#';      // default values given to data members
  x = 1;         // because none were specified
  y = 1;
}

//*********************
point::point(char ch1, int x1, int y1)  // constructor #2
{
  ch = ch1;      // initialize data members
  x = x1;
  y = y1;
}

//*********************
void point::display()
{
  gotoxy(x, y);
  cout << ch;
}

//*********************
void point::erase()
{
  gotoxy(x, y);
```

```
    cout << ' ';
}

void main()
{
  point pt1;                  // use constructor #1
  point pt2('*', 40, 13);   // use constructor #2

  pt1.display();
  getch();
  pt1.erase();

  pt2.display();
  getch();
  pt2.erase();

}
```

This program creates two instances of the class, as follows:

```
point pt1;
point pt2('*', 40, 13);
```

The first instance of the class, pt1, is not passed any parameters. The compiler recognizes this and automatically calls the constructor that has no parameters, in which we initialize the data elements to default values.

The second instance of the class, pt2, is passed three values. Again, the compiler recognizes this and calls the constructor that can accept three variables passed to the class.

After instances of the classes are declared, the points are displayed on the screen to test the functionality of the class.

Destructors

You have seen how a constructor is automatically called when an instance of a class is first created. There is another type of function that is automatically called when an object is destroyed: a destructor.

A *destructor* is a function that is given the same name as the class (similar to a constructor), but the destructor is preceded by a tilde. Destructors are used for any housecleaning that may be necessary when a class goes out of scope. They are frequently used to return any memory that was originally allocated in the constructor. Listing 21.7 shows how a destructor is declared.

Listing 21.7. Program to declare a destructor.

```
/*********************************************
  PTS7.CPP--Use destructors.
  Do It Yourself Turbo C++ by Paul J. Perry
  *********************************************/

#include <iostream.h>
#include <conio.h>

class point
  {
  private :
    char ch;                            // data
    int x, y;
  public :
    point(char ch1, int x1, int y1);   // constructor
    ~point();                          // destructor
    void display();                    // member functions
    void erase();
  };

//*********************
point::point(char ch1, int x1, int y1)  // constructor
{
  ch = ch1;
  x = x1;
  y = y1;
}

//*********************
point::~point()
{
  // This destructor does nothing.
}
```

```
//**********************
void point::display()
{
    gotoxy(x, y);
    cout << ch;
}

//**********************
void point::erase()
{
    gotoxy(x, y);
    cout << ' ';
}


void main()
{
  point pt('*', 40, 13);   // constructor call

  pt.display();            // display point

  getch();                 // wait for keypress
  pt.erase();              // erase point

}
```

This sample program shows how a destructor is declared. Like constructors, destructors do not have a return value. Different from a constructor, destructors take no arguments. The most common use of destructors is to deallocate memory that was allocated when the class was active.

The best way to actually see when constructors and destructors are called is to single step through your program using the Integrated Debugger. You can really learn a lot by single stepping through the examples and noting when and how constructors and destructors are called.

This chapter introduced you to the basic elements of object-oriented programming. You learned about encapsulation of code and data. You saw how member functions work. You learned about two special types of functions, called constructors and destructors.

The next chapter continues the journey of object-oriented programming by looking at inheritance.

What You Have Learned

The following important topics were covered in this chapter:

- The lowest level of programming is that of machine language, in which you use low-level instructions that accomplish very little.

- Procedural languages are used to program the computer using high-level statements that handle the looping, decision making, and subroutines of your programs.

- Structured programming expands on procedural languages, in that subroutines of procedural languages are structured programming's functions, which are isolated from the main program. Each function has its own variables and each function is an independent modules.

- Object-oriented programming is the obvious next evolutionary step of programming technology. Object-oriented programming combines program code and data into one self contained unit called a class.

- Some of the benefits of object-oriented programming include simplification of program code, reusability of objects, and the ability to change objects easily.

- Encapsulation enables program code and data to be combined into one self-contained unit.

- When the body of a member function is outside of the class, you must include a prototype of the member function inside the class and then use the scope resolution operator (::) to tell the compiler which class the body of the function belong to.

- The difference between a class and a struct is that within a class every element is private by default. In a struct, every element is public by default.

- A constructor is a special type of function that is called automatically when an object is declared.

- A destructor is a special type of function that is called automatically when an object goes out of scope or when a program ends.

22

Creating an Object Hierarchy

Goals

After reading this chapter, you will

- Understand what an object hierarchy is.

- Recognize inheritance and how it helps the programmer be more productive with C++.

- Know how to use inheritance in C++ programs.

- Understand how to call member functions of inherited classes using the scope resolution operator.

- Know what the three access specifiers are and how they are used.

● Be able to directly call a member function of an inherited class inside a class definition.

● Understand what multiple inheritance is and how to declare a class that uses multiple inheritance.

An *object hierarchy* is the creation of new classes based on existing classes. This process is known as *inheritance.* The existence of inheritance greatly expands the power and expandability of C++.

Computer scientists borrowed the term *inheritance* from biologists. You probably have heard the term used in reference to children. You might hear somebody say "he received his father's eyes." Inheritance in terms of object-oriented programming is similar. A class can receive (or inherit) variables and member functions from a parent class.

This chapter examines the aspects of C++ that allow for inheritance. You will learn how classes inherit other classes, and you will find out about a related topic, called multiple inheritance.

More About Inheritance

Inheritance offers an important advantage—it allows for code reusability. Once a base class is written and debugged, the source code for that class does not need to be modified or changed. However, its functionality can be changed by deriving a new class that inherits its functionality.

By reusing existing code, a programmer saves time and money. Furthermore, program reliability is improved, because the core functionality of the class already knows how to operate. It is only the new behavior that needs to be tested.

Definitions

A class inherits the variables and member functions of another class through inheritance. The class that members are borrowed from is known as the *base class.* The class that inherits the trait of another class is called the *derived class.*

Because classes can inherit more than one class, any classes that are inherited are also referred to as *ancestor classes*. A class that inherits functionality from a class is also referred to as a *descendant class*.

Through inheritance, an object type inherits all the characteristics of an existing type and also adds some specific functionality of its own. Examples of inheritance are common. You know that many times children inherit specific traits from their parents. Or you might describe a wolf as being "like a dog, except it is wild and has larger teeth." This statement says that a wolf is a descendant of a dog, and the wolf therefore inherits all the abilities and attributes of the dog. In addition, the wolf has a new attribute, that of large teeth.

When you declare a derived class, the name of the base class is listed immediately after the name of the derived class and before the opening brace of the class definition.

An Object Hierarchy

To examine how inheritance works, let's start with a basic class definition. Listing 22.1 is a program that creates a simple windowing system. The program is based on a class called `WinClass`. The class includes variables for the coordinates of the upper left and lower right corners of the window and the character that is to mark the interior rectangle of the window.

Listing 22.1. Program to show the start of an object hierarchy.

```
/***********************************************
WIN1.CPP--Show a simple windowing system.
Do It Yourself Turbo C++ by Paul J. Perry
***********************************************/

#include <iostream.h>
#include <conio.h>
```

continues

427

Listing 22.1. continued

```cpp
class WinClass
  {
  private :
    int x1, y1, x2, y2;
    char ch;
  public :
    WinClass();                              // constructor #1
    WinClass(int xx1, int yy1, int xx2, int yy2, char cch);
            // constructor #2
    void display();
    void changewindow(char chto);
    void closewindow();
  };

//************************************************************
void WinClass::WinClass()
{
  x1 = 20;        // default window positions
  y1 = 5;
  x2 = 60;
  y2 = 20;
  ch = 176;
}

//************************************************************
void WinClass::WinClass(int xx1, int yy1, int xx2, int yy2,
                        char cch)
{
  x1 = xx1;
  y1 = yy1;
  x2 = xx2;
  y2 = yy2;
  ch = cch;
}

//************************************************************
void WinClass::display()
{
  for (int column=x1; column<x2; column++)
    {
    for (int row=y1; row<y2; row++)
```

```
        {
        gotoxy(column, row);
        cout << ch;
        }
      }
}

//*************************************************************
void WinClass::changewindow(char ch2)
{
  ch = ch2;
  display();   // redisplay window
}

//*************************************************************
void WinClass::closewindow()
{
  for (int column=x1; column<x2; column++)
    {
    for (int row=y1; row<y2; row++)
      {
      gotoxy(column, row);
      cout << " ";
      }
    }
}

//*************************************************************
void main()
{
   clrscr();

   WinClass win;                        // first instance
   WinClass win2(1, 1, 4, 5, '#');      // second instance

   win.display();                  // display the windows
   win2.display();

   getch();
```

continues

Listing 22.1. continued

```
win.changewindow('¦');     // change character of first window

getch();

win.closewindow();         // erase windows
win2.closewindow();
}
```

Two constructors are declared in the class. If you do not pass any parameter, default values are used for the class. Otherwise, you can specify your own data values when the class is declared and the second constructor will be called. Member functions are included that display the window, change the background character of the window, and close the window. The output of the program appears in Figure 22.1.

Figure 22.1. Output of WIN1.CPP.

Reusing Code

In regular C programming, if you wanted to modify the code to draw a frame around the window, you must modify the source code directly. However by using C++, we can simply inherit the class we already have and expand on its functionality. Listing 22.2 shows how this might be done. It adds the capability of drawing a frame around the perimeter of the window area.

Listing 22.2. Program showing class that displays a frame.

```
/***********************************************************
  WIN2.CPP--Create an inherited class that has a frame.
  Do It Yourself Turbo C++ by Paul J. Perry
  ***********************************************************/


#include <iostream.h>
#include <conio.h>

class WinClass    // base class
  {
  public :          // notice that all members are now public
    int x1, y1, x2, y2;
    char ch;

    WinClass()  // constructor #1
      {x1 = 20;   y1 = 5;   x2 = 60;   y2 = 20;   ch = 176; }

    WinClass(int xx1, int yy1, int xx2, int yy2, char cch)
      {x1=xx1; x2=xx2; y1=yy1; y2=yy2; ch=cch; }
        // constructor #2

    void display();
    void changewindow(char chto);
    void closewindow();
  };

//***********************************************************
void WinClass::display()
{
  for (int column=x1; column<=x2; column++)
    {
    for (int row=y1; row<=y2; row++)
      {
      gotoxy(column, row);
      cout << ch;
      }
    }
}
```

continues

431

Listing 22.2. continued

```cpp
//************************************************************
void WinClass::changewindow(char ch2)
{
  ch = ch2;
  display();  // redisplay window
}


//************************************************************
void WinClass::closewindow()
{
  for (int column=x1; column<=x2; column++)
    {
    for (int row=y1; row<=y2; row++)
      {
      gotoxy(column, row);
      cout << " ";
      }
    }
}


//////////////////////////////////////////////////////////////
class WinClass2 : public WinClass      // derived class
  {
  public :
    WinClass2() : WinClass() { };  // constructors call base class

    WinClass2(int xx1, int yy1, int xx2, int yy2, char cch) :
      WinClass(xx1, yy1, xx2, yy2, cch) { };

    void display();                    // new functionality
    void changewindow(char cch);   // new functionality
  };


//************************************************************
void WinClass2::display()
{
  const char UL = 218;  // upper left corner
  const char UR = 191;  // upper right corner
  const char LL = 192;  // lower left corner
  const char LR = 217;  // lower right corner
```

```
const char HL = 196;   // horizontal line
const char VL = 179;   // vertical line

WinClass::display();   // call base class member function

gotoxy(x1,y1);
cout << UL;          // draw upper left corner

gotoxy(x1, y2);
cout << LL;          // draw lower left corner

gotoxy(x2, y1);
cout << UR;          // draw upper right corner

gotoxy(x2, y2);
cout << LR;          // draw lower right corner

for(int temp=x1+1; temp<x2; temp++) // draw horizontal lines
   {
   gotoxy(temp,y1);
   cout << HL;

   gotoxy(temp,y2);
   cout << HL;
   }

 for(temp=y1+1; temp<y2; temp++) // draw vertical lines
   {
   gotoxy(x1, temp);
   cout << VL;

   gotoxy(x2, temp);
   cout << VL;
   }
}

//************************************************************
void WinClass2::changewindow(char cch)
{
  ch = cch;
  display();
```

continues

Listing 22.2. continued

```
}

//************************************************************
void main()
{
    clrscr();

    WinClass2 win;                          // first instance
    WinClass2 win2(1, 1, 4, 5, '#');        // second instance

    win.display();
    win2.display();

    getch();

    win2.changewindow('W');

    getch();

    win.closewindow();
    win2.closewindow();
}
```

Notice that we have pretty much left the original class the same. It is now referred to as the base class. The inherited class is called `WinClass2`. The definition of the base class may look a little different so that the program listing would not be as long. Figure 22.2 shows the output of the new program.

The only reason that the base class was compacted was so it would not be as long. Look at the definition for the constructors:

```
WinClass()
    { x1 = 20;   y1 = 5;   x2 = 60;   y2 = 20;   ch = 176; }

WinClass(int xx1, int yy1, int xx2, int yy2, char cch)
    { x1=xx1; x2=xx2; y1=yy1; y2=yy2; ch=cch; }
```

The code is the same, except that it has been moved into the class definition and put on the same line. The C++ compiler (just like the C compiler) does not force you to insert spaces or carriage returns in any specific sequence or order. You can format the program however you like, much as you did in the previous class declarations.

Figure 22.2. *New WinClass2 window.*

Access Specifiers

Look at the definition for the second (derived) class:

```
class WinClass2 : public WinClass
  {
  public :
    WinClass2() : WinClass() { };

    WinClass2(int xx1, int yy1, int xx2, int yy2, char cch) :
      WinClass(xx1, yy1, xx2, yy2, cch) { };

    void display();
    void changewindow(char cch);
  };
```

On the first line we declare the class, then insert a colon and the access specifier keyword, followed by the name of the base class. The new derived (WinClass2) class inherits all the variables and member functions from the base class. The function is then free to modify the functions and data or add more.

The keyword public between the colon and the name of the base class enables you to control access to base class members. You have three choices, as follows:

- public—This allows both member functions and variables of inherited class members to be treated as public members of the class. They can then be used (when they are data members) or called (when they are member functions) by any function in the class.

- private—This allows member functions and variables of inherited class members to be used or called only by member functions of the same class.

- protected—Class members declared as protected can be used only by member functions of the same class or by member functions of another class derived from the original class.

These three keywords are called *access specifiers.* The access specifiers control access to class members. They are meant to guard class members against accidental change. Any one of them can be used in specifying the class that is being inherited.

Two new constructors have been declared for the class. However, these constructors do not need to do any additional tasks. We can therefore call the constructors of the base class. This is done as follows:

```
WinClass2() : WinClass() { };

WinClass2(int xx1, int yy1, int xx2, int yy2, char cch) :
   WinClass(xx1, yy1, xx2, yy2, cch) { };
```

The colon tells the compiler that the base class should be called. In the second case, we must pass appropriate parameters, so the same parameters that are passed to WinClass2's constructor are then passed to WinClass's constructor. This move makes it very easy to access code from the base class without writing any new code.

The new member function, display(), adds new functionality by drawing a frame around the window. However, as you know, the functionality of the base class can still be used to draw the background of the window.

Within the WinClass2::display member function, this background drawing is accomplished by calling the base class member function, as follows:

```
WinClass::display();
```

The scope resolution operator (: :) is used to specify that we want to execute the display() function from the base class. The compiler automatically calls it for you. Therefore, we use the previously written code to display the interior of the window. We then continue on in our display() function by drawing the frame of the box.

You can clearly see that none of the original class was modified in order to take advantage of its functionality in the derived class. To show how this can be carried out to another level, the next program inherits WinClass2's functionality. This time, we add a title to the window. Take a look at Listing 22.3. The actual code for the program is not that much more substantive than in the previous examples, except both of the inherited classes are included in the listing. Don't let it intimidate you.

Listing 22.3. Program to demonstrate even more functionality in a window.

```
/****************************************************
WIN3.CPP--Inherit another class to add a title.
Do It Yourself Turbo C++ by Paul J. Perry
****************************************************/

#include <iostream.h>
#include <conio.h>
#include <string.h>

class WinClass    // base class
  {
  public :
    int x1, y1, x2, y2;
    char ch;

    WinClass()  // constructor #1
      {x1 = 20;   y1 = 5;   x2 = 60;  y2 = 20;   ch = 176; }

    WinClass(int xx1, int yy1, int xx2, int yy2, char cch)
      { x1=xx1; x2=xx2; y1=yy1; y2=yy2; ch=cch; }
        // constructor #2

    void display();
    void changewindow(char chto);
    void closewindow();
```

continues

Listing 22.3. continued

```cpp
  };

//*************************************************************
void WinClass::display()
{
  for (int column=x1; column<=x2; column++)
    {
    for (int row=y1; row<=y2; row++)
      {
      gotoxy(column, row);
      cout << ch;
      }
    }
}
//*************************************************************
void WinClass::changewindow(char ch2)
{
  ch = ch2;
  display();   // redisplay window
}


//*************************************************************
void WinClass::closewindow()
{
  for (int column=x1; column<=x2; column++)
    {
    for (int row=y1; row<=y2; row++)
      {
      gotoxy(column, row);
      cout << " ";
      }
    }
}


/////////////////////////////////////////////////////////////
class WinClass2 : public WinClass      // derived class
  {
  public :
    WinClass2() : WinClass() { };  // constructors call base class
```

```
    WinClass2(int xx1, int yy1, int xx2, int yy2, char cch) :
      WinClass(xx1, yy1, xx2, yy2, cch) { };

    void display();                 // new functionality
    void changewindow(char cch);    // new functionality
  };

//*************************************************************
void WinClass2::display()
{
  const char UL = 218;  // upper left corner
  const char UR = 191;  // upper right corner
  const char LL = 192;  // lower left corner
  const char LR = 217;  // lower right corner
  const char HL = 196;  // horizontal line
  const char VL = 179;  // vertical line

  WinClass::display();  // call base class member function

  gotoxy(x1, y1);
  cout << UL;

  gotoxy(x1, y2);
  cout << LL;

  gotoxy(x2, y1);
  cout << UR;

  gotoxy(x2, y2);
  cout << LR;

  for(int temp=x1+1; temp<x2; temp++) // draw horizontal lines
    {
    gotoxy(temp,y1);
    cout << HL;

    gotoxy(temp,y2);
    cout << HL;
    }

  for(temp=y1+1; temp<y2; temp++) // draw vertical lines
```

continues

22

Listing 22.3. continued

```
      {
      gotoxy(x1, temp);
      cout << VL;

      gotoxy(x2, temp);
      cout << VL;
      }
}

//*********************************************************
void WinClass2::changewindow(char cch)
{
  ch = cch;
  display();
}

///////////////////////////////////////////////////////////
class WinClass3 : public WinClass2
  {
  public :
    char title[81];

    WinClass3();   // constructor #1

    WinClass3(int xx1, int yy1, int xx2,         // constructor #2
            int yy2, char cch, char name[81]);

    void display();
    void changewindow(char cch, char name[81]);
  };

//*********************************************************
WinClass3::WinClass3()  // constructor #1 (default values)
{
  WinClass2::WinClass2();
  strcpy(title, "Default Window\0");
}

//*********************************************************
WinClass3::WinClass3(int xx1, int yy1, int xx2, int yy2, char cch,
                   char name[81])
```

```
{
  WinClass2::WinClass2(xx1, yy1, xx2, yy2, cch);
                          // call previous class constructor
  strcpy(title, name);
}

//***********************************************************
void WinClass3::display()
{
  WinClass2::display();  // call previous class definition

  int midpoint = x1 + ( (x2-x1) / 2 );        // midpoint of window
  int at = midpoint - ( strlen(title) / 2 ); // where to start
                                                     title

  gotoxy(at, y1);
  cout << title;
}

//***********************************************************
void WinClass3::changewindow(char cch, char name[81])
{
 ch = cch;
 strcpy(title, name);

 display();
}

//***********************************************************
void main()
{
   clrscr();

   WinClass3 win;  // First Instance uses default values
   WinClass3 win2(1, 1, 5, 5, '#', "WIN");    // second Instance

   win.display();
   win2.display();

   getch();  // wait for keypress
```

continues

441

Listing 22.3. continued

```
    win2.closewindow();  // close this window
    win.changewindow('*',"No Longer Using Default Values");

    getch();  // wait for keypress

    win.closewindow();
}
```

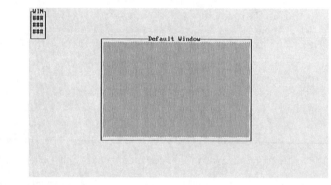

Figure 22.3. *Output of WIN3 program.*

Figure 22.3 shows the output of this program. The new class (called WinClass3) inherits the member functions and variables of WinClass2, which already inherits the functionality of WinClass. This program adds a character array variable type to hold the title of the window. It also declares two constructors and redefines the display() and changewindow() member functions.

In the code for the constructors, you will notice that we use the scope resolution operator to call the constructor of the previous class. We then add any code that is needed for the functionality of this class. In the case of the constructor that takes no parameters, the new constructor looks like this:

```
WinClass3::WinClass3()
{
  WinClass2::WinClass2();
  strcpy(title, "Default Window\0");
}
```

The strcpy() function is provided in the standard C library to copy a string into a character array. It is convenient to be able to inherit code from the base class. You can see that the object-oriented approach saves several lines of typing code that was used in the base class.

In more complex programs, object-oriented program design is even more desirable, because once a base class is tested and debugged, you can be certain that the code being inherited works correctly. If something does not work as expected in a derived class, you can be almost certain that the bug is in that class and not in the base class.

You can see that the scope resolution operator is used in the second constructor as well as in the display() function to use code from the previous class. The only thing the new code does is inside the display() function, where the center point of the upper window frame is calculated, so that the window title can be displayed.

As was recommended in the last chapter, if some of this seems rather daunting to you, you might want to use the Integrated Debugger to single step through the code. Once you do so, you will see exactly how code is executed.

Multiple Inheritance

A class can be derived from more than one base class, a situation known as *multiple inheritance*. In multiple inheritance a class receives member functions and variables from several classes.

Listing 22.4 is an example of a program that uses multiple inheritance.

Listing 22.4. Program using multiple inheritance.

```
/***********************************************************
MULTINH.CPP--Use multiple inheritance in a program.
Do It Yourself Turbo C++ by Paul J. Perry
***********************************************************/

#include <iostream.h>
```

continues

Listing 22.4. continued

```cpp
/////////////////////////////////////////////////
class first
  {
  public :
    int numb1;
    first()               { numb1 = 0; }          // constructor #1
    first(int defvalue) { numb1 = defvalue; } // constructor #2
    void show()           { cout << numb1 << endl; }
  };


/////////////////////////////////////////////////
class second
  {
  public :
    int numb2;
    second()               { numb2 = 0; }          // constructor #1
    second(int defvalue) { numb2 = defvalue; } // constructor #2
    void show()           { cout << numb2 << endl; }
  };


/////////////////////////////////////////////////
class third : public first, public second
  {
  public :
    int numb3;
    third();                                                      // construc-
                                                                  tor #1
    third(int default1, int default2, int default3); // construc-
                                                                  tor #2

    void show();
  };

//*******************************************************
third::third()
{
  first::first();    // call base class constructor
  second::second();  // call base class constructor
  numb3 = 0;         // initialize variable
}
```

```
//********************************************************
third::third(int default1, int default2, int default3)
{
   first::first(default1);    // call base class constructor
   second::second(default2);  // call base class constructor
   numb3 = default3;          // initialize variable
}

//********************************************************
void third::show()
{
  first::show();             // call base class member function
  second::show();            // call base class member function
  cout << numb3 << endl;
}
//********************************************************
void main()
{
  third x(1,2,3);   // create instance of class third
  third y;

  cout << "First Instance data values " << endl;
  x.show();

  cout << "Second Instance data values " << endl;
  y.show();

}
```

The program assigns a value to three integer variables and then displays them with the show( ) member function. The output of the program looks similar to this:

First Instance data values
1
2
3
Second Instance data values
0
0
0

Initially, two classes are declared called `first` and `second`. The `third` class inherits functions from the previous two classes. The base classes from which `third` are derived are listed following the colon in the class specification separated by commas, as follows:

```
class third : public first, public second
  {
...
  };
```

In the constructor for the `third` class, we save ourselves some work by calling the constructor for both of the inherited classes. The same is done for the `show()` member function.

Can you see how inheritance can make programming easier? In the examples presented in this chapter, we have saved a couple of lines of code by inheriting member functions. Imagine if you were using inheritance for a larger project involving hundreds or thousands of lines of code. Instead of saving the trouble of typing a couple of lines of code, you would save more work. It is in large-scale, long-term situations when inheritance really shines.

What You Have Learned

Inheritance is one of the key concepts of C++. It gives programmers more control over their code and how it is written. Some of the topics covered in this chapter were:

- Inheritance allows for the creation of new classes based on existing classes. A class receives the variables and member functions from another class, and can then add or change to the functionality already present in the other class.

- The advantage of inheritance is that it fosters code reusability. Program code can be used without having to modify the original source code.

- A class that members are borrowed from is known as a base class. The class that inherits the traits of another class is called the derived class.

- To access member functions of inherited classes, use the scope resolution operator to specify the class and member function you wish to call.

- There are three access specifiers: `public`, `private`, and `protected`. They control how classes inherit the code and variables from base classes.

- Multiple inheritance allows a class to be derived from more than one base class. When this occurs, a class receives member functions and variables from several classes.

23

Operator Overloading

Goals

After reading this chapter, you will

- Understand the term operator overloading.
- Know why operator overloading was included as part of the C++ language.
- Recognize the types of operators that can be overloaded.
- Understand how to overload the unary operators.
- Know how to force a unary operator to return a value, so it can be used inside an expression.
- Be able to overload the + operator.

● Be capable of creating a class of strings. You'll know how to overload the + arithmetic operator to combine strings without using any special function calls.

You already know from Chapter 6 that operators are symbols that cause a program to do something to variables. C and C++ include a large number of operators that you use for operations with the built-in data types.

With the operator overloading feature of C++, you can change the way an operator works for a class. Operator overloading actually enables you to redefine how an operator interacts with class members. Each class can redefine the meaning of how an operator works for its data members. Operator overloading is a powerful aspect of the C++ language. With it you give special meaning to an operator relative to each class you declare.

This chapter examines how to use operator overloading. You will see several examples of how operator overloading works inside a program. By the end of this chapter you should see the power and benefits of operator overloading.

Introduction to Operator Overloading

Because C++ enables you to create your own classes, it also enables you to define the behavior of operators as they affect the new classes you create. By now, you are accustomed to using an operator on a variable. For example, to increment an integer variable using the increment (++) operator, you can use a statement like this:

```
int count = 0;  // declare variable and initialize to zero

++count;        // increment variable
```

You know that the value of count will be equal to 1 after the statements are carried out.

Suppose you have declared a class representing the English system of measurement. It might be declared something like this:

```
class length
  {
  int feet;
  int inches;
  ... // list of constructors, destructors, and member functions
  };
```

and an instance is created like this:

```
length len;
```

At this point, if we tried to increment the class member with the increment operator using the statement:

```
++len;
```

the compiler would not know what to do. It has no method of incrementing the class members. It is through operator overloading that we tell the compiler how to react to the operator.

When an operator is overloaded, a special function must be written that is executed when the compiler encounters the operator used with an instance of the class. It is through this function that we define how the operator acts on the class instance.

How Operator Overloading Works

As was illustrated earlier, if you do not declare the behavior of an operator as related to a specified class, you cannot use the operator on that class. Therefore it is up to you as the programmer to extend a class by defining the function that is executed when the compiler runs into the operator.

Following are some of the operators that accept additional meanings with operator overloading:

+	-	*	/	%	^	&	¦	~
!	=	<	>	+=	-=	*=	/=	%=
++	--	&&	¦¦	=	[]	+=	<<	>>

When you overload an operator, you should be careful that you assign a function to the operator that is consistent with how the operator works with built-in variables.

For example, if you overload the decrement operator (--) you can give it any functionality you want (including the ability to increment variables). However, to make your code easier to read you would want the operator to have the same basic operation as is defined in the language—that of incrementing a class data member.

Overloading Unary Operators

Unary operators—those operators that work on one variable—are the easiest type of operator to override. Let's take a look at how to override the increment operator (++). A similar procedure would be used for the decrement operator (--). Listing 23.1 shows an example of a class that counts up by two.

Listing 23.1. Program example of overloading the increment operator.

```
/**********************************************************
OPOVL.CPP--Show operator overloading for unary operator.
Do It Yourself Turbo C++ by Paul J. Perry
**********************************************************/

#include <iostream.h>
#include <conio.h>

class count
  {
  private :
    unsigned int count;     // Positive values only

  public :
    count()                 { count = 0; }      // constructor
    int curvalue()          { return count;  } // return current
                                                             value
```

```
      void reset()          { count = 0; }      // reset value to
                                                //   zero
      void operator ++ ()    { count += 2; }    // for prefix
                                                //   notation
      void operator ++ (int) { count += 2; }    // for postfix
                                                //   notation
    };

void main()
{
  clrscr();
  count a;

  cout << "a equals " << a.curvalue() << endl;

  a++;  // increment with postfix notation
  ++a;  // increment with prefix notation

  cout << "a equals " << a.curvalue() << endl;

  a.reset();  // set class member equal to zero

  cout << "a equals " << a.curvalue() << endl;

}
```

The output of the program looks something like this:

```
a equals 0
a equals 4
a equals 0
```

In the program, an instance of the class count is created. The single data member is initialized to zero in the constructor. In the main() function the data member is incremented twice using both postfix and prefix notation using the overloaded ++ operator. Then the result is displayed on the screen. Another member function resets the data member and the value is displayed on the screen again.

To tell the compiler to override the increment operator, we use a special keyword, operator, that tells the compiler which function to call when it runs into the specified operator. The declaration of the overloaded operator functions looks like this:

```
void operator ++ ()    { count += 2; }    // for prefix notation
void operator ++ (int) { count += 2; }    // for postfix notation
```

The return type (void in this case) comes first, followed by the keyword operator, followed by the operator itself, and finally the argument list enclosed in parentheses. In this example, the body of the function is listed after the declaration. You can always declare the body of the program at a different point in the program using the scope resolution (::) operator.

The only way the compiler has determined which function to associate with postfix or prefix notation is by taking a single int variable as a parameter to the function that is to be used as the postfix operator. The declaration tells the compiler to call the member function when the specified operator is encountered, assuming the operand is an instance of the class.

When the compiler finds the increment operator in the main() section of the program, it knows to call the appropriate function. We use the increment operator just as we would with any type of variable, like this:

```
a++;  // increment with postfix notation
++a;  // increment with prefix notation
```

Although calling the overloaded operator in the above fashion makes the most sense, it is the same as calling the function using the notation:

```
a.operator ++ ();
a.operator ++ (i);
```

where *i* is a previously declared integer variable. Obviously, the previous methods are preferred, because they are easier to read and easier to understand.

Returning Values

If you modify the previous program to force the statement to return a value, you will notice a small quirk. If you use the following statement:

```
count b;  // define another instance of the class

b = a++;  // assign the result of incrementing a to b
```

in your program, the compiler will not accept your code. The reason is that when the increment operator was declared it was not declared to have a return type. This assignment statement is asking the function to return a variable. The type of variable it expects is of type count.

In order to use the ++ operator in the previous code, we must provide a way for it to return a value. Listing 23.2 does the trick for us.

Listing 23.2. Program example of increment operator returning a value.

```
/*****************************************************************
OPOVL2.CPP--Show increment operator overloading by returning
            a value.
   Do It Yourself Turbo C++ by Paul J. Perry
*****************************************************************/

#include <iostream.h>
#include <conio.h>

class count
  {
  private :
    unsigned int number;    // positive values only

  public :
    count()               { number = 0; }     // constructor
    int curvalue()        { return number;  } // return current
                                                         value
    void reset()          { number = 0; }     // reset value to
                                                         zero

    count operator ++ ();
    count operator ++ (int);
  };

//********************************
count count::operator ++()
{
 number += 2;
 count temp;
 temp.number = number;
```

continues

Listing 23.2. continued

```
  return temp;

}

//********************************
count count::operator ++(int)
{
 number += 2;
 count temp;
 temp.number = number;

 return temp;

}

//********************************
void main()
{
  clrscr();
  count a, b;

  cout << "a equals " << a.curvalue() << endl;
  cout << "b equals " << b.curvalue() << endl << endl;

  a++;       // Increment a

  b = a++;   // Increment a and return value to b

  cout << "a equals " << a.curvalue() << endl;
  cout << "b equals " << b.curvalue() << endl;


}
```

This is the output of the new program:

```
a equals 0
b equals 0
```

```
a equals 4
b equals 4
```

In this program, the `operator++()` function creates a new object of type `count`, called `temp`, to use as a return value. It increments the count data in its own object as before, then creates the new `temp` object and assigns count to the new object of the same value as its own object. Finally it returns the `temp` object to the calling part of the program.

This has the desired result. We can now use an expression like

```
b = a++;
```

in our program. This returns the value of class a after it has been incremented and assigns that value to b.

The body of the new function looks like this:

```
number += 2;
count temp;
temp.number = number;

return temp;
```

We first increment the data member of the class. A temporary class is created inside the function and we assign that function the value of the class data member. That temporary class is then returned to the calling routine.

By creating a temporary instance of the class inside the member function it gives us the flexibility of creating overloaded functions that return a value. You will see this method of returning values from an overloaded function used in other examples in this chapter, too.

Overloading Arithmetic Operators

At the beginning of this chapter, you saw an example of adding lengths together. We discussed there that lengths, heights, or any distance based on the English system of measure are difficult to add together, because they are not a base-10 mathematical operation.

Listing 23.3 creates a class called `height`. It includes an example of the + arithmetic operator used to add heights together.

Listing 23.3. Program example of overriding the assignment operator.

```
/*****************************************************
 ASSGNOVL.CPP--Show how to override the + operator.
 Do It Yourself Turbo C++ by Paul J. Perry
 *****************************************************/

#include <iostream.h>
#include <conio.h>

class height
  {
  private :
    int feet;
    float inches;
  public :
    height()                   { feet=0; inches=0; }    // con-
                                                           structor
                                                           #1

    height(int fe, float in)  { feet=fe;   inches=in; } // con-
                                                           structor
                                                           #2

    height operator + (height);
    void set(int fe, float in);
    void display();
  };

//***************************************************
height height::operator + (height l)
{
  int temp = feet + l.feet;
  float temp2 = inches + l.inches;

  if (temp2 >= 12.00)
    {
    temp2 -= 12.00;       // subtract 12 inches from temp2
    temp++;               // add one foot to temp
    }

  return height(temp, temp2);  // return appropriate values
}
```

```
//**********************************************************
void height::set(int fe, float in)
{
  feet=fe;
  inches=in;
}

//**********************************************************
void height::display()
{
  const char apostrophe = 39; // ' character
  const char quote       = 34; // " character

  cout << feet << apostrophe << inches << quote;
}

//**********************************************************
void main()
{
  height myheight(6,1); //  6'1"
  height urheight(5,6); //  5'6"

  height rheight;       //  combined height (for result)
  clrscr();

  rheight = myheight + urheight;  // + operator

  myheight.display();
  cout << endl;

  urheight.display();
  cout << endl;

  cout << "----------" << endl;
  rheight.display();

}
```

The main() section of this program creates three instances of the class. It then adds two of the heights together and returns that value into the third instance of the class. Finally, it displays the two heights along with the result.

Sample output of the program looks like this:

```
6'1"
5'6"
----------
11'7"
```

In the class `height`, the prototype for `operator +()` looks like this:

```
height operator + (height);
```

This function has a return type of `height` and takes one parameter of type `height`. Here is the call to the function in the `main()` section of the program:

```
rheight = myheight + urheight;
```

At first glance, it might be rather confusing to understand how the compiler translates this call to the previous function declaration. What you want to remember is that the argument on the left side of the operator (`myheight` in this case) is the instance of the class of which the operator is a member. The object on the right side of the operator (`urheight`) is furnished as an argument to the operator. The operator returns a value, which would be assigned to `rheight`.

Inside the body of the `operator + ()` function, the left operand is accessed directly as the class member. The right operand (`urheight`) is accessed as the functions arguments.

The body of the `operator + ()` function looks like this:

```
height height::operator + (height l)
{
  int temp = feet + l.feet;
  float temp2 = inches + l.inches;

  if (temp2 >= 12.00)
    {
    temp2 -= 12.00;        // subtract 12 inches from temp2
    temp++;                // add one foot to temp
    }

  return height(temp, temp2);  // return appropriate values
}
```

This function works by adding together the feet members of the classes. The `inches` members are added together at the same time. A loop is then created in which 12 is subtracted from the inches and 1 is added to the foot until the inches is less than 12. The total feet and inches is returned to the calling routine at the end of the function.

A String Class

As you know, the C language does not accept the + operator for character arrays (string variables). With some languages (like BASIC) you simply use a statement with this format:

```
str1 = str2 + str3;
```

where *str1*, *str2*, and *str3* are all declared as string arrays. However, by using C++'s operator overloading feature, we can create our own class, which allows us to add strings together.

Take a look at Listing 23.4 which shows an example of a simple string class.

Listing 23.4. Program example of a string class.

```
/****************************************************
STRING.CPP--Show a string class.
Do It Yourself Turbo C++ by Paul J. Perry
****************************************************/

#include <stdlib.h>
#include <iostream.h>
#include <string.h>
#include <conio.h>

class string
   {
   public :
     char *s;                          // data member
   public :
     string();                         // constructor #1
     string(char st[]);                // constructor #2
```

continues

461

Listing 23.4. continued

```
      ~string();                          // destructor
      string(const string& str);          // copy constructor
      void show();
      string operator + (string st);
   };

//***********************************************
string::string()      // constructor #1
{
   s = NULL;
}

//***********************************************
string::string(char st[])    // constructor #2
{
   s = strdup(st);
}
//***********************************************
string::~string()              // destructor
{
   delete(s);
}

//***********************************************
string::string(const string& str)         // copy constructor
{
   s = strdup( str.s );
}

//***********************************************
void string::show()        // display string
{
   cout << s;
}

//***********************************************
string string::operator + (string st)   // operator overloading
{
   string temp;
```

```
    temp.s = new char[ strlen(st.s) + strlen(s)+1];
    strcpy(temp.s, s);
    strcat(temp.s, st.s);
    return temp;
}

//************************************************
void main()
{
    clrscr();

    string str1("This is a test");
    string str2(" of the emergency broadcast system");
    string str3;

    str3 = str1 + str2;

    str3.show();

}
```

The main() section of this program declares three strings. It assigns values to the first two. Internally, we use a pointer to a character to store the variable. In the constructor to the program, we allocate memory for the character array that is passed to the constructor. We then use the overloaded + operator to add the two strings together.

Output of the program looks like this:

```
This is a test of the emergency broadcast system
```

You will notice some new notation used in this program. If you do not pass any parameters to the constructor, the pointer to a character is declared to be NULL. However, if you do declare a string, the strdup() function is used to allocate memory for a string and copy one string to another location. This is a handy routine available in both C and C++ which makes allocating memory space for strings easy.

This program uses a destructor to clean up after itself. Inside the destructor the delete() function is used to restore the memory that was declared with the strdup() function.

The `operator + ()` function takes a parameter of type `string` and returns a `string`. The body of the function looks like this:

```
string string::operator + (string st)   // operator overloading
{
    string temp;

    temp.s = new char[ strlen(st.s) + strlen(s)+1];
    strcpy(temp.s, s);
    strcat(temp.s, st.s);
    return temp;
}
```

> The `delete()` function is used in C++ only to restore previously allocated memory. It is used instead of the `free()` function when you are programming in C++, although you can still use `free ()` if you like.

C++ uses the `new` statement to allocate memory. It is an alternative to `malloc()` but is much easier to use, because the compiler takes care of calculating the size of the memory you want to allocate. This function starts by allocating memory to store the size of the combined string plus one (for the terminating zero). The `operator + ()` function then combines the two operands of the expression to form a string and returns that string to the calling point of the program.

In the listing you will notice a new type of constructor, called a *copy constructor*. This type of constructor is used in classes that rely on pointers as data members. Inside the `operator + ()` function, the copy constructor is automatically called when we create a temporary instance of the class. When working with pointer variables as is done in this program, it is mandatory to create a copy constructor that copies the value of what we pass it when we create temporary values.

By overloading the + operator in Listing 23.4, we were actually able to expand the language. Operator overloading enable your programs to actually add new meaning to C++.

Although the examples in this chapter did not go through every operator that the C++ language enables you to override, you probably now understand why operator overloading is used and how to make use of it in your own programs. The notation of operator overloading for other operators is similar to the ones we looked at here.

Be careful not to overuse overloaded operators. Only include overloaded operators when they help to clarify the result of what you are coding. You don't want to use them just because they are there. If you overuse overloaded operators in contexts that are not meaningful, you create unnecessary confusion in your program that could lead to bugs.

What You Have Learned

In this chapter, you learned how operator overloading makes the C++ language even more versatile. We took a look at specific examples of overloading. In particular, the following topics were covered:

- Operator overloading enables you to change the way an operator works with different classes.

- Almost any operator can be overridden and given new functionality.

- To overload an operator use the keyword operator followed by the symbol of the operator you want to overload in your class declaration.

- To use an operator in an expression, make sure that you declare it to return a class of the type you are declaring the operator to be.

- A copy constructor is used in class declarations when dealing with pointer variables to allow temporary data members to be created.

24

Using C++ Streams

Goals

After reading this chapter, you will

- Understand what C++ streams are and when to use them.

- Know the file creation types available in C++ to open a file stream.

- Be able to read and write characters using C++ streams and be familiar with the get() and put() stream member functions.

- Know how to read and write strings using C++ streams and know how to use the getline() stream member function.

- Be able to read and write binary data using C++ streams, and be familiar with the write() and read() stream member functions.

● Know how to read and write instances of classes using the stream member functions.

We first examined file input and output in Chapter 17 using straight C code. In this chapter we are going to examine how file input and output work using C++ objects.

This chapter examines file input and output using objects. You will see how to read and write characters and strings to a file, how to create binary files, and how to save your own objects to disk.

Because C++ is a superset of C, you can still use all the C input and output functions in your C++ code. However, C++ streams do offer some advantages over the regular C library—they are object oriented, and therefore work with the rest of the C++ language a little better.

Input and Output Streams

In C++, a file is opened by linking it to a stream. A *stream* is a method of linking the input or output of a file to a C++ class. We're going to explore two types of streams: input and output. To open an input stream, you must declare the stream to be of class `ifstream`. To open an output stream, you declare it as class `ofstream`.

You must include the header file FSTREAM.H in any programs that use C++ file input or output. You associate a stream with a file when you declare it by passing the constructor information about the file you wish to open. You include the path and filename along with a constant that determines how the file is to be opened. Valid constants are listed in Table 24.1.

You can combine two or more mode specifiers together by ORing the values together. For example, to open a file for input in binary mode, you use something like this:

```
ios::in | ios::binary
```

Including `ios::nocreate` causes the constructor to fail if the file does not already exist. The `ios::noreplace` value causes the constructor to fail if the file already exists. The `ios::trunc` mode causes the contents of the preexisting file of the same name to be destroyed and the file to be truncated to zero length before carrying out any file operations on it.

Table 24.1. File creation modes.

Mode	Action
`ios::in`	Open for input.
`ios::out`	Open for output.
`ios::app`	Open for append mode, writes to end of file.
`ios::ate`	Open and relocate to end of file.
`ios::binary`	Open in binary mode.
`ios::trunc`	Create file; if it already exists, truncate it to length 0.
`ios::nocreate`	Do not create file if no file exists.
`ios::noreplace`	Do not truncate to length of 0 if file exists.

Notice the use of the logical OR (¦) symbol to combine the contents of the values. The most commonly used values are `ios::in` and `ios::out`. However, if you declare a class of type `ifstream`, the compiler automatically knows that you are using mode `ios::in` and it is not necessary to include the specifier (although it doesn't hurt to include it). The same is true if you use an instance of `ofstream`—the `ios::out` flag is assumed and need not be included.

To learn how C++ streams work, let's look at some simple programs that read and write disk files, starting with character values.

Character Input and Output

Character input and output use two special member functions called `get()` and `put()` to retrieve and write characters. Listing 24.1 shows how these functions output a character array to a file, one character at a time.

Listing 24.1. Program to show character streams for file output.

```
/******************************************************
CHAR_O.CPP--Show character stream output in C++.
Do It Yourself Turbo C++ by Paul J. Perry
******************************************************/

#include <iostream.h>
#include <fstream.h>
#include <process.h>
#include <string.h>

char str[] = "Now \nis \nthe \ntime";  // include carriage returns
                         // make sure each word is on
                         // a separate line
void main()
{
  ofstream outfile("TEST.DAT", ios::out);  // open file for output
  if (!outfile)             // error opening file
    {
    cout << "Error opening file " << endl;
    exit(0);
    }

  for (int x=0; x<strlen(str); x++)  // set up loop for character
array
    outfile.put(str[x]);                // write a single character

  outfile.close();   // close output file

}
```

When you run this program, it creates an ASCII text file that looks like this:

```
Now
is
the
time
```

In this program, an instance of ofstream is created. The filename is specified along with the access mode ios::out. If the constructor was not successful, a FALSE value is returned. We test the return value, and if the file open was not successful, we display an appropriate message and exit the program, as listed here:

```
if (!outfile)
  {
  cout << "Error opening file " << endl;
  exit(0);
  }
```

We then find the length of the string with the `strlen()` function. For each character in the string we make a call to the `put()` member function within the `for` loop.

When we break out of the `for` loop, we use the `close()` member function to close the file. When we exit the program, any open files are automatically closed; however, it is good practice to always close any open files when we are done with them.

We can read the file contents back in with the `get()` member function. The CHAR_I.CPP file in Listing 24.2 shows how this is done.

Listing 24.2. Program example of character stream input.

```
/*****************************************************
CHAR_I.CPP--Show character stream input in C++.
Do It Yourself Turbo C++ by Paul J. Perry
*****************************************************/

#include <iostream.h>
#include <string.h>
#include <fstream.h>
#include <process.h>

void main()
{
  char ch;

  ifstream infile("TEST.DAT", ios::in);  // open file for input
  if (!infile)                // error opening file
    {
    cout << "Error opening file " << endl;
    exit(0);
    }
```

continues

Listing 24.2. continued

```
while (infile.get(ch))   // read a single character
  cout << ch;            // display character on screen

infile.close();


}
```

This program reads in the file that was created with the earlier program and displays it on the screen. The program uses about the same structure as the one that was used to write the file. You will notice the instance is of type ifstream (instead of ofstream). We still check the return value to ensure that the open was successful. Finally, we use a while loop to check the return value of the get() function to display each character on the video display. The program ends by closing the file.

String Input and Output

String input and output is easier than character I/O was. The C++ language enables us to use the << operator to direct string output to an instance of the ofstream or ifstream class.

Listing 24.3. Program to write strings to an output file.

```
/****************************************************
STR_O.CPP--Show stream string output.
Do It Yourself Turbo C++ by Paul J. Perry
****************************************************/

#include <iostream.h>
#include <fstream.h>
#include <process.h>

void main()
{
  ofstream outfile("TEST.DOC", ios::out);
```

```
if (!outfile)              // error opening file
  {
  cout << "Error opening file " << endl;
  exit(0);
  }

outfile << "This is the full length" <<  endl;
outfile << "of the text to be output" << endl;
outfile << "into the streamed file." << endl;
outfile.close();

}
```

Once we open the file and check the return value we simply use the insertion (<<) operator to insert text into the text stream. We output several lines of text and then close the file with the close() member function. You can see that the designers of the ofstream class had to use operator overriding to create a new use for the << operator.

Listing 24.4 shows the program we use to read in the strings we just wrote to the disk file.

Listing 24.4. Program example of stream string input.

```
/****************************************************
   STR_I.CPP--Show stream string input.
   Do It Yourself Turbo C++ by Paul J. Perry
 ****************************************************/

#include <iostream.h>
#include <fstream.h>
#include <process.h>

void main()
{
  ifstream infile("TEST.DOC", ios::in);

  if (!infile)              // error opening file
    {
    cout << "Error opening file " << endl;
```

continues

Listing 24.4. continued

```
    exit(0);
    }

const int MAXLEN = 80;
char currentline[MAXLEN];

while (infile.getline(currentline,MAXLEN))
    cout << currentline << endl;   // must add CR/LF sequence
                                              ourselves

infile.close();

}
```

This time, after we open the file for input and check the return value, a while loop is set up. Then we use the getline() class member function to read in each line of the file. The function takes a buffer in which to store the line of text it reads in and the maximum number of characters to read in as parameters.

We then send the text we just read in from the file to the video display. Notice that we must include the endl specifier to send the carriage return/ linefeed sequence to the screen. This is because the getline() function reads everything in a line up to the CR/LF sequence or the maximum length you specify in your call. It does not read the CR/LF sequence.

Binary Input and Output

We can still work with binary input and output in C++. To accomplish this, we must use the ios::binary flag when we open the file. When a file is saved in binary, it is unreadable as text by people. However, the form in which the data is stored on disk is stored in a more efficient manner. With lots of data, it would take less time to read the data in or save it out.

Listing 24.5 is an example of a program that uses binary input and output. It opens a file and writes four integer values from an array into the file and then closes the file. We then proceed to open the file again and read the contents of the file into a different array.

Listing 24.5. Program example of binary stream input and output.

```
/****************************************************
 BIN_IO.CPP--Show binary stream input and output.
 Do It Yourself Turbo C++ by Paul J. Perry
 ****************************************************/

#include <iostream.h>
#include <fstream.h>
#include <process.h>

int arr[] = {345, 678, 987, 321};    // what we will write out to
                                         disk
int arr2[4];                          // input buffer

void main()
{
  cout << "Opening file for write..." << endl;

  ofstream outfile("TEST.DOC", ios::out | ios::binary);
  if (!outfile)              // error opening file
    {
    cout << "Error opening file " << endl;
    exit(0);
    }

  // Write array elements to disk
  outfile.write( (char *) arr, sizeof(arr) );

  cout << "Closing file that was written to" << endl;
  outfile.close();       // Close file
  //--------------------------------------------------//
  // Now, open the file and display it on screen
  cout << "Opening file for read..." << endl;

  ifstream infile("TEST.DOC", ios::in | ios::binary);
  if (!infile)              // error opening file
    {
    cout << "Error opening file " << endl;
    exit(0);
    }
```

continues

475

Listing 24.5. continued

```
infile.read( (char*) arr2, sizeof(arr2)); // read array elements
for (int x=0; x<4; x++)
  cout << arr2[x] << endl;  // display them on screen

cout << "Closing file" << endl;
infile.close();

}
```

Output of the program should look like this:

```
Opening file for write...
Closing file that was written to
Opening file for read...
345
678
987
321
Closing file
```

This shows the steps the program took to open and close files, along with the data values that were read back in.

The `write()` class member function is used to write the data out to disk. The function is passed the array to be written to disk along with the number of characters to output. In the program, the line used to write the text to the file looks like this:

```
outfile.write( (char *) arr, sizeof(arr) );
```

Notice the use of the cast (`char *`), which is used because the function is expecting a pointer to a character. We are using an integer value, so we must tell the compiler that we are aware of the situation and know that what we are doing is correct.

To read the data in, we use the `read()` member function:

```
infile.read( (char*) arr2, sizeof(arr2));
```

This function takes the array that the data is to be read into and the number of bytes to read in as parameters. Once the function is carried out, we go into a loop to display the integer values on the screen.

To prove it to yourself, you might want to try bringing the text file that was created by this program into the editor and examining it. Notice that you cannot read the data stored in the file, whereas if you examine the file after using some of the earlier programs in this chapter, the file can easily be read because it is stored as ASCII data.

Object Input and Output

The first thought that might have come to your mind regarding C++ streams is their ability to read and write an object to disk. It is one of the primary reasons you would want to use the stream input and output classes. Listing 24.6 shows a program that outputs a class to a disk file.

Listing 24.6. Program example of stream output of objects.

```
/******************************************************
OBJ_O.CPP--Show stream output of an object.
Do It Yourself Turbo C++ by Paul J. Perry
******************************************************/

#include <iostream.h>
#include <fstream.h>
#include <string.h>
#include <process.h>

class person
  {
  private :
    char name[80];
    int age;

  public :
    person();
    person(char * nam, int ag);  // constructor
    void display();
  };


//*****************************************
```

continues

477

Listing 24.6. continued

```
person::person()
{
  strcpy(name, "    ");
  age = 0;
}


//****************************************
person::person(char * nam, int ag)
{
  strcpy(name, nam);
  age = ag;
}


//****************************************
void person::display()
{
  cout << name << endl;
  cout << age << endl;
}


//****************************************
void main()
{
  person neighbor("Bob", 35);

  neighbor.display();
  cout << "Writing class to disk";

  ofstream outfile("TEST.DOC", ios::out);
  if (!outfile)              // Error opening file
    {
    cout << "Error opening file " << endl;
    exit(0);
    }

  outfile.write( (char *)&neighbor, sizeof(neighbor) ); // write
                                                        it out

  outfile.close();

}
```

The program starts out by defining a class that includes two data members, two constructors, and one member function. The member function displays the values of data items to the screen, and the constructors initialize the data members.

Inside the main() section of the program, an instance of the class is declared and initialized at the same time. Then an instance of ofstream is declared. We check to ensure that we were able to open the file. We then use the write() member function to output the contents of the class to the file. The code that writes the class out to disk looks like this:

```
outfile.write( (char *)&neighbor, sizeof(neighbor) );
```

This tells the write() function the name of the instance of the class to write out as well as the number of bytes to write out. We close the file as we have done all along.

The inverse program—the one to read a class from disk—follows, as Listing 24.7.

Listing 24.7. Program to show stream input using objects.

```
/***************************************************
OBJ_I.CPP--Show stream input using objects.
Do It Yourself Turbo C++ by Paul J. Perry
***************************************************/

#include <iostream.h>
#include <fstream.h>
#include <string.h>
#include <process.h>

class person
  {
  private :
    char name[80];
    int age;

  public :
    person();                      // constructor #1
    person(char * nam, int ag);   // constructor #2
    void display();
  };
```

continues

Listing 24.7. continued

```cpp
//****************************************
person::person()
{
  strcpy(name, "   ");  // initialize values
  age = 0;
}

//****************************************
person::person(char * nam, int ag)
{
  strcpy(name, nam);
  age = ag;
}

//****************************************
void person::display()
{
  cout << name << endl;
  cout << age << endl;
}

//****************************************
void main()
{
  person neighbor;

  ifstream infile("TEST.DOC", ios::in);
  if (!infile)                // error opening file
    {
    cout << "Error opening file " << endl;
    exit(0);
    }

  infile.read( (char *)&neighbor, sizeof(neighbor) ); // read it
                                                          in

  infile.close();

  cout << "Class read in from disk" << endl;
```

```
    neighbor.display();

}
```

If you use this program on the data file that was created in the previous program, the output of the program looks like this:

```
Class read in from disk
Bob
35
```

Basically, the same class is declared in this program. We then use the read() member function to input the data from the file. The line looks like this:

```
infile.read( (char *)&neighbor, sizeof(neighbor) );
```

This code takes the name of the class, along with the number of bytes to read in. Once the data is retrieved, we use the display() member function to display the data on the screen. That is all that is required to read data from disk into an instance of a class.

As you can see, once you learn how they are used, the C++ file streams offer more flexibility than the regular C file input and output methods. They help you to create your program faster and more efficiently.

What You Have Learned

This chapter explored the stream file input and output system that comes as part of C++. You learned how to use the C++ functions to replace most of the regular C file functions.

Although this is the last chapter of this book, it is by no means the last word on the subject of the C and C++ languages. I encourage you to continue your study of these languages. There is no possible way a single book could cover every aspect of both languages. After all, the manuals for Borland C++ (Turbo C++'s big brother) span seven volumes. Therefore, never think that you have learned everything there is to learn. I hope this has only been a beginning for you.

In this chapter the following topics were covered:

● A stream is a method of linking the input or output of a file to a C++ class. We looked at two types of streams in this chapter: input and output.

● When you declare an instance of a stream, you must specify the filename to associate with the stream and a file creation mode. The most common file creation modes are ios::in and ios::out.

● To use any of the file streams, you must include the FSTREAM.H header file at the beginning of your program.

● Character streams enable you to input or output a character at a time. The put() member function is used to write the character to the file, and the get() member function is used to read the character from the file.

● String stream input or output works by reading or writing an entire string to a file. To output a string to a stream, you follow the instance name of the stream with the insertion operator followed with the data you want to write to the stream.

● The getline() member function is used to read an entire line of text (up to the carriage return/line feed sequence or the maximum length you specify) into a buffer. It does not return the CR/LF sequence, so you must provide this processing yourself.

● To work on binary files, remember to include the ios::binary access specifier when you declare an instance of the class.

● Binary input and output use the write() and read() member functions to output to a file or to read in from a file. Binary file input and output is more efficient then regular text input and output because the data is stored on disk in a more efficient manner.

● To read or write objects to a disk file, use the write() and read() member functions in the stream library.

ASCII Table

This appendix shows the ASCII (American Standard Code for Information and Interchange) character code values in hex and decimal. The original ASCII character set is composed of only the first 127 characters and are composed of a 7-bit value. The additional codes (128 to 255) are called the IBM extended ASCII character set because they are stored in 8 bits (one full byte).

Character	Hex Code	Decimal Code
◘	8	8
○	9	9
◙	a	10
♪	d	13
	20	32
!	21	33

continues

Character	Hex Code	Decimal Code
"	22	34
#	23	35
$	24	36
%	25	37
&	26	38
'	27	39
(	28	40
)	29	41
*	2a	42
+	2b	43
'	2c	44
-	2d	45
.	2e	46
/	2f	47
0	30	48
1	31	49
2	32	50
3	33	51
4	34	52
5	35	53
6	36	54
7	37	55
8	38	56
9	39	57
:	3a	58
;	3b	59
<	3c	60

Character	Hex Code	Decimal Code
=	3d	61
>	3e	62
?	3f	63
@	40	64
A	41	65
B	42	66
C	43	67
D	44	68
E	45	69
F	46	70
G	47	71
H	48	72
I	49	73
J	4a	74
K	4b	75
L	4c	76
M	4d	77
N	4e	78
O	4f	79
P	50	80
Q	51	81
R	52	82
S	53	83
T	54	84
U	55	85
V	56	86

A

continues

Character	Hex Code	Decimal Code
W	57	87
X	58	88
Y	59	89
Z	5a	90
[	5b	91
\	5c	92
]	5d	93
^	5e	94
–	5f	95
`	60	96
a	61	97
b	62	98
c	63	99
d	64	100
e	65	101
f	66	102
g	67	103
h	68	104
i	69	105
j	6a	106
k	6b	107
l	6c	108
m	6d	109
n	6e	110
o	6f	111
p	70	112
q	71	113

Character	Hex Code	Decimal Code
r	72	114
s	73	115
t	74	116
u	75	117
v	76	118
w	77	119
x	78	120
y	79	121
z	7a	122
{	7b	123
¦	7c	124
}	7d	125
~	7e	126
⌂	7f	127
╟	80	128
ff	81	129
Θ	82	130
Γ	83	131
Σ	84	132
α	85	133
σ	86	134
τ	87	135
Ω	88	136
δ	89	137
Φ	8a	138
η	8b	139

continues

Character	Hex Code	Decimal Code
∈	8c	140
∞	8d	141
−	8e	142
✝	8f	143
╔	90	144
μ	91	145
╞	92	146
∫	93	147
÷	94	148
≥	95	149
√	96	150
·	97	151
	98	152
╥	99	153
■	9a	154
ó	9b	155
ú	9c	156
Ñ̃	9d	157
ρ	9e	158
−	9f	159
β	a0	160
Ø	a1	161
≤	a2	162
	a3	163
±	a4	164
╤	a5	165
¬	a6	166

Character	Hex Code	Decimal Code
‖	a7	167
¬	a8	168
_	a9	169
¼	aa	170
⌐	ab	171
⌐	ac	172
¡	ad	173
½	ae	174
⫪	af	175
▓	b0	176
▓	b1	177
▓	b2	178
│	b3	179
┤	b4	180
╡	b5	181
╢	b6	182
╖	b7	183
╕	b8	184
╣	b9	185
║	ba	186
╗	bb	187
╝	bc	188
╜	bd	189
╛	be	190
¬	bf	191
└	c0	192

continues

Character	Hex Code	Decimal Code
⊥	c1	193
⊤	c2	194
├	c3	195
─	c4	196
┼	c5	197
╞	c6	198
╟	c7	199
╚	c8	200
╔	c9	201
╩	ca	202
╦	cb	203
╠	cc	204
═	cd	205
╬	ce	206
╧	cf	207
╨	d0	208
╤	d1	209
╥	d2	210
╙	d3	211
╘	d4	212
╒	d5	213
╓	d6	214
╫	d7	215
╪	d8	216
┘	d9	217
┌	da	218
█	db	219

Character	Hex Code	Decimal Code
■	dc	220
▌	dd	221
▐	de	222
▬	df	223
–	e0	224
■	e1	225
–	e2	226
–	e3	227
–	e4	228
–	e5	229
⌐	e6	230
–	e7	231
–	e8	232
–	e9	233
–	ea	234
–	eb	235
–	ec	236
–	ed	237
–	ee	238
–	ef	239
–	f0	240
▌	f1	241
–	f2	242
–	f3	243
–	f4	244
–	f5	245

continues

A

Character	Hex Code	Decimal Code
≈	f6	246
_	f7	247
▓	f8	248
⊤	f9	249
⊤	fa	250
_	fb	251
n	fc	252
▌	fd	253
_	fe	254
	ff	255

Memory Models

Memory models confuse many programmers who must deal with compilers based on the 8086 family of computers. You can compile a Turbo C++ program using one of six different memory models. Each memory model organizes the memory of the computer differently and governs the size of the code or data that your program can use.

This appendix refers to the 8086 microprocessor. However, the information applies equally to all processors in this family: the 8088, 80286, 80386, and 80486. The x286, x386, and x486 have another mode of operation that is different than what we are going to look at here. However when you run these processors under DOS, they operate as discussed here.

The purpose of this appendix is to familiarize you with the different memory models available and explain when they should be used.

Background Information

A memory model is used to tell how much memory different parts of a program can occupy. The six possible options are tiny, small, medium, compact, large, and huge. To understand what the different memory models are used for, you must understand the way the 8086 family of microprocessors addresses memory.

The microprocessor registers (or memory locations) in which information is placed for processing or for program control. The registers are 16 bits large (2 bytes). The 8086 uses a *segmented* memory management architecture. This means that the total amount of memory that can be addressed by the microprocessor is 1 megabyte (MB). However, this address space is divided into 64KB sections, or *segments*.

Each register can hold a memory address up to FFFF hex, (decimal 65,536) or 64KB. A single register can only access a section (or segment) of memory 64KB in size. To access addresses outside of this segment, the processor must use two registers.

The first register, called the *segment register,* holds the starting address of a 64K segment of memory. The other register holds the number of bytes from the beginning of the segment to the point in which you want to access. This is called the *offset address.*

Therefore, the address of any specific byte within the computer's memory is accessed with a combination of the segment address and the 16-bit register. To calculate the actual memory location referred to by the combination of the segment and offset registers, the number in the segment register is shifted left four bits, and added to the offset address. This results in a 20-bit address.

This 20-bit address permits addressing FFFFF hex (decimal 1,048,576) bytes or the one megabyte of addressable memory space. Most addresses are referred to in the 8086 using segment:offset notation. Using this notation, the segment is listed first followed by a colon and ending with the offset address, such as 5379:FFF4. This describes the two parts of a memory address. Using this notation, you can refer to the same memory location using different combinations of numbers because segments and offset pairs overlap.

Types of Memory Models

Turbo C++ compiles your program in a way specific to the type of memory model you choose. Each memory model organizes the way your program accesses memory differently. Table B.1 summarizes the memory model specifications. We will take a closer look at each memory model available.

Table B.1. Memory model specifications.

Memory Model	Meaning
Tiny	All code and data must reside in a 64KB of memory.
Small	Your code has 64KB available to it, and your data has 64KB available to it.
Medium	1MB is available to your code, and 64KB is available to your data.
Compact	64KB is available to your code, and 1MB is available to your data.
Large	Your code has 1MB available to it, and your data has 1MB available to it.
Huge	Same as the large model, but address arithmetic is performed in such a way that an array can span multiple segments.

Tiny Model

The tiny memory model is the smallest of all the memory models. All segment registers are set to the same value. You have a total of 64KB for all of your code and data. All addressing is done using a single 16-bit register. Programs such as those using the Borland Graphics Interface (BGI) cannot be compiled in the tiny memory model because of its limitations. The tiny memory model is best used for small utility programs.

Small Model

If the code for your program fits inside 64KB of memory and the data fits inside a separate 64KB, you will want to use the small memory model. Because it is the default memory model for the compiler, it is the most commonly used memory model in Turbo C++. The maximum size of a compiled program is 128KB. As with the tiny model, all addressing is done using a 16-bit address. The small memory model uses different segments for code and data.

Medium Model

Most programs don't require more code or data space than the small memory model provides. However, if the code for your program is larger than 64KB, but the data fits in 64KB, you would use the medium memory model. It makes 1MB of memory available to your code and 64KB or your data.

Compact Model

The reverse of the medium model is the compact memory model. This is used when code is smaller than 64KB but the data is larger. This memory model is suited to programs with little code and large amounts of data. It makes 64KB of memory available to your code and 1MB available to your data.

Large Model

The large model combines the medium and compact models. If both your code and data require more than 64KB each, the large model is for you. It allows code and data to use multiple segments. With it, your code has 1MB available to it, and your data has 1MB available as well. Programs compiled with the large memory model take longer to execute, because the microprocessor is using a segment:offset address pair whenever it accesses memory.

Huge Model

The huge memory model is the same as the large model, except it provides for the special case of a single data item such as an array, which is larger than 64KB. The huge memory model makes the speed of your program even slower, so it should only be used when absolutely necessary.

Choosing a Memory Model

Each memory model involves a trade-off. Programs written in memory models other than tiny or small will take longer to execute and the size of the resulting executable (.EXE) file will be larger. Examine your specific program to determine the size of your program and the amount of data it is manipulating. Then make a reasonable decision. You will use the small memory model most often. Keep the information in Table B.1 handy until you have it memorized, because it gives you information about the six memory models and how they use memory.

Usually, if you write a program under a smaller memory model, you can move it up to a larger memory model. The result is usually that the program will require more memory to run and will execute slower than before.

You specify a memory model by choosing one of the six selections from the dialog box displayed when you select Options, then choose

Compiler, and finally select the Code Generation option. Once you specify the type of memory model to use, the compiler automatically creates the correct memory addressing. The appropriate library functions will be linked into your program.

Make sure you specified the appropriate memory models when you installed Turbo C++, because compiling a program for a specific memory model requires library files that were created especially for that memory model. If you didn't install the library files for a specific memory model and decide later that you want to use it, you must reinstall Turbo C++ so the appropriate library files can be copied to your hard drive.

C

ANSI C Language Summary

This appendix provides a reference to some of the more fundamental constructions in the C and C++ programming language. The goal here is not to cover every aspect of the language. Instead, it is meant to provide a quickly accessible guide to the essential elements of the C language that will be most important to you.

General Language Information

1. Program execution always begins at the main() function:

```
void main()
{
  statement1;
  statement2;
```

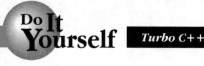

```
          .
          .
          .
        statementX;
}
```

2. Command-line arguments can be passed to your program by passing parameters to the `main()` function:

```
void main(int argc, char *argv[])
{
  int counter;

  printf("Number or arguments: %d\n", argc);

  for (counter=0; counter<argc; counter++)
  printf("Argument %d is : %s\n", counter, *(argv+counter) );
}
```

3. C language comments begin with /* and end with */. In C++ you can also use single line comments with // notation:

```
/* This is a comment in both C and C++. */
// This is a single line C++ comment.
```

Data Types

1. The basic integer type occupies 2 bytes on PC computers:

```
int value;                /* basic integer data type */
long longintvalue;        /* occupy four bytes of memory */
short int number;         /* same as int on the PC */
unsigned int posnumber;   /* only positive values */
int p = 23;               /* initialize integer value */
```

2. Floating-point numbers include a decimal point:

```
float bignumber;          /* basic floating-point variable */
double evenbiggernumber;  /* double-precision floating-point
                             value */
```

3. Character variables are a single byte. They can be treated as integers in most situations:

```
char ch1;              /* character variable, ranging from
                          -128 to 127 */
unsigned char ch2;     /* unsigned character, ranging from 0
                          to 255 */
char ch3 = 'A';        /* initialize using character value */
char ch4 = 65;         /* initialize using decimal value */
```

4. Quick reference table of data types size and ranges:

Type	Size	Range of Values
int	2 Bytes	-32,768 to 32,767
float	4 bytes	3.4×10^{-38} to 3.4×10^{38} (7-digit precision)
double	8 bytes	1.7×10^{-308} to 1.7×10^{308} (15-digit precision)
long double	10 bytes	3.4×10^{-4932} to 3.4×10^{4932} (19-digits precision)
char	1 byte	-128 to 127
unsigned char	1 byte	0 to 255
short int	2 bytes	-32,768 to 32,767
long	4 bytes	-2,147,483,648 to 2,147,483,647
unsigned int	2 bytes	0 to 65,535
unsigned long	4 bytes	0 to 4,294,967,295

Operators

1. Assignment operators assign the value on the right side of an expression to the value on the left side of an expression:

Name	Symbol(s)	Example
Equals	=	x = y;
Addition	+=	x += y (equal to x = x + y)
Subtraction	-=	x -= y (equal to x = x - y)
Multiplication	*=	x *= y (equal to x = x * y)
Division	/=	x /= y (equal to x = x / y)
Modulus	%=	x %= y (equal to x = x % y)

2. Arithmetic operators carry out math operations:

Name	Symbol	Example
Addition	+	1 + 2
Subtraction	-	5 - 2
Multiplication	*	7 * 9
Division	/	6 / 2
Remainder (modulus operator)	%	5 % 4

3. Relational operators compare value on the left side of an expression to value on the right side of an expression:

Operator	Description	Example
<	Less than	1 < 2
>	Greater than	2 > 1
==	Equal to	10 == 10

!=	Not equal to	1 != 2
<=	Less than or equal to	10 <= 10 or 5 <= 10
>=	Greater than or equal to	20 >= 20 or 20 >= 10

4. Logical operators carry out logical operations:

Operator	Description
&&	AND
¦¦	OR
!	NOT

5. Unary operators operate on a single variable:

Operator	Description	Example
++	Increment variable	++i or i++
--	Decrement variable	--i or i--
-	Negation	-6

6. Bitwise operators or binary operators operate on the binary values of values:

Operator	Description	Example
&	AND	x & y
^	XOR (exclusive or)	x ^ y
¦	NOR (inclusive or)	x ¦ y
~	Complement	~ x
<<	Shift left	x << 2
>>	Shift right	y >> 2

7. The conditional operator is used to replace the `if...else` statement in marking simple decisions. It has the format

```
condition ? expression1 : expression2
```

and is equivalent to

```
if (condition)
    expression1;
else
    expression2;
```

8. Table of operator precedence:

Operator Type	Operators	Associativity
Groups	() []	Left to Right
Unary	- ~ ! &	Right to Left
Unary	++ --	Right to Left
Multiplication	* / %	Left to Right
Addition	+ -	Left to Right
Shift	>> <<	Left to Right
Relational	< <= > >=	Left to Right
Relational (Equality)	== !=	Left to Right
Bitwise AND	&	Left to Right
Bitwise XOR	^	Left to Right
Bitwise NOR	¦	Left to Right
Logical AND	&&	Left to Right
Logical OR	¦¦	Left to Right
Conditional	exp1 ? exp2 : exp3	Right to Left
Assignment	= += -=	
	*= /= %=	Right to Left
Comma	,	Left to Right

Conditional Statements

1. The `if` statement has this format:

```
if (expression)
  statement;
```

2. The multistatement `if` expression has this format:

```
if (expression)
  {
  statement1;
  statement2;
  statement3;

    .
    .
    .

  statementX;
  }
```

3. Nested `if` statements take this form:

```
if (expression1)
  if (expression2)
    statement;
```

4. The `if...else` statement follows this format:

```
if (expression)
  statement1;
else
  statement2;
```

5. Nested `if...else` statements:

```
if (expression1)
  if (expression2)
    statement
  else
      statement;
else
  statement;
```

The important point to remember about nested if...else statements is that the C programming language always associates an else with the *closest* preceding if statement.

6. The switch statement follows this form:

```
switch (expression)
  {

  case constant1 :
    statement1;
    break;

  case constant2 :
    statement2;
    break;

  case constant3 :
    statement3;
    break;
         .
         .
         .
  case constantX :
    statementX;
    break;

  default :
    default statement;
  }
```

Program Control Statements

1. The for loop uses this format:

```
for (initialization; condition; increment)
  statement;
```

2. Multistatement `for` loops follow this form:

```
for (initialization; condition; increment)
   {
   statement1;
   statement2;
      .
      .
      .
   statement3;
   }
```

3. The `while` loop takes this form:

```
while (expression)
   statement;
```

4. Nested `while` statements use this format:

```
while (expression1)
   {
   while(expression2)
      {
      statement;
      }
   }
```

5. The `do...while` loop follows this form:

```
do
   {
   statement1;
   statement2;
      .
      .
      .
   statementX;
   } while (expression);
```

6. The `goto` statement used with labels looks like this:

```
goto label;
      .
      .
      .
label:
   statement;
```

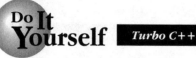

C Functions

1. The following is a simple function definition:

```
void functionname();        /* prototype   */

void functionname()         /* name of function */
{
  statement1;               /* body of function */
  statement2;
}

functionname();             /* function call */
```

2. This is a model for returning values from a function:

```
int number9();              /* prototype   */

int number9()               /* function name */
{
  return(9);                /* returns an integer value */
}
int value;                  /* variable to store result in */

value = number9();          /* function call */
```

3. The following format is used for passing arguments to a function:

```
int addnumbersfunc(int a,b);        /* prototype */

int addnumbersfunc(int a,b)         /* function name */
{
  return(a+b);
}

printf(" a plus b equals %d", addnumbersfunc() ); /* function
                                                     call */
```

Data Constructions

1. Array declarations are as follows:

```
int data[10]            /* one-dimensional integer array with
                           10 elements */
data[1] = 99;           /* array element */
float table[4][5];      /* two-dimensional array, four rows,
                           five columns */

int initarray[] =
    { 2, 4, 6, 8 };     /* initialize array */
```

2. String variables follow this form:

```
char stringvariable[45];             /* string with length
                                        of 45 */
char strarray = "Now is the time..."; /* initialize string
                                         array */
```

3. Structures enable you to store groups of different types of information together:

```
struct structname
    {
    datatype element1;
    datatype element2;
    datatype element3;
    .
    .
    .
    datatype elementX;
    };
```

Pointers

1. To declare a pointer variable, use this format:

```
datatype *ptrname;
```

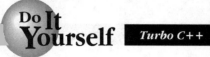

2. To return the address of a pointer variable:

   addr = &ptrname;

3. To return the value of the variable located at an address:

   *contents = *addr;*

Input and Output Format Codes

1. Format specifiers for printf() function are as follows:

Format Specifier	*Output Type*
%d	Signed decimal integer
%f	Floating-point
%e	Floating-point with exponential notation
%x	Unsigned hexadecimal integer
%o	Unsigned octal integer
%c	Character
%s	String

2. Special character escape sequences are as follows:

Code	*Description*
'\\'	Backslash
'\b'	Backspace
'\r'	Carriage return
'\"'	Double quotes
'\f'	Formfeed
'\n'	Newline
'\0'	Null value

`'\''`	Single quote
`'\t'`	Tab
`'\v'`	Vertical Tab

3. `Scanf()` conversion codes:

Character	*Description*
`%c`	Single Character
`%d`	Signed decimal integer
`%e`	Floating-point value in exponential format
`%f`	Floating-point value
`%h`	Short integer
`%i`	Integer
`%o`	Octal integer
`%s`	String value
`%u`	Unsigned decimal integer
`%x`	Hexadecimal integer

Classes

1. To declare a class, enter the following:

```
class clname
   {
   private :        /* private member items  */
      datamembers;
      memberfunctions();
```

```
              .
              .
              .

    public :         /* public member items   */
       clname();     /* constructor   */
       ~clname();    /* destructor   */
       datamembers;
       memberfunctions();

              .
              .
              .

    };

  clname::clname()   /* body of function outside of class

  declaration */
```

2. Declare a class that inherits elements from other classes in this way:

```
class first
   {
   public :
      int number;
      first(int n)   { number = n;   }    /* constructor */
   };

class second : public first       /* inherit members of first
                                      class */

   {
   public :
      int number2;
      second(int n1, int n2)
         {
         first::first(n1);
         number2 = n2;
         }
   };
```

3. Use multiple inheritance within this framework:

```
class first
   {
```

```
  public :
    int numb1;
    first()     { numb1 = 0; }                   // constructor #1
    first(int defvalue)\{ numb1 = defvalue; }
          // constructor #2
    void show()         { cout << numb1 << endl; }
  };

class second
  {
  public :
    int numb2;
    second()   { numb2 = 0; }                    // constructor #1
    second(int defvalue){ numb2 = defvalue; }// constructor #2
    void show()          { cout << numb2 << endl; }
  };

class third : public first, public second
  {
  public :
    int numb3;
    third();                            // constructor #1
    third(int default1, int default2, int default3);
          // constructor #2
    void show();
    };

 third::third()
 {
   first::first();     // call base class constructor
   second::second();  // call base class constructor
   numb3 = 0;         // initialize variable
 }

 third::third(int default1, int default2, int default3)
 {
    first::first(default1);     // call base class constructor
    second::second(default2);   // call base class constructor
    numb3 = default3;           // initialize variable
```

```
     }

     void third::show()
     {
       first::show();              // call base class member
                                      function
       second::show();             // call base class member
                                      function

       cout << numb3 << endl;
     }
```

Error Messages

This appendix lists the Turbo C++ compiler error messages. The list is split into two parts: error messages and warning messages. Error messages indicate program syntax errors, whereas warning messages indicate program code that is suspicious but will still compile.

This appendix is meant to inform you about the great number of messages that the Turbo C++ compiler can report. It is not intended to be all-inclusive documentation for what each message means. Most messages are self-explanatory.

Error Messages

```
( expected
) expected
, expected
: expected after private
```

: expected after protected
: expected after public
< expected
{ expected
} expected
286/287 instruction not enabled
Access can only be changed to public or protected
Address of overloaded function doesn't match type
Ambiguity between firstfunction and secondfunction
Ambiguous member name
Array allocated using new may not have an initializer
Array bounds missing]
Array must have at least one element
Array of references is not allowed
Array size is too large
Assembler statement too long
Assignment to this not allowed, use X::operator new instead
Attempt to grant or reduce access to identifier
Attempting to return a reference to a local object
Attempting to return a reference to local variable identifier
Bad define directive syntax
Bad file name format in include directive
Bad file name format in line directive
Bad #ifdef directive syntax
Bad #undef directive syntax
Bad syntax for pure function definition
Base class is included more than once
Base class is initialized more than once
Base initialization without a class name is now obsolete
Bit field cannot be static
Bit field too large
Bit fields must be signed or unsigned int
Bit fields must contain at least one bit
Bit fields must have integral type
Body has already been defined for function
Call of nonfunction
Cannot access an inactive scope
Cannot add or subtract relocatable symbols
Cannot allocate a reference
identifier cannot be declared in an anonymous union
function1 cannot be distinguished from function2
Cannot call near class member function with a pointer of type

Cannot cast from type1 to type2
Cannot convert type1 to type2
Cannot create instance of abstract class
Cannot define a pointer or reference to a reference
Cannot find class:class (class &) to copy a vector
Cannot find class::operator=(class&) to copy a vector
Cannot find default constructor to initialize array elements of
type class
Cannot find default constructor to initialize base class
Cannot find default constructor to initialize member identifier
Cannot generate function from template function template
Cannot have a near class member in a far class
Cannot have a non-inline function in a local class
Cannot have a static data in a local class
Cannot initialize a class member here
Cannot initialize type1 with type2
Cannot modify a const object
Cannot overload 'main'
function cannot return a value
identifier cannot start an argument declaration
Case bypasses initialization of a local variable
Case outside of switch
Case statement missing :
Class may not contain a pure function
Class member declared outside its class
Compiler could not generate copy constructor for class
Compiler could not generate default constructor for class
classname
Compiler could not generate operator = for class
Compound statement missing }
Conflicting type modifiers
Constant expression required
Constant member in class without constructors
Constant variable must be initialized
constructor cannot be declared const or volatile
constructor cannot have a return type specification
Conversion of near pointer not allowed
Conversion operator cannot have a return type specification
Conversion to type will fail for members of virtual base class
Could not find a match for argument(s)
Could not find file filename
Declaration does not specify a tag or an identifier

Declaration is not allowed here
Declaration missing ;
Declaration syntax error
Declaration terminated incorrectly
Declaration was expected
Declare operator delete (void*) or (void*, size_t)
Default argument value redeclared for parameter
Default expression may not use local variables
Default outside of switch
Default value missing
Default value missing following parameter
Define directive needs an identifier
Delete array size missing]
Destructor cannot be declared const or volatile
Destructor cannot have a return type specification
Destructor for class is not accessible
Destructor for class required in conditional expression
Destructor name must match the class name
Division by zero
do statement must have a while
do...while statement missing (
do...while statement missing)
do...while statement missing ;
Duplicate case
Enum syntax error
Error writing output file
Expression expected
Expression of scalar type expected
Expression syntax
extern variable cannot be initialized
Extra argument in template class name template
Extra parameter in call
Extra parameter in call to function
File must contain at least one external declaration
File name too long
For statement missing (
For statement missing)
For statement missing ;
Friends must be functions or classes
Function call missing)
Function calls not supported
Function defined inline after use as extern

Function definition cannot be a Typedef'ed declaration
Function functionname cannot be static
Function should have a prototype
Function should return a value
Functions function1 and function2 both use the same dispatch
number
Functions may not be part of a struct or union
Global anonymous union not static
Goto bypasses initialization of a local variable
Goto statement missing label
Group overflowed maximum size:
Specifier has already been included
Identifier expected
Identifier cannot have a type qualifier
If statement missing (
if statement missing)
Illegal character
Illegal initialization
Illegal parameter to __emit__
Illegal pointer subtraction
Illegal structure operation
Illegal to take address of bit field
Illegal use of floating point
Illegal use of member pointer
Illegal use of pointer
Ill-formed #pragma
Implicit conversion of type1 to type2 not allowed
Improper use of typedef identifier
Incompatible type conversion
Incorrect command line option:
Incorrect configuration file option:
Incorrect number format
Incorrect use of default
Inline assembly not allowed in inline and template functions
Invalid combination of opcode and operands
Invalid indirection
Invalid macro argument separator
Invalid pointer addition
Invalid register combination
Invalid template argument list
Invalid template qualified name template::name
Invalid use of dot

Invalid use of template

Irreducible expression tree

base is an indirect virtual base class of class

identifier is assigned a value that is never used

constructor is not a base class of class

identifier is not a member of struct

identifier is not a non-static data member and can't be **initialized here**

identifier is not a parameter

identifier is not a public base class of classtype

member is not accessible

Last parameter of operator must have type int

Linkage specification not allowed

LeftValue required

Macro argument syntax error

Macro expansion too long

main must have a return type of int

Matching base class function for function has different dispatch **number**

Matching base class function for function is not dynamic

Member cannot be used without an object

Member function must be called or its address taken

Member identifier expected

Member has the same name as its class

Member is ambiguous: member1 and member2

Member is initialized more than once

Member pointer required on right side of .* or ->*

Memory reference expected

Misplaced break

Misplaced continue

Misplaced decimal point

Misplaced #elif directive

Misplaced else

Misplaced #else directive

Misplaced #endif directive

Multiple base classes require explicit class names

Multiple declaration for identifier

identifier must be a member function

identifier must be a member function or have a parameter of class **type**

identifier must be a previously defined class or struct

identifier must be a previously defined enumeration tag

function must be declared with no parameters
function must be declared with one parameter
operator must be declared with one or no parameters
operator must be declared with one or two parameters
function must be declared with two parameters
Must take address of a memory location
Need an identifier to declare
No : following the ?
No base class to initialize
No file name ending
No file names given
No type information
Nonportable pointer conversion
Nontype template argument must be of scaler type
Non-virtual function declared pure
Not a valid expression format type
Not an allowed type
Numeric constant too large
Objects of type cannot be initialized with {}
Only member functions may be 'const' or 'volatile'
Only one of a set of overloaded functions can be "C"
Operand of delete must be non-const pointer
Operator [] missing]
operator -> must return a pointer or a class
operator delete must return void
Operator must be declared as function
operator new must have an initial parameter of type size_t
operator new must return an object of type void*
Operators may not have default argument values
Out of memory
Overlays only supported in medium, large, and huge memory models
Overloadable operator expected
Overloaded function name ambiguous in this context
Overloaded function resolution not supported
Parameter names are used only with a function body
Parameter number missing name
Pointer to structure required on left side of -> or ->*
Reference initialized with type1, needs lvalue of type type2
Reference member in class without constructors
Reference member is not initialized
Reference member needs a temporary for initialization
Reference variable must be initialized

Register allocation failure
Repeat count needs an lvalue
Side effects are not allowed
Size of identifier is unknown or zero
sizeof may not be applied to a bit field
sizeof may not be applied to a function
Size of the type is unknown or zero
identifier specifies multiple or duplicate access
Statement missing ;
Structure required on left side of . or .*
Structure size too large
Subscripting missing]
Switch selection expression must be of integral type
Switch statement missing (
Switch statement missing)
Template argument must be a constant expression
Template class nesting too deep: 'class'
Template function argument not used in argument types
Template function may only have type-arguments
Templates can only be declared at file level
Templates must be classes or functions
The constructor is not allowed
The value for identifier is not within the range of an int
'this' can only be used within a member function
Too few arguments in template class name
Too few parameters in call
Too few parameters in call to function
Too many decimal points
Too many default cases
Too many error or warning messages
Too many exponents
Too many initializers
Too many storage classes in declaration
Too many types in declaration
Too much global data defined in file
Trying to derive a far class from the huge base
Trying to derive a far class from the near base
Trying to derive a huge class from the far base
Trying to derive a huge class from the near base
Trying to derive a near class from the far base
Trying to derive a near class from the huge base
Two consecutive dots

Two operands must evaluate to the same type
Type mismatch in default argument value
Type mismatch in default value for parameter
Type mismatch in parameter
Type mismatch in parameter number in call to function
Type mismatch in parameter
Type mismatch in parameter in call to function
Type mismatch in parameter in template class name
Type mismatch in redeclaration of identifier
Type name expected
Type qualifier identifier must be a struct or class name
Unable to create TURBOC.#IN
Unable to execute command
Unable to open include filename
Unable to open input file
Undefined label
Undefined structure
Undefined symbol
Unexpected }
Unexpected end of file in comment started on line number
union cannot be a base type
union cannot have a base type
Unions cannot have a virtual member functions
Unknown language
Unknown preprocessor directive:
Unterminated string or character constant
Use . or -> to call function
Use . or -> to call member, or & to take its address
Use :: to take the address of a member function
User break
v86 task without vcpi
Value of type void is not allowed
Variable has been optimized
Variable is initialized more than once
'virtual' can only be used with a member function
Virtual function conflicts with base class
virtual specified more than once
void & is not a valid type
function was previously declared with the language
While statement missing (
While statement missing)
Wrong number of arguments in call of macro

Warning Messages

Ambiguous operators need parentheses
Array size for 'delete' ignored
Array variable identifier is near
Assigning type to enumeration
Base class is inaccessible because also inclass
Bit fields must be signed or unsigned int
Both return and return with a value used
Call to function with no prototype
Code has no effect
Condition is always false
Condition is always true
Constant is long
Constant member is not initialized
Constant out of range in comparison
Conversion may lose significant digits
Declare type prior to use in prototype
identifier is declared but never used
Division by zero
Function should return a value
Functions containing local destructors are not expanded inline in
function
Functions containing reserved are not expanded inline
Hexadecimal value contains more than 3 digits
function1 hides virtual function
Ill-formed #pragma
Initializing enumeration with type
identifier is assigned a value that is never used
identifier is declared as both external and static
Maximum precision used for member pointer type
Mixing pointers to signed and unsigned char
No declaration for function
Non-const function called for const object
Nonportable pointer comparison
Nonportable pointer conversion
Non-volatile function called for volatile object
overload is now unnecessary and obsolete
Overloaded prefix 'operator operator' is used as a postfix
operator

Parameter is never used
Possible incorrect assignment
Possible use of identifier before definition
Redefinition of macro is not identical
Structure passed by value
Style of function definition is now obsolete
Superfluous & with function
Suspicious pointer conversion
Temporary used for parameter number
Temporary used for parameter number in call to function
Temporary used for parameter parametername
Temporary used for parameter parametername in call to function
Temporary used to initialize identifier
This initialization is only partly bracketed
Undefined structure identifier
Use qualified name to access nested type
void functions may not return a value

Library Reference

This appendix contains a quick reference to the functions found in the Turbo C++ runtime library (RTL) that were referenced in this book. This appendix is not meant to be an all-inclusive reference to every function in the library. Rather, it is meant as a quick reference that you can flip through when you are looking for the parameters to a specific function which you remember was used in this book.

RTL Functions Referenced in This Book

asctime

Declaration: `char *asctime(const struct tm *tblock);`

Include: TIME.H

Description: Returns the string representation of a time that is stored in a time (tm) structure.

bar

Declaration: void bar(*int left*, *int top*, *int right*, *int bottom*);

Include: GRAPHICS.H

Description: Draws a filled rectangular figure in graphics mode.

bar3d

Declaration: void bar3d(*int left*, *int top*, *int right*, *int bottom*, *int depth*, *int topflag*);

Include: GRAPHICS.H

Description: Draws a three-dimensional filled rectangular figure in graphics mode.

biosequip

Declaration: int biosequip(void);

Include: BIOS.H

Description: Returns information about the current computer system.

biosmemory

Declaration: int biosmemory(void);

Include: BIOS.H

Description: Returns amount of conventional memory available on the current computer system.

circle

Declaration: `void circle(int x, int y, int radius);`

Include: GRAPHICS.H

Description: Displays a circle in graphics mode.

closegraph

Declaration: `void closegraph(void);`

Include: GRAPHICS.H

Description: Restores the text mode screen and deallocates any memory used for the Borland Graphics Interface.

clreol

Declaration: `void clreol(void);`

Include: CONIO.H

Description: Clears the text screen to the end of line (EOL).

clrscr

Declaration: `void clrscr(void);`

Include: CONIO.H

Description: Clears the screen in text mode.

cprintf

Declaration: int cprintf(*const char *format* [, *argument*, ...]);

Include: STDIO.H

Description: Writes character strings and values of C variables in the current color to the standard output stream, stdout, which is normally set to the screen.

delay

Declaration: void delay(*unsigned milliseconds*);

Include: DOS.H

Description: Halts execution of your program for a specified number of milliseconds.

delline

Declaration: void delline(void);

Include: CONIO.H

Description: Deletes the current text screen line.

diftime

Declaration: double difftime(*tim_t*, *time2*, *time_t time1*);

Include: TIME.H

Description: Returns the difference between two times.

ellipse

Declaration: void ellipse(*int x*, *int y*, *int stangle*, *int endangle*,
int xradius, *int yradius*);

Include: GRAPHICS.H

Description: Draws an elliptical arc figure in graphics display mode.

exit

Declaration: void exit(*int status*);

Include: PROCESS.H

Description: Terminates the current program.

fclose

Declaration: int fclose(*FILE *stream*);

Include: STDIO.H

Description: Closes the specified stream.

fgetc

Declaration: int fgetc(*FILE *stream*);

Include: STDIO.H

Description: Returns the next character in the specified stream.

fgets

Declaration: `char *fgets(char *s, int n, FILE *stream);`

Include: STDIO.H

Description: Reads characters from the specified string into a string.

fopen

Declaration: `FILE *fopen(const char *filename, const char *mode);`

Include: STDIO.H

Description: Opens a disk file and associates a C stream with it.

fprintf

Declaration: `int fprintf (FILE *stream, const char *format [, argument, ...]);`

Include: STDIO.H

Description: Sends formatted output to the specified stream.

fputs

Declaration: `int fputs(const char *s, FILE *stream);`

Include: STDIO.H

Description: Outputs a string to the specified stream.

fread

Declaration: size_ fread(*void *ptr, size_t size, size_t n,* FILE
streams);

Include: STDIO.H

Description: Reads binary data from a stream.

free

Declaration: void free(*void *blocks*);

Include: STDLIB.H

Description: Frees previously allocated memory.

fscanf

Declaration: int fscanf(*FILE *stream, const char *format* [, *argument,*
...]);

Include: STDIO.H

Description: Gets formatted input from the specified stream.

fseek

Declaration: int fseek(*FILE *stream, long offset, int whence*);

Include: STDIO.H

Description: Moves the file pointer to any position within a stream.

ftell

Declaration: `long ftell(FILE *stream);`

Include: STDIO.H

Description: Returns the current file pointer position for the specified stream.

fwrite

Declaration: `size_t fwrite(const void *ptr, size_t size, size_t n,`
`FILE *stream);`

Include: STDIO.H

Description: Writes specified number of bytes to a stream.

getch

Declaration: `int getch(void);`

Description: CONIO.H

Include: Reads a single character from the keyboard without echoing it to the screen.

getchar

Declaration: `int getchar(void);`

Include: STDIO.H

Description: Returns the next character in the standard input stream (stdin) usually defined as the keyboard.

getche

Declaration: `int getche(void);`

Description: CONIO.H

Include: Reads a single character from the keyboard and echoes it to the screen.

getpixel

Declaration: `unsigned getpixel(int x, int y);`

Include: GRAPHICS.H

Description: Returns the color of the specified screen pixel.

gets

Declaration: `char *gets(char *s);`

Include: STDIO.H

Description: Enables the user to enter a string of characters into the standard input stream (stdin), which is usually defined as the keyboard.

gettextinfo

Declaration: `void gettextinfo(struct text_info *r);`

Include: CONIO.H

Description: Gets information about the current text mode.

gotoxy

Declaration: `void gotoxy(int x, int y);`

Include: CONIO.H

Description: Moves the text cursor to a new position.

graphresult

Declaration: `int far graphresult(void);`

Include: GRAPHICS.H

Description: Returns the error code for the last graphics operation that resulted in an error. Graphics error message is reset after a call to this function.

highvideo

Declaration: `void highvideo(void);`

Include: CONIO.H

Description: Selects high-intensity video display characters.

initgraph

Declaration: `int initgraph(int *graphdriver, int *graphmode, char *driverpath);`

Include: GRAPHICS.H

Description: Initializes the Borland Graphics Interface (BGI) System.

insline

Declaration: `void insline(void);`

Include: CONIO.H

Description: Inserts a blank line at the current position in text mode.

line

Declaration: `void line(int x1, int y1, int x2, int y2);`

Include: GRAPHICS.H

Description: Draws a line between two points in graphics mode.

lineto

Declaration: `void lineto(int x, int y);`

Include: GRAPHICS.H

Description: Draws a line from the current position (CP) to the specified point.

localtime

Declaration: `struct tm *localtime(const time_t *timer);`

Include: TIME.H

Description: Converts a time in a structure `time` to a structure of `tm`.

lowvideo

Declaration: void lowvideo(void);

Include: CONIO.H

Description: Selects low-intensity video display characters.

malloc

Declaration: void *malloc(*size_t size*);

Include: STDLIB.H

Description: Allocates a block of memory.

moveto

Declaration: void moveto(*int x*, *int y*);

Include: GRAPHICS.H

Description: Moves the current position (CP) to the specified point.

normvideo

Declaration: void normvideo(void);

Include: CONIO.H

Description: Selects normal-intensity video display characters.

outtext

Declaration: void outtext(*char *textstring*);

Include: GRAPHICS.H

Description: Displays a string of text characters at the current position (CP) on the graphics display.

outtextxy

Declaration: `void outtextxy(int x, int y, char *textstring);`

Include: GRAPHICS.H

Description: Displays a string of text characters at the specified X and Y coordinates on the graphics display.

perror

Declaration: `void perror(const char *s);`

Include: STDIO.H

Description: Displays a system error message on the standard error stream, usually defined as the screen.

printf

Declaration: `int printf(const char *format [, argument, ... ]);`

Include: STDIO.H

Description: Writes character strings and values of C variables, to the standard output stream, stdout, which is normally set to the screen.

putc

Declaration: `int putc(int c, FILE *stream);`

Include: STDIO.H

Description: Outputs a character to the specified stream.

putchar

Declaration: int putchar(*int c*);

Include: STDIO.H

Description: Puts the specified character to the standard output stream (stout), usually the screen.

putpixel

Declaration: void putpixel(*int x, int y, int color*);

Include: GRAPHICS.H

Description: Plots a point on the graphics display screen.

rectangle

Declaration: void rectangle(*int left, int top, int right, int bottom*);

Include: GRAPHICS.H

Description: Draws a rectangle figure in graphics display mode.

scanf

Declaration: int scanf(*const char *format* [, *address*, ...]);

Include: STDIO.H

Description: Reads formatted characters from the standard input file, stdin, usually the keyboard.

setcolor

Declaration: void setcolor(*int color*);

Include: GRAPHICS.H

Description: Sets the current drawing color in graphics mode.

setfillstyle

Declaration: void setfillstyle(*int pattern*, *int color*);

Include: GRAPHICS.H

Description: Sets the current fill pattern and color in graphics mode.

setlinestyle

Declaration: void setlinestyle(*int linestyle*, *unsigned pattern*, *int thickness*);

Include: GRAPHICS.H

Description: Sets the current line style in graphics display mode.

settextstyle

Declaration: void settextstyle(*int font*, *int direction*, *int charsize*);

Include: GRAPHICS.H

Description: Sets current text characteristics when displaying text in graphics display mode.

sound

Declaration: void sound(*unsigned frequency*);

Include: DOS.H

Description: Turns the PC speaker on at the specified frequency.

spawnl

Declaration: int spawnl(*int mode, char *path, char *arg0, ..., NULL*);

Include: PROCESS.H

Description: Allows your program to execute another program and give control to it. When the other program is done executing, control will return to your program.

stime

Declaration: time_t stime(*time_t *tp*);

Include: TIME.H

Description: Returns the system time and date measured in Greenwich Mean Time (GMT).

strcpy

Declaration: char *strcpy(*char *dest, const char *source*);

Include: STRING.H

Description: Copies a source string to a destination string.

strdup

Declaration: char *strdup(*const char *s*);

Include: STRING.H

Description: Allocates memory for a string and copies the string to the memory space.

strlen

Declaration: size_t strlen(*const char *s*);

Include: STRING.H

Description: Returns the length of a string.

textattr

Declaration: void textattr(*int attr*);

Include: CONIO.H

Description: Selects a new text attribute in text display mode.

textbackground

Declaration: void textbackground(*int color*);

Include: CONIO.H

Description: Selects a new background text color in text display mode.

textcolor

Declaration: void textcolor(*int newcolor*);

Include: CONIO.H

Description: Selects a new text color in text display mode.

time

Declaration: time_t time(*time_t *timer*);

Include: TIME.H

Description: Returns the seconds passed since 00:00:00 Greenwich Mean Time (GMT).

textmode

Declaration: void textmode(*int mode*);

Include: CONIO.H

Description: Changes the current text screen mode in text display mode.

tolower

Declaration: int tolower(*inc ch*);

Include: CTYPE.H

Description: Converts an ASCII character to lowercase.

toupper

Declaration: int toupper(*int ch*);

Include: CTYPE.H

Description: Converts an ASCII character to uppercase.

E

Glossary

ANSI C—The version of the C programming language that was standardized by the American National Standards Institute.

Arguments—Those parameters that are passed to a function.

ASCII—Abbreviation for the American Standard Code for Information Interchange. ASCII is a standard code for representing characters in a computer's memory.

ASCIIZ—A string of ASCII characters followed by a zero.

Assignment—The process of taking one variable and setting another variable equal to it.

Bit—One binary digit. A bit can receive the value of either 1 or 0, values that are usually represented by humans as TRUE or FALSE. The bit is the basic method of representing information in memory.

Bitwise operator—An operation that only affects individual bits of a binary representation of an integer value.

Buffering—The process of storing up characters before they are read or written to a device. Using buffering, a system can work much more efficiently.

Byte—Eight bits of information.

C programming language—General purpose programming language developed by Brian Kernighan and Dennis Ritchie.

C++ programming language—A superset of the C programming language developed by Bjarne Stroustrup.

Character—A single letter, number, or symbol that occupies 1 byte in memory and has the range of 0 to 127. In C, characters are assigned using single quotes.

Class—The combination of code and data into a unit. The code is usually in the form of member functions that operate on the data members.

Command line—The instruction that the operator types at the DOS prompt.

Conditional operator—A special type of operator in C that enables you take one of several actions. It is used in making choices.

Control constructions—Statements that are used to control program flow in software.

CPU—Abbreviation for central processing unit. The main "brain" inside your computer.

Decrement—To subtract one from a variable. C uses the symbols $--$ to represent the decrement operator.

DOS—Abbreviation for disk operating system. The program that controls disk input and output. DOS also takes care of a large portion of communications between application programs and the computer.

Double integer—Double-precision floating-point numbers that occupy eight bytes of memory. The exponent has a range of 10^{-308} to 10^{308} power.

Enumerated types—A type of variable that gives the programmer a way to limit what values the variable can have.

Expression—A combination of constants, variables, and operators that can be evaluated to yield a value. An entire expression can be used almost anyplace a variable can.

FALSE—One of two boolean states that some variable may take on. In C, the logical state of FALSE is represented by the integer number zero (0).

Floating Integer—Floating-point numbers occupy four bytes of memory. The exponent has a range of 10-38 to the 1038 power.

Header file—A separate source code file with the extension .H that usually contains function prototypes. Header files are usually found at the beginning of a C or C++ program.

Increment—Add one to a variable. In C, the increment operator (++) will add one to a variable.

Inheritance—The ability of classes to share common characteristics. A class that shares attributes with other classes is called a *derived class.* The original class is called the *base class.*

Integer—Any positive or negative whole number including zero.

K byte—1024 bytes. It is often shortened to KB or K (for example 64K).

Lifetime—The lifetime of a variable is the length of time it retains a value.

Logical operator—An operator that enables you to choose between two different truths.

Logical operators—The operators used when a program uses multiple choices in tests for truth.

Memory model—A features used to tell the compiler how much memory different parts of a program can occupy. There are six memory models: tiny, small, medium, compact, large, and huge. Memory models are used only on DOS-based versions of C and C++.

Modulo—A type of division in which the modulo is the remainder of two numbers divided together.

Offset—A special term applied to the 8086 series of microprocessors that, when combined with a segment value, lets the microprocessor represent all available memory with less than the required address width.

Operand—The variable that an operator uses.

Operator—A word or symbol that causes a program to do something to a variable.

Pointer—A pointer provides a way of accessing a variable without referring to the variable directly. The way a program statement can refer to a variable indirectly is using the address of a variable. Pointers are used in situations when passing actual values is difficult or undesirable.

Polynomial—In algebra, an expression consisting of more than two terms. Usually in the form of X2 + 4X + 5.

Precedence level—The order in which operator expressions are evaluated. If an operator has a higher precedence level, it is evaluated before other operators.

RAM—*See* Random-access memory.

Random-access memory—A type of memory that changes. This is what the programs you create are stored in. An acronym for random-access memory is RAM.

Read-only memory—A type of memory that is permanent and cannot be changed. An acronym for read-only memory is ROM.

Recursion—The ability for a function to call itself.

Relational operators—Operators that are used in testing a value. Relational operators are the vocabulary the program uses to ask questions about variables.

ROM—See Read Only Memory

ROM BIOS—The program stored in your computer's read-only memory that starts the computer and loads the disk operating system. ROM BIOS is actually an acronym for read-only memory basic input/output system.

Scope—*See* Visibility.

Segment—A special term applied to the 8086 microprocessor that, when combined with an offset value, lets the microprocessor represent all available memory with less than the required address width.

Signed—When a variable can have either a positive or negative value.

Stderr—A stream that is usually attached to display errors.

Stdin—A stream that is usually defined as the keyboard.

Stdout—A stream that is usually attached to the display.

Stream—Sequences of contiguous character values. The header text file STDIO.H must be included in a program file to use this facility.

Strings—The form of data used in programming languages for storing and manipulating text. In C, a string is an array of characters.

Structure—A special kind of array that contains variables of different types.

System program—The class of programs that forms a portion of an operating system.

TRUE—One of two boolean states that some variable may take on. In C, the logical state of TRUE is represented by the integer number one (1).

Type definitions—A feature that the programmer uses to create a new type from an existing type and to give it a special name. Generally, type definitions are used to clarify the role a variable will play in a program.

Unions—A data structure that allows many different variables to share one space in memory.

UNIX—An operating system written in the C programming language. The C language gets much of its background from this operating system.

Unsigned—A variable that can only take on positive values.

Visibility—The visibility (or scope) of a variable refers to which parts of a program will be able to recognize it. A variable may be visible in a block, a function, a file, a group of files, or an entire program.

Word—A unit of measure that is 2 bytes long, or equal to 16 bits.

Index

Symbols

! (NOT) logical operator, 110
!= (not equal to)
  operator, 106
% (remainder) operator, 103
%= (modulus division)
  extended assignment
  operator, 226
& (ampersand)
  AND logical operator,
    227-232
      truth table, 230
    passing variables by
      reference with, 390
    pointer operator, 268
&& (AND) logical
  operator, 110

(XOR) logical operator,
  229-232
    truth table, 230
* (asterisk)
  indirection operator, 267
  multiplication
    operator, 103
  pointer operator, 268
*= (multiplication) extended
  assignment operator, 226
+ (addition) operator, 103
++ (increment)
  operator, 108
    overloading, 452-453
+= (addition) extended
  assignment operator, 226
- (subtraction) operator, 103
-- (decrement) operator, 108
-= (subtraction) extended
  assignment operator, 226

... (ellipsis marks), 23
/ (division) operator, 103
// (double slashes) in
  comments, 388
/= (division) extended
  assignment operator, 226
:: (scope resolution operator),
  411-412, 437
    with constructors, 416-417
< (less than) operator, 106
<< operator
  insertion, 392-393
    cascading, 393-394
    manipulators, 394-396
  left-shift, 232-235
<= (less than or equal to)
  operator, 106
= (assignment) operator, 100
== (equal to) operator, 106

553

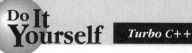

Order Your Program Disk Today!

You can save yourself hours of tedious, error-prone typing by ordering the companion disk to *Do It Yourself Turbo C++*. The disk contains the source code for all the programs in the book.

You will get code that shows you how to use all the basic and advanced features discussed in the book. Every complete program listing is included on the diskette. With the companion disk you will be able to spend your valuable time learning the essential elements of C and C++ programming rather than straining your eyes trying to find a mistake in your typing.

Disks are available in both 5-1/4" and 3-1/2" format. The price of $20 includes shipping to USA addresses. (Foreign orders please add $5 for shipping and handling in USA funds only.) Make checks and money orders payable to Perry Software Development.

Just make a copy of this page, fill in the blanks, and mail with check or money order only to:

Do It Yourself Turbo C++ Diskette
Perry Software Development
P.O. Box 66841
Scotts Valley, CA 95067

Please **print** the following information:

Payment method: Check _____   Money Order _____

Name: _____

Street Address: _____

City: _____

State: _____   ZIP: _____

Disk Size: 5-1/4" _____   3-1/2" _____

(This offer is made by the author, not by the publisher)

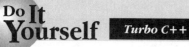

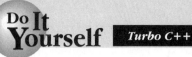